INSTITUTE OF CLASSICAL ARCHITECTURE & ART
20 West 44th Street, Suite 310, New York, NY 10036-6603
telephone (212) 730-9646 facsimile (212) 730-9649 institute@classicist.org

WWW.CLASSICIST.ORG

EDITOR
Richard John

DESIGNER
Tom Maciag
Dyad Communications *design office*
Philadelphia, Pennsylvania

MANAGING EDITOR
Henrika Dyck Taylor

PRINTER
Crystal World Printing
Manufactured in China

ISBN 978-0-9642601-3-9
ISSN 1076-2922

FRONT AND BACK COVERS
David Ligare, *Ponte Vecchio/ Torre Nova*, 1996, Oil on Canvas, 40 x 58 inches. Private Collection, San Francisco, CA. ©D. Ligare. This painting was created for a solo exhibition at The Prince of Wales's Institute of Architecture in London in 1996. David Ligare described his intentions in the following terms: "The old bridge has been painted countless times by artists who have utilized every style and manner of painting imaginable. I was not interested in making yet another 'new' view of it. What I wanted to do instead was to imagine what the Ponte Vecchio would have been like if the early Renaissance architect, Filippo Brunelleschi (1377-1446) had designed a new tower for it. Brunelleschi, like the poet Petrarch (1304-1374) used ancient art to create an alternate modernity."

END PAPERS
Giambattista Piranesi, *Le Antichità Romane* (Rome: Angelo Rotilj, 1756), Vol. III, Plates LIII and LIV.

SECTION OPENING IMAGES
PAGE 6: Eduard Gaertner, Detail from *Panorama of Berlin*, Oil on Canvas, 1832-6. The view is from the roof of Schinkel's Friedrichswerder Church showing the Bauakademie under construction. PAGES 26-27: Ferguson & Shamamian Architects, A New Residence in Malibu, CA. Photograph by Scott Frances. PAGE 48: Detail of façade, Pan American Union Building by Paul Cret and Albert Kelsey. Photograph by John Collier (Prints and Photographs Division, Library of Congress). PAGES 58-59: Nicole Bernal-Cisneros, Proposed Redevelopment, Chelsea Barracks, London, UK, Aerial perspective. PAGE 78: Demetri Porphyrios, Interamerican Headquarters, Athens, Greece, 2000-02. PAGES 96-97: *Vermont Landscape* by Ken Salaz, 2010 Hudson River Fellow, Oil on Linen, 18 x 24 inches. PAGES 106-107: Pavilion, Seaside, FL, by Eric Watson, Architect, P.A. PAGES 122-123: The Castel Sant'Angelo and the Aelian Bridge, Rome. Photograph by Patrizia Ferri.

The generous contributions of individuals and institutions who provided images for publication and the invaluable assistance of the anonymous peer reviewers of the academic articles in the Essay sections are very gratefully acknowledged.

THE CLASSICIST

№ 9: 2010-2011

THE CLASSICIST AT LARGE 4

CANON AND INVENTION: THE FORTUNA OF VITRUVIUS' ASIATIC IONIC BASE

ESSAY 7

SCHINKEL'S ENTWÜRFE ZU STÄDTISCHEN WOHNGEBÄUDEN:
LIVING ALL'ANTICA IN THE NEW BOURGEOIS CITY
Jean-François Lejeune

FROM THE OFFICES 28

ESSAY 49

PAUL CRET AND LOUIS KAHN:
BEAUX-ARTS PLANNING AT THE YALE CENTER FOR BRITISH ART
Sam Roche

FROM THE ACADEMIES 60

EDUCATION AND THE PRACTICE OF ARCHITECTURE
Michael Lykoudis

NOTRE DAME/GEORGIA TECH/MIAMI/JUDSON/YALE/COLLEGE OF CHARLESTON/THE ICAA

ESSAY 79

DEMETRI PORPHYRIOS: REFUTATIONS AND CONJECTURES
Kyle Dugdale

THE ALLIED ARTS 98

GRAND CENTRAL ACADEMY OF ART

MISCELLANEA 106

REFLECTIONS ON PRACTICE
Scott Merrill

ARCHITECTURAL DRAWING IN THE DIGITAL AGE
Jacob Brillhart

ICAA ADMINISTRATION, MEMBERSHIP, AND SPONSORS 124

The Classicist at Large

CANON AND INVENTION: THE *FORTUNA* OF VITRUVIUS' ASIATIC IONIC BASE

One of the many challenges facing those architects who were trying to revive *all'antica* classicism in the Renaissance was how to resolve the discrepancy between what they read in Vitruvius, the only architectural treatise to survive from antiquity, and what they could see in the ancient Roman remains around them. A perfect example of this problem can be found in the response to Vitruvius' account of the Ionic order where he gave detailed descriptions of two alternative bases for an Ionic column: First, the Attic base in which two convex moldings (toruses) sandwiched between them a concave molding (the scotia or trochilos); and, secondly, what he called the Ionic base with two scotias placed below a torus [FIGURE 1]. The latter we now refer to as the Asiatic Ionic base because in antiquity it was rarely seen outside Asia Minor (perhaps the most notable example being Pytheos' temple of Athena Polias at Priene [FIGURE 2]). Because Vitruvius gave no description of a base for the Doric order—following Greek practice he had presumably intended it to be baseless as at the Theater of Marcellus—most Renaissance architects assigned his Attic base to the Doric, a decision which would suggest that the other type of base, the Asiatic one, should be used for the Ionic order. However almost all the ancient examples of Ionic columns surviving in Rome used some variant of the Attic base (perhaps the sole exception being recorded by Antonio da Sangallo in his study drawing of the temples in the Forum Holitorium, UA 1174r) and so architects were left with a conundrum: Should they follow what they saw with their own eyes or what they read in the notoriously corrupted text of Vitruvius?

The issue was further complicated by the fact that the Asiatic Ionic base, as described by Vitruvius, could make a column look rather unstable because of the deep concave moldings, the two large scotias separated only by small astragals, placed right at the bottom of the column.

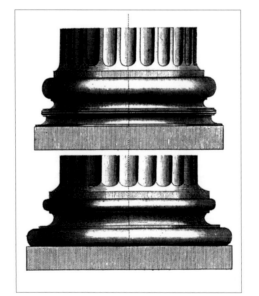

This awkwardness was summed up in 1650 by Roland Fréart who described the Asiatic base as never having "had the approbation of the ablest modern masters, who upon examination have greatly wondered that Vitruvius should impose so vast a Torus upon so small Cinctures, charging the strong upon the weaker, which being totally repugnant to the order of Nature, is very offensive to the eyes of the Curious." (*Parallèle de l'architecture antique avec la moderne*, trans. John Evelyn).

The canon of the classical orders was codified in the form in which we know it today through the publications of three architects: Serlio (1537), Vignola (1562), and Palladio (1570). We can gain some understanding of the haphazard process through which codification occurred by examining the approach each of them took to the base of the Ionic order. Serlio repeated Vitruvius' description and illustrated it, but then commented that it "does not satisfy many people because of the very large torus with very small moldings underneath" and so he proposed a visual adjustment—keeping the same number and sequence of moldings, but changing their proportions so that the two scotias with their projecting astragals now appear large enough to support the torus above. Vignola, on the other hand, followed Vitruvius' account of the Asiatic Ionic base very closely, both in his *Regola delli cinque ordini d'architettura* and in his practice (for instance in the cortile of the Palazzo Farnese at Caprarola [FIGURE 3]). Yet elsewhere in his treatise, Vignola did not hesitate to depart from Vitruvian authority whenever he saw fit, most notably in his total omission of the Attic base from his account of the orders. Finally, Palladio took a middle route, paying due respect to the ancient Roman author, but making clear his own preferences: "These are the dimensions of the Ionic base according to Vitruvius. But because in many antique buildings we see this order used with Attic bases, which please me greatly, I have drawn the Attic base . . . though I have not neglected to also make a drawing of the type about which Vitruvius taught us."

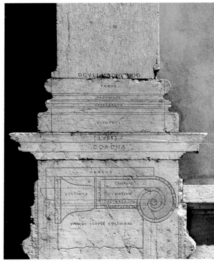

Figure 1 (opposite page): Attic and Asiatic Ionic Bases, Claude Perrault, *Les dix livres d'architecture de Vitruve* (Paris: Coignard, 1673).

Figure 2 (above): Asiatic Ionic base, Temple of Athena Polias at Priene by Pytheos (from the reconstructed bay at the Pergamon Museum, Berlin).

Figure 3 (far left): Cortile of the Palazzo Farnese, Caprarola by Vignola.

Figure 4 (left): Detail of the façade of the Casa Bertani, Mantua.

Despite the enthusiastic endorsement by Vignola, Vitruvius' Asiatic Ionic base did not gain much popularity in practice, even though a number of other sixteenth- and seventeenth-century theorists embraced it. Giovan Battista Bertani, the commentator on Vitruvius famous for a tortured attempt to interpret the problematic *scamilli impares* (unequal steps), included it in the masonry diagrams of the ionic order which he placed on the façade of his house in Mantua [FIGURE 4]. More significantly Claude Perrault adopted it in his *Ordonnance,* but noted that it partook of "something of the bizarre" and admitted that "it is no surprise that it was rejected by the ancients."

One might have thought that rehabilitation could be at hand when the first archaeological example of the Asiatic base was published in the eighteenth century: Pytheos' Temple of Athena Polias which appeared in the Dilettanti Society's *Ionian Antiquities* of 1769. However the drawings were erroneous, grossly exaggerating the upper torus and making the base appear even more ill-proportioned than previously thought. When the corrected profile was finally substituted it was already too late, the Asiatic base had failed to earn its place in the canon and had become a mere footnote to the classical tradition.

The point of this excursus into the obscure world of Vitruvian exegesis is to demonstrate that the classical canon is not unchanging like a holy writ but is customary and relative, building continuously on what has gone before in order to address contemporary issues and concerns. It is crucial for us to appreciate the way in which it has advanced in the past so that it can again develop in the future. The ever evolving minutiae of the orders are what give them their character and individuality, and make them unique from place to place, and from time to time. This ninth volume of *The Classicist* shows the extraordinary progress that is being made by the modern classical movement both in recovering the whole richness of the tradition and in taking it forward to new heights. The subtleties and nuances which once engaged Raphael and Bramante engage us once again. —RTJ

Schinkel's *Entwürfe zu städtischen Wohngebäuden*

LIVING *ALL'ANTICA* IN THE NEW BOURGEOIS CITY[1]

By Jean-François Lejeune

From 1819 until his death in 1841, Karl Friedrich Schinkel published his own work in a series of periodical portfolios entitled the *Sammlung architektonischer Entwürfe* (Collection of Architectural Projects). Almost all of the schemes included were of a public, religious, or princely nature, with the notable exception of a group of five projects for urban houses for Berlin (*Entwürfe zu städtischen Wohngebäuden*), which appeared in 1826.[2] The number of plates alone—ten—suggests how important Schinkel must have considered these projects within his vision of the architecture of the city. Although his official responsibilities in the Prussian Ober-baudeputation did not allow him to devote much time to private construction, he could not but be mindful of the burgeoning demographic needs of the growing city—Berlin expanded from 200,000 residents in 1820 to 330,000 in 1840, a trend which translated into the construction of about one hundred multi-storey houses per year [FIGURE 2].[3] Likewise he must have been aware of the changes in lifestyle that accompanied this growth for the well-to-do urban classes.

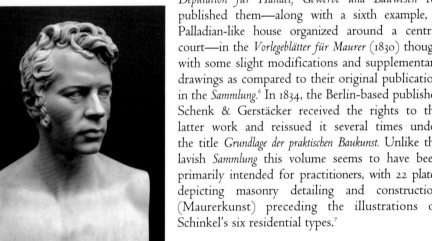

The five projects can be divided into two distinct typologies: The first, consisting of Houses I and V (plates 62-63 and 71-72) [FIGURES 9, 10, 12, AND 13], are detached buildings aligned on the street, surrounded by a garden on three sides to provide the delights of the countryside within the city proper. They are examples of the new type of houses that appeared on the fringes of major European capitals at the beginning of the nineteenth century. The second type, Houses II, III, and IV, are more traditional urban buildings, which share a party wall with their neighbors on either side. House III (plates 67-68) [FIGURES 14 AND 15], depicted on a tight site surrounded by dense buildings, is a U-shaped reinterpretation of the Pompeian house around a colonnaded atrium; Houses II and IV (plates 64-65 and 69-70) [FIGURES 23-26] are set on narrow lots and organized around bright courtyards in order to provide the best compromise between urban

density and requirements for privacy, light, and functionality. Sandwiched between the plates for Houses II and III, Schinkel inserted another unrealized project: a summer house (Lusthaus) on a lakefront in Potsdam.[4] None of the five urban house projects were built, though Schinkel's Feilner House of 1828 (separately published on plates 113-114 in 1831) shared a common typology with Houses II and IV.

According to Georg Peschken, Schinkel published the designs for these urban houses himself in the *Sammlung* because publication by the state would have taken too long.[5] Four years later, the *Technisches Deputation für Handel, Gewerbe und Bauwesen* re-published them—along with a sixth example, a Palladian-like house organized around a central court—in the *Vorlegeblätter für Maurer* (1830) though with some slight modifications and supplementary drawings as compared to their original publication in the *Sammlung*.[6] In 1834, the Berlin-based publisher Schenk & Gerstäcker received the rights to the latter work and reissued it several times under the title *Grundlage der praktischen Baukunst.* Unlike the lavish *Sammlung* this volume seems to have been primarily intended for practitioners, with 22 plates depicting masonry detailing and construction (Maurerkunst) preceding the illustrations of Schinkel's six residential types.[7]

THE SAMMLUNG AS AN URBAN TREATISE: THE INDIVIDUAL AND THE CITY

Following the introduction of the new Prussian Land Law (Allgemeine Preußische Landrecht) in 1794, individual property rights were increasingly protected and recognized in the state: "As a rule every property owner is authorized to occupy his land property

---

Opposite: Eduard Gaertner, Detail from *Panorama of Berlin*, 1832-6.

Figure 1 (above): Bust of Schinkel by Christian Friedrich Tieck. Photograph by Giopuo.

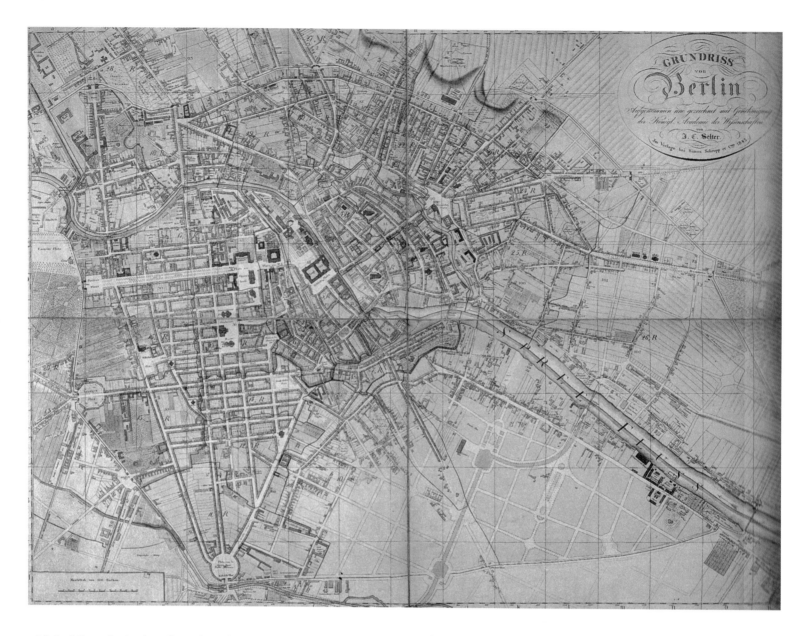

with buildings; he is also allowed to alter his buildings."[8] As a public official, Schinkel was particularly well-placed to comprehend the impact of the new and freer play of economic forces in planning the city, and it is probably within this context that one must understand and analyze the projects for the five urban houses. As Paul Ortwin Rave wrote, "the projects were in no way conceived for pedagogical or academic reasons, nor were they planned 'in the air'." On the contrary, "they resulted from specific needs and were clearly based upon the conditions of the lots."[9] We do not know where the programs for the five houses originated, but it is obvious that the projects, for the first time in an architectural treatise, were being studied and represented within the context of the new property rights for individuals. Although Rave focused on the specificity of the site conditions as illustrating particular cases, it is also possible to interpret Schinkel's site-specific

projects in a more theoretical way as an attempt to outline a potential typology of the bourgeois house in the emerging modern city. Wolfgang Büchel discusses the *Sammlung* as "a public podium" where the "possible" can be shared and explained, in other words, "as a discussion forum established by Schinkel to reach not only a specialized public but also a critical one, and to impart knowledge of what is possible for every project."[10] At the same time, he was "the inventor of a new and singularly successful format of promotion, the *oeuvre complète*."[11]

Figure 2 (above): J. C. Selter, Map of Berlin, 1843.

Figure 3 (opposite top): Sir John Soane's House, 13 Lincoln's Inn Fields, London.

Figure 4 (opposite bottom): Schinkel, Redern Palace, Berlin. Photograph c. 1900.

With the *Sammlung architektonischer Entwürfe* Schinkel put forth a new type of corpus, which, like sections of his fragmentary and unpublished *Lehrbuch*, intertwines theory and practice or, rather, *practice seen as theory* within the context of the new industrial city.[12] The period of ideal sites and utopian cities organized according to the geometrical rules of Renaissance perspective can be seen to have passed (although new life would be breathed into those concepts with the ascent of powerful nation states and their representative capital cities at the end of the nineteenth century). From this perspective, Schinkel was perhaps the first architect to set aside the acontextual presentation of both public and private works as seen in the treatises of Andrea Palladio, Claude-Nicolas Ledoux or Jean-Nicolas-Louis Durand, and to systematically present architectural works in their real urban and legal context. To do so he systematically drew "in situ" perspectives of his buildings, described in details their programmatic and legal conditions, and also included numerous plans for more extensive urban intervention. In Schinkel's city the context interacts with the architecture and helps mold and interpret it. The ideal solution is the one that fits the site as it is or as it can be reasonably modified to permit the project—such as for the Bauakademie (plate 116), the Schauspielhaus (plates 7, 11, 14), or the Friedrichswerderkirche (plate 85). Schinkel's unique mode of graphic presentation uses a type of "graphic redundancy" to pursue "a didactic goal, namely to communicate the corporeality of the architecture... and to make evident the reality of the building in relation to its site."[13] When Palladio presented the Palazzo Thiene and other projects in the heart of Vicenza, he published them as he had planned them—complete and without context—and not as he built them—incomplete and modified according to the urban circumstances.

Schinkel chose to represent two of the five urban house projects in the context of their streets: Houses III and V. This decision was deliberately taken to make these two highly individualistic houses stand out from their more conventional neighbors on the street. Schinkel's strategy here could be compared to John Soane's 1812 design for the façade of his own house at 13 Lincoln's Inn Fields [FIGURE 3]. Soane's astonishing addition of a projecting frontispiece was found by some contemporaries to be "a palpable eyesore" but Soane justified it "in terms of the picturesque, envisaging it as an eye-catcher in the center of the uniform building of the north side of Lincoln's Inn Fields."[14]

Schinkel took this individualistic approach further in 1828 with his renovation proposal for the Redern Palace at Pariser Platz (plate 126) [FIGURE 4]. His asymmetrical Renaissance-style project was so unusual that it was transferred to the highest authorities of the Oberbaudeputation for an opinion on "whether the proposed building would diminish or enhance the beauty of the whole square and the entrance to Unter den Linden."[15] The latter strongly criticized Schinkel's proposal and the architect was forced to issue a response: "The stylistic uniformity of residences has become quite universal in modern times, and Berlin is being subjected to the same plight; there is something unpleasant in these regular arrangements, even when they are made up of good architecture. Everyone feels how contrived it is to force upon owners of very different professions and financial means, and even more so with contrasting individual philosophies of life, such

a similar form of housing."[16] Alluding to the irregularity of his proposal, he defended the appropriateness of creating variations in the profile of the street: "... it would be desirable for the beautification of a city to see such things more often, because too straight an alignment of identical houses along a street creates a very tiring impression; the identity and effect of the architecture of the streets could best be achieved through allowing some parts of buildings with interesting forms to stand out and project out of the regular arrangement."[17] Here, in counterpoint to the concept of Baroque unity and order, Schinkel put forth "the architectonic self-representation of the individual, who longs to express his individuality within the public space of the city."[18]

While clearly concerned with external representation, Schinkel did not neglect internal disposition: his house projects demonstrate great care for the comfort of the residents, with a particular emphasis on clear circulation systems. Schinkel's use of long horizontal corridors breaks with the palatial tradition of room to room movement; the interior distribution of the rooms is functionalized, going along with a "privatization" of the rooms (every room is clearly labeled "his" or "her" room, etc.); and, finally, the concerns for quality and quantity of light in a dense urban fabric are manifest in his solution for the angle room of the courtyard (the so-called "Berlin room") as seen in House IV and the Feilner House.

The emphasis on "practicality" and "economy" in the descriptions of these house projects reflected a major shift in values from those of the aristocracy to the bourgeoisie. The *Sammlung* clearly reflects the transformation of Berlin into a city of "flâneurs" where commerce and business predominate in the organization and perception of urban life. Schinkel presents his architecture and the city as seen by a regular spectator or pedestrian in movement rather than in a static frontal view as was the case in most previous architectural treatises.[19] Correspondingly,

Schinkel's interest in commercial life and structures set him quite apart from most treatise authors before him. It also reflected the particular condition of Berlin where industrial structures such as the Packhof (Arsenal) neighbored the palace, the Altes Museum, and other royal structures. His Kaufhaus (Department Store) project would have introduced a large U-shaped structure facing Unter den Linden [Figure 5], with retail stores and residential units for artisans and store-owners on two independent levels around a central planted garden—yet another expression of Schinkel's vision of a new bourgeois society "as a politically motivated urban planner ... who not only cared for the aesthetic image of the city, but was equally motivated by the particular social conditions of Berlin."[20] A similar principle guided the Bauakademie project with the pragmatic inclusion of retail spaces all around the ground floor of the freestanding structure with the offices of the Oberbaudeputation and an apartment for Schinkel himself on the upper floors [Figure 6]. As regards the house projects, it must be noted that four of the proposed residential types—three urban (Houses II, III, IV) and one suburban (House V)—included commercial or business-related uses in the tradition of the antique and medieval house. Some of them, like Houses II and IV, even made provision for a diversity of apartment types.

In the 1830s, Schinkel and Peter Joseph Lenné were involved in the master-planning of the large-scale district of Luisenstadt, setting up an urban model that would endure, with all its merits and defects, until World War II [Figure 7]. They were well aware of the burgeoning problems of the metropolis, especially the lack of public parks and the increasing distances between residences, workplaces, and the different social classes. The success of Lenné's final plan for Luisenstadt was due to his adoption of a dense, mixed-use urban fabric made up of large blocks and an extensive network of green spaces and public buildings.[21]

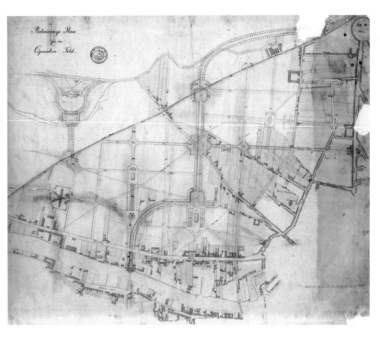

In 1862, the Prussian urban planner, James Hobrecht, who had experienced the strict "separation of classes" in neighborhoods in England explained why it was preferable for the growing city of Berlin to develop along different lines rather than following the English practice of "zoning:"

> It is known that our way of life stands on an opposite principle to that of the English way of living. In the so-called Mietshaus (apartment building) there is on the first floor a flat for a rent of 500 taler; on the ground floor and on the second floor there are two flats each for 200 taler; on the third there are two flats each for 150 taler; on the fourth, three flats each costing 100 taler; in the cellar, the garret, the rear courtyard building, or in similar spaces, there are several other units rented for 50 taler. In English towns, situated close together, there are villas and single houses of the wealthy classes to be found in the western areas and elsewhere, while in the other districts of the town, the houses of the poorer population are to be found, put together in groups according to the fortunes of the owners… Who wants to doubt that the reserved areas of the wealthy classes and their houses offer enough comfort, but who can close his eyes to the fact that the poorer classes lose many benefits. Not 'seclusion' but 'integration' seems to me requisite for ethical and therefore political reasons.[22]

For Hobrecht, the coexistence of classes and professions, the frequenting of similar schools and gymnasia raised social consciousness and responsibility. In contrast, the English model separated the groups as "working-class districts," were entered only by "the policeman and the writer seeking sensation." The middle and high classes shied away, they shuddered at "the evil and the crime seen everywhere as a companion of poverty which is left to its fate." The lady "returns home in order not to witness this horrible area again and salves her soul by paying money destined for a pauper-commission."[23]

Figure 5 (opposite): Schinkel, Project for Kaufhaus, Unter den Linden, Berlin.

Figure 6 (top left): Schinkel, Bauakademie, Berlin. Oil painting by Eduard Gaertner, 1868.

Figure 7 (top right): Peter Joseph Lenné, Plan for Luisenstadt, Berlin.

Figure 8 (above): John Wood the Elder, The Circus, Bath (1754-68). Photograph by grahamc99.

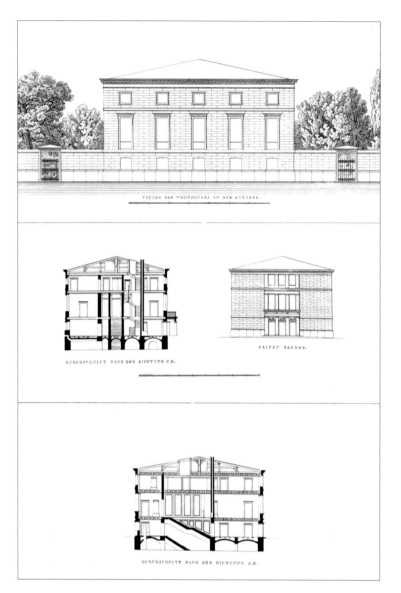

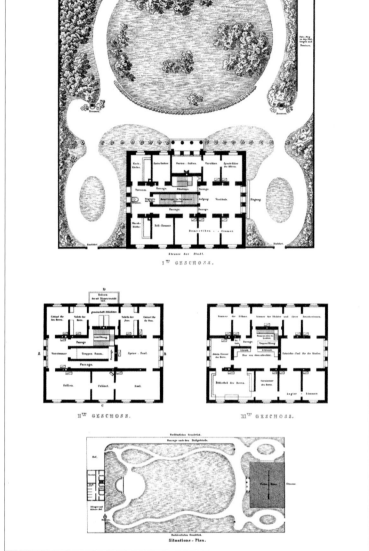

Figure 9 (top left): House I, plate 62 of the *Sammlung.*

Figure 10 (top right): House I, plate 63 of the *Sammlung.*

Figure 11 (right): Schinkel, Schauspielhaus, Berlin. Photograph by Joseph A.

Schinkel's five projects for urban houses in Berlin reflect a similar vision of a bourgeois city where the rich would reside in close proximity to lower classes, often living under the same roof. Private houses would also continue, whenever possible, to function as places of business for the owner or include rental spaces for dwelling or commerce.[24]

URBAN CORE AND SUBURBAN FRINGES

For a modern day visitor to Berlin, it is hard to comprehend the context within which Schinkel developed his residential proposals.[25] Until the Wars of Liberation of 1813-14, house construction within the city was primarily implemented at the King's initiative and followed the Baroque concept of *Immediatebauten* (literally "instant constructions")— a kind of serial and party-wall construction developed in relation to the concept of "embellishment of the city" and the highly regulated façade of which served as primary definer of the architecture.[26] They were generally two-stories high, with some usable space in the roof and a ground floor that often accommodated shops or workrooms; a passage typically led into a courtyard where all production activities took place. Berlin like most cities in the eighteenth century followed the principles of the absolutist planning where strict aesthetic regulations were imposed on individual properties by the ruler, or, in cities like London by the developer. In Berlin, like in London, Bath, Karlsruhe, Nancy, or Turin, the single-house rarely appeared as such [FIGURE 8]. In Friedrichstadt for instance, the private house materialized "as a section, as a piece of a larger whole under a single roof," abandoning its individuality for the benefit or the control of the whole. "The whole street as a single house" could therefore be stated as the leading motto of the period.[27]

This morphology, which originated in seventeenth-century practice, found theoretical support in Marc Antoine Laugier's *Essai sur l'architecture*: "If one wants a well-built town the façades of houses must not be left to the whim of private persons. Every part that faces the street must be determined and governed by public authority according to the design which will be laid down for the whole street."[28] Unity and proportion were the principles of Baroque and, later, neoclassical street design.[29] In the particular case of Absolutist Berlin, houses were usually built on the immediate order of the King for people in trade or commerce who were not empowered to build a house for themselves.[30] David Leatherbarrow has argued that the homogeneous architecture of Friedrichstadt went beyond the esthetic conception of the city but functioned practically as a symbol of toleration: "The city prospered because its citizens feared neither for their lives nor their property. Each citizen patiently tolerated his neighbors no matter how irregular each one's way of life was. . . . Because the buildings of Friedrichstadt tolerated one another by keeping their distinguishing characteristics from public view, this 'style' reduced civil discord and the aggravation of opposite sentiments in the city."[31]

With the elaboration of the concept of the picturesque in England and the rise of romanticism in Germany, such a homogeneous vision of residential architecture was increasingly put into question. Wolfgang von Goethe and Johann Gottlieb Fichte, among others, were definitive influences on Schinkel's intellectual development and they helped him discover the "characteristic of the self."[32] Unsurprisingly, Schinkel later followed Goethe in taking a stand against the "lack of character and style…which many new buildings suffer"[33] and regularly decried the "regularity, monotony and excessive resemblance" of Baroque street architecture, which not only did not express the functional content of the buildings but created excessive uniformity at a time of increasing individualism.[34] During his travels to Paris and England, he saw in neo-classical Paris or London the early-nineteenth-century product of mass-housing: "Often one sees long rows of palaces which are but private houses pushed all together, three or four windows wide, to which one has given a global architectural form."[35] Interestingly, Laugier himself had guarded against excessive monotony stating: "Long streets where all houses seem to be one single building, because one has observed a rigorous symmetrical scheme, are a thoroughly boring sight. It is there-fore necessary that in the same street the façades are free of this ugly uniformity."[36] Yet his advice to look for "variation in design" continued to imply collective control over sections of streets, a far cry from the picturesque expression of the individual.[37] One of Schinkel's later sketches for the elaborate project designed in 1835 for a Prince's Residence showcases the "vernacular" fabric of the avenue leading to the Palace's main gate. There is no great alignment "à la rue de Rivoli," but rather a varied, almost chaotic assemblage of individual houses— perhaps a graphic critique of the impersonality of "mass-housing" as he experienced it in neoclassical Paris or London.[38]

For Schinkel, the fundamental principle of any construction was "the best possible representation of the ideal of functionality," meaning its character, its individuality, its non-repeatability, and everything that allowed it to break away from the Baroque street regularity.[39] Schinkel, in this author's view, was not so much concerned with a compositional system in the manner of Jean-Nicolas-Louis Durand, but departed from the Baroque fusion of types behind the façade as a homogenizing screen in order to create a more complex typology of architecture. Accordingly, the housing types discussed in this essay can be viewed as a challenging attempt to rediscover the physical and symbolic corporeality of the house in the context of the new metropolis.[40] Moreover, if Houses II, III and IV were designed for relatively tight urban sites within the tradi-tional structure of the city, his Houses I and V were, on the other hand, designed for large and deep garden plots likely to be located on the new fringes of the developing bourgeois city.

It was in Paris and Versailles during the second half of the seventeenth century that a new suburban building type appeared, which was made up of a main house with no setback from the street but surrounded on three sides by walls and gardens.[41] This new type was adopted in Germany during the eighteenth century, located on access roads and first rings of expansion in cities like Frankfurt or as a constituent type of the Residenz Neustadt fabric in Darmstadt, Ludwigsburg, Nymphenburg-Munich, and Potsdam, the summer residence of Prussian rulers. In Berlin it appeared more sporadically, along the Tiergarten or along the Chaussée near the Oranienburg Tor.[42] Located on smaller plots of land and of relatively small size if compared with former aristocratic residences outside of the city limits, this new type of house appealed increasingly to the new class of wealthy nineteenth-century citizens. In his essay "The Picturesque

Bourgeois House at the Edge of the Neoclassical City" Philippe Gresset has discussed the appearance of new "suburbs of the bourgeois which claimed to be able simultaneously to enjoy the advantages of both the city and the countryside in dwellings of relatively modest size."[43] Schinkel used almost the same words to describe House V and what could be considered a "romantic desire" to combine city and country life in a single type close to the heart of the city.[44] This nascent aspiration of the bourgeoisie was an undeniable element of urban modernity; it slowly reshaped Berlin at the same time as the first smokestacks of the Borsig Locomotive factory would rise in the landscape to the north of the Spreebogen.

Schinkel was cognizant of this new planning context and was clearly interested to find a solution specific to Berlin for the type (Houses I and V). While Ludwig Persius, his former student and collaborator, devised an Italianate picturesque landscape for his houses in Potsdam in the late 1830s and 1840s, Schinkel's projects were in complete continuity with the classical tradition of the urban center. Moreover, whereas in English, French, and many German residences, the new suburban type was primarily residential, Schinkel's houses integrated an unusual mix of residential and commercial/business functions, which paralleled his own vision of the development of Berlin's new extension to the East, the Köpenicker Field, and reflected his overall vision of the future of Berlin as Peter Beuth's "Fabrikstadt," a modern capitalist city of integrated business and residence.[45]

LIVING ALL'ANTICA: THE FIVE PROJECTS FOR URBAN HOUSES
Schinkel's types had no real antecedents in the context of Berlin and he presented them as specific solutions to contemporary problems. Yet, in spite of their important differences in program, plans, sections, and lot sizes, Schinkel's five projects for urban houses share a common vision of urban living that supersedes all practical and economic considerations. In a certain sense, what Schinkel was looking for was a modern way for the bourgeois family to "live all'antica" in the developing industrial city.[46] This can be understood more precisely through the two typological categories into which we have divided the five houses: Houses I and V as new types of the suburban villa, and Houses II, III, and IV as courtyard houses for the urban core. All three in the latter category are organized around a well-lighted and primarily residential courtyard that could be seen as a metropolitan equivalent of the cortile of a Renaissance palace or the peristyle court of a Roman domus. Let us now examine each of the types independently.

HOUSE I
Plates 62 and 63 of the Sammlung [FIGURES 9 AND 10] illustrate the "Project for the residence of a wealthy man in Berlin, who occupies and lives in the house by himself with his family, and for that reason has selected a garden-like plot 200-feet-long along the street and 490-feet-deep between two adjacent lots."[47] The five-bay urban villa has no entrance fronting the street yet is designed as an urban house with no setback from the alignment line. Most remarkable is the division of the rectangular plan in three equal, parallel parts. The first row of rooms facing the street has services on the ground floor, salons and other public rooms upstairs, and the private rooms of the owner at the top. The second

row of rooms, at the back facing the garden, contains more services on the ground floor, the owners' bedrooms on the second floor with the master bedroom opening onto a balcony over the portico, and the childrens' bedrooms on the top floor. In-between, Schinkel inserts a wide, eighty-foot-long hallway that serves as a large vestibule with a straight staircase leading to the second floor. There, two passages lead to the private staircase and to the central dining room; on the third floor, the central bay, lit by a large skylight, becomes a schoolroom for children and the owners' workrooms. The façades reflect the unusual organization. To the neoclassical street front Schinkel opposes a more "modern" side façade: the blank walls correspond to the two rows of rooms and the fully-glazed central section provides ample light to the core of the house. Its three bays of superimposed windows framed by simple rectangular pilasters clearly appear as a residential application of the composition system adopted by Schinkel for the lateral sections and side facades at the Schauspielhaus in Berlin (1821) [FIGURE 11].[48] For the later republication of this house (plates 27 and 28 in the Grundlage der praktischen Baukunst), Schinkel left the plans and sections unchanged but narrowed the width of the lot and drew a detail of the street façade showing the adjacent building.

HOUSE V
At the urban level, the last house in the series (plates 71-72) [FIGURES 12-13], is morphologically similar to House I. Detached and placed at the center of a large lot located "in a lively part of the city," it was planned for a well-to-do businessman "whose business is so confined to the city, that, even in the summer, it does not allow him to live in the countryside." The very large site—238-feet-long along the street and 462-feet-deep—allows the owner to build "a comfortable residence in such a way that it substitutes, to some degree, for a house built in the countryside."[49] The house is not only surrounded by its own private park, but it directly enjoys the liveliness of the street, realizing, like House I, the synthesis between urban and rural. Schinkel makes clear that both the quiet of the garden and the life of the street are key elements of a project that also needs rental space to be economically feasible. As a result he proposes a remarkable synthesis of utility and function—mixing industry and comfort. The three structures—two on the edges of the site in party wall conditions and one larger one isolated at the center—are built on the street line and contain large shops, storage rooms, and other service spaces on the first floor with large windows down to the ground. Colonnades connect the main building to the accessory buildings on either side creating an unusual series of alternating high and low interconnected volumes.[50] As we have already noted, Schinkel's attempt to combine new suburban aspirations with the continuity of the mixed-use structure of the city has no equivalent in other European capitals. Here, each side building contains an apartment for the store owners on the second floor while the central house contains not only a full ground floor for business and storage but also two potentially rentable apartments on the third floor. To facilitate such a mix of functions, the central pavilion is designed as a courtyard house with a glass-roofed metal staircase in its center. At the same time as he reduces or eliminates the emphasis on a large central salon or living room familiar from the

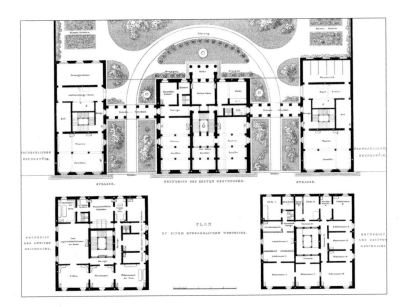

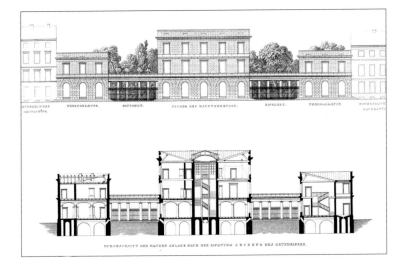

HOUSE III: THE "POMPEIAN"

"In big cities, it is often a challenge to design houses on tight sites. Frequently, adjacent tall buildings generate dark places and make it difficult for the architect to create pleasant dwellings, thus forcing him to deviate completely from traditional solutions."[52] This is how Schinkel initiates his description of House III, the "Pompeian" residence (plates 67-68) [FIGURES 14-15]. He writes that, because of the constricted lot (100 x 104.5 feet with high buildings on three sides) and issues of lighting, he had to reverse the location of the courtyard and open it up to the front, an innovative solution that organizes the house around a sort of urban atrium open to the street and which provides light for the entire house. In spite of Schinkel's functional arguments it is easy to figure out that his solution was essentially a typological and architectonic one: a courtyard of 50 feet by 50 feet (as shown in the plan) would have been very generous at the back of the lot and capable of providing good lighting while allowing the main living rooms direct access to the street. To some extent Schinkel's project is related to the typology of the Parisian *hôtel particulier* but unlike its French counterpart the court is not accessible to horses and carriages. It is instead a pedestrian-oriented realm, the world of a rich bourgeois family trying to merge *otium* and *negotium* in a Roman-like house at the heart of Berlin and the closest example of an *"all'antica* living" strategy in Schinkel's residential work.[53]

The plans and sections are ingenious and provide a unique spatial experience where circulation and movement are paramount and create an experimental *promenade architecturale.* The ground floor is primarily reserved for business and domestic activities and as such recalls the front section of the House of the Faun in Pompeii: "the inclusion of small shops makes it profitable and gives the whole a most friendly character."[54] A small hallway with shops on the sides opens into an open court decorated with vases, flowers, and antique statues: "The downstairs courtyard is enclosed and surrounded by columns, making the entrance appear like an antique atrium."[55] On the second floor, a continuous terrace surrounds the void of the atrium and a flowered pergola connects both wings along the street front. The family visitor or the resident must pass through the Doric atrium to enter a hallway leading to the back wall where two straight staircases ascend to the second floor, casually distributing the house into two symmetrical parts. Access to the third floor is gained via two circular staircases that rise from the ground floor in the middle of each wing. In section, Schinkel completes this bold *parti* with a glazed roof that floods the formal stairs with light and also illuminates the third floor catwalk. As in Pompeii, the main living rooms are removed from the street by being pushed behind the atrium, and, taking the analogy further, the grand salon is placed like a tablinium on the central axis [FIGURE 16]. The axiality of its placement

great eighteenth-century traditions of France and England, Schinkel inventively addresses new ways of living for this new class of urban citizens.[51]

It is worth noting, however, that in the later republication of this type (Plates 23-26 of the *Grundlage der praktischen Baukunst*), Schinkel made significant modifications which diminish somewhat the functional inventiveness of the house. Leaving the central building unchanged, he reduced both the depth and the width of the lateral structures (in the updated description he indicates a width of only 200 feet for the lot). As a result, they do not reach the street edge and are separated from it by a strip of garden; moreover, they lose their business-based uses and are labeled as a house for the gardener (left) and stables (right). Interestingly, Schinkel no longer shows the complete street elevation and instead illustrates the garden façade and two elegant perspectives of the vaulted atrium-like entry vestibule and the library on the second floor.

is reinforced by terminating the room with a curved rear wall, which frames a fitted sofa on an elevated platform. From this vantage point, set at the very back of the house, the distance to the street puts the city into a deliberate perspective, in the same way as Schinkel choreographed the view of the garden at the Neuer Pavillon (Gartensaal) at Charlottenburg from the blue sofa.[56]

Of exquisite proportions but unfortunately unrealized, Schinkel's atrium was his sole attempt at introducing in the fabric of the city the concept of the *Außenwohnraum* (outdoor living space) with which he was experimenting in Potsdam at the very same time.[57] The atrium became a rare and essentially suburban idea, as can be seen from the Roman Baths at the Gardener's House of Schoß Charlottenhof or the Atrium of the Paradiesgärtlein built by Friedrich Ludwig Persius at Sanssouci in 1841-44 [FIGURES 17-18]. The latter was an architectonic fragment in the garden exemplifying Karl Boetticher's "Greek manner"

and recalling Aloys Hirt's reconstruction of the Roman House in *Die Geschichte der Baukunst bei den Alten* (Berlin, 1827).[58] Another rare manifestation of this theme was the *Pompeianum* built by Friedrich von Gärtner in Aschaffenburg (1842-43) for Louis I of Bavaria; conceived as a reconstruction of the Castor and Pollux House in Pompeii it was dramatically centered on an open atrium [FIGURE 19]. At the urban scale of Berlin, Schinkel's concept of the front atrium had virtually no follow-up, although it is possible to see it as a precedent for the recessed courtyards of Paul Mebes' Beamten-Wohnungs-Verein at Schöneberg (1906-07) and Peter Behrens' workers housing at Henningsdorf for the AEG (1910-11)—a multi-family typology that was intensely used until the late 1930s.[59] Another suburban example is the entry atrium of Haus Wiegand in Berlin-Dahlem, the house that Peter Behrens designed in 1911-12 for the archeologist and director of the Department of Antiquity at the Berlin Museum, Theodor Wiegand

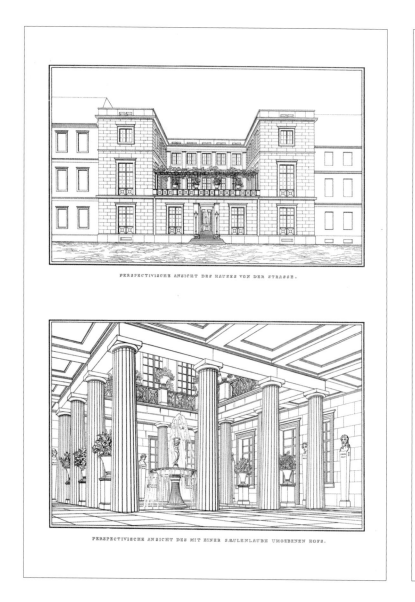

PERSPECTIVISCHE ANSICHT DES HAUSES VON DER STRASSE.

PERSPECTIVISCHE ANSICHT DES MIT EINER SÄULENLAUBE UMGEBENEN HOFS.

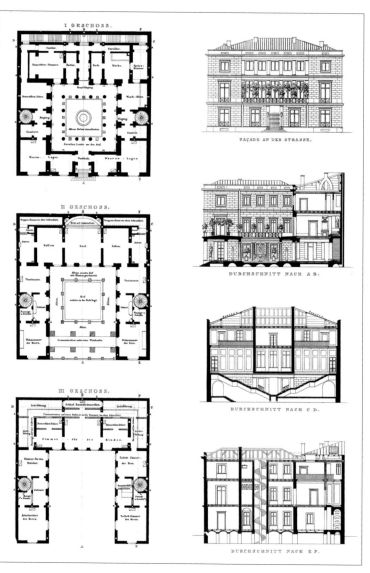

[FIGURE 20-21]. On a large lot in the planned suburb of Dahlem, Behrens designed, like Schinkel, an urban house in the garden. Although the main body is somewhat recessed, the square entrance atrium—in fact an open-air room covered with a coffered ceiling made up of glass bricks—is aligned with the edge of the sidewalk, a marked departure from other houses in the neighborhood. The Doric order and the proportions are clearly reminiscent of Schinkel's project, but according to Wiegand its source was the peristyle of House 33 in Priene, dating from the Hellenistic period. As for the rest of the house, its clever balance of symmetry and asymmetry, the use of a pergola and a back pavilion, as well as the water garden show clear affinities with Schloß Charlottenhof in Potsdam.[60]

Schinkel's insertion of the unbuilt Lusthaus (summer house, plate 66) at the center of the houses' portfolio, immediately before the Pompeian house, may appear at first incongruous [FIGURE 22]. Yet, what is interesting in the succession of these two projects is the possible reading of the Lusthaus as the "inversion" of the Pompeian house. The Lusthaus is symmetrical although Schinkel's perspective reveals the asymmetry of the landscape around it. Entry is by water or through the fenced garden, both of which involve a sophisticated sequence of movement along the *promenade architecturale* that reveals the symmetrical house through carefully framed picturesque snapshots. The high living room, ventilated by small clerestory windows, corresponds to the atrium of the Berlin house. To the projecting bedroom wings the Lusthaus responds with open loggias. The same antique character of statues and Capri-like pergolas present in the "Pompeian" House III permeates the general atmosphere. Although one is a party-wall structure and the other an isolated villa along one of the lakes in Potsdam, they both express a modern interpretation of antiquity. Typological invention goes hand in hand with programmatic wit; for instance, the idea of a country house shared by four owners with four individual reading rooms in connection with the great salon and its two candelabra.

House II

Of the three "party-wall" projects, House II shows the most complex structure (plates 64-65) [FIGURE 23-24]. The task was to design a town-house the main floor of which was the owner's apartment, whereas the courtyard level floor and the upper floor were to be rented out with two apartments per floor. All vertical circulations were independent to maintain absolute privacy. Its dimensions of 88-feet-wide by 170 feet allow the program to be arranged around a large courtyard surrounded by continuous balconies on the two upper floors—a rare type in Berlin but one that can be found in aristocratic palaces in Vienna. Like a Renaissance or Baroque palace, the court, here lowered to maintain privacy, provides another passage to access the two apartments at the rear. Its façade, traditionally articulated with drafted stucco base and piano nobile, expresses the clear division in functions. The irregular octagonal shape of the courtyard allows Schinkel to introduce on each floor four rooms organized on the diagonal and lit through the small sides of the irregular octagon—he described this solution for the bedroom with the bed in a semi-circular alcove in relation to house IV. Architecturally, the court is quite original, with its horizontal emphasis

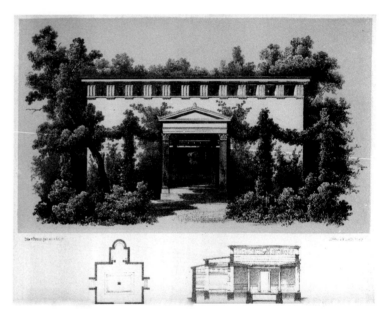

Figure 14 (opposite left): House III, plate 67 of the *Sammlung.*

Figure 15 (opposite right): House III, plate 68 of the *Sammlung.*

Figure 16 (top): View from the atrium to the tablinum of the House of the Faun, Pompeii. Photograph by Kudumomo.

Figure 17 (bottom): Friedrich Ludwig Persius, Atrium of the Paradiesgärtlein, Sanssouci, 1841-44.

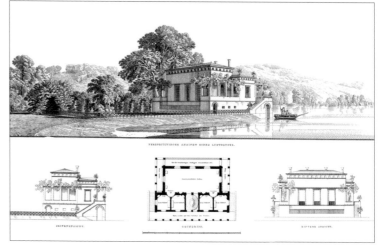

created by the long bands of metallic balconies; likewise the grouping of windows separated by squat pilasters accentuates the horizontality—another application to domestic design of the frame motif Schinkel experimented with at the Schauspielhaus in Berlin. As if the building was a real commission, Schinkel indulges in the unusually precise description of the entrance hall—an urban version of the Pavilion at Charlottenburg. The slightly vaulted ceiling, strong blue with golden yellow dividing lines, suggests an outdoor entrance, almost as an arbor, and, above the glass doors at the back, a painting of children playing on a blue background suggests the family-based domestic character of the house. The rest is an explosion of colors and senses: "The walls are in light stone color; the panels between pilasters are bordered by friezes with colored arabesques on a reddish brown background; floating figures are brilliant colored on white background; the sides of the vestibule are made of an imitation green marble; the floor is tiled in red, brown and yellow colors."[61]

HOUSE IV

A townhouse that according to Schinkel "causes many difficulties for the architect" occupies a narrow urban lot, 60 feet along the street and 167 feet in depth (plates 69-70) [FIGURES 25-26]. It is the most speculative of all types as it provides for three identical apartments, presumably to be rented. In this house more than in his other projects, Schinkel shows great attention to practical issues of modern bourgeois life. Three large and almost identical apartments occupy its footprint, yet it is easy to imagine that each plan could be split to create more housing units, thus making the presence of the rear courtyard essential. The corner of the courtyard is cut on the diagonal (as in House III and in the Feilner House) to allow for the placement of full windows in the main bedroom; the staircases are in iron and lit from above; the long distribution corridors receive light from adjacent rooms through glass doors and high windows. This brings not only light but, more poetically, substantiates "his desire to bestow a genuine 'inner life' to the dwelling."[62] Furthermore, in section and in elevation, the concept of piano nobile, still visible in Houses I and II, has disappeared. All floors have approximately the same height, a condition that Schinkel emphasized through the strongly marked floor bands and eaves line and the general gridding of the façade through bands and windows.[63]

Figure 18 (opposite bottom left): Friedrich Ludwig Persius, Atrium of the Paradiesgärtlein, Sanssouci, 1841-44.

Figure 19 (opposite top): Friedrich von Gärtner, Pompeianum, Aschaffenburg, 1842-43. Photograph by Henk van der Eijk.

Figure 20 (top left): Peter Behrens, Haus Wiegand, Berlin-Dahlem, 1911-12.

Figure 21 (left): Peter Behrens, Haus Wiegand, Berlin-Dahlem, 1911-12.

Figure 22 (opposite bottom right): Lusthaus, plate 66 of the *Sammlung.*

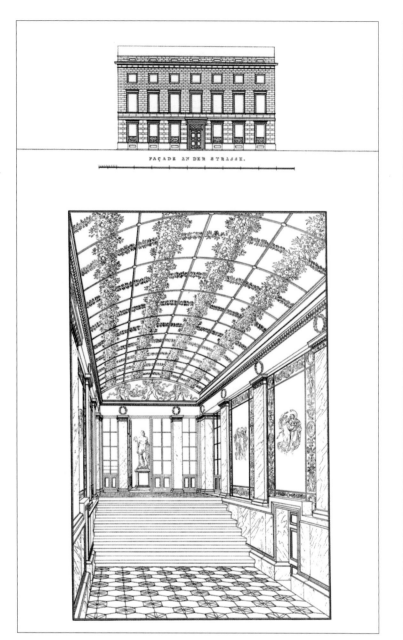

FAÇADE AN DER STRASSE.

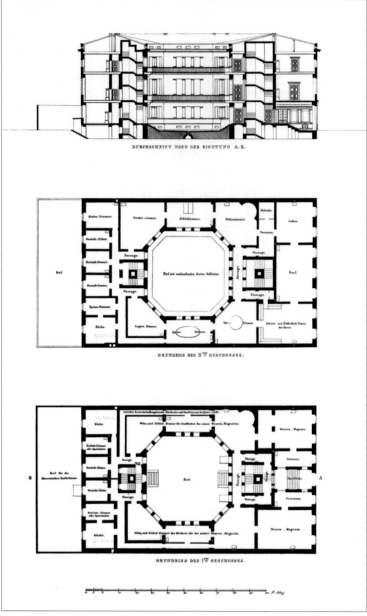

DURCHSCHNITT NACH DER RICHTUNG A.B.

GRUNDRISS DES II.ᵗᵉⁿ GESCHOSSES.

GRUNDRISS DES I.ᵗᵉⁿ GESCHOSSES.

"House VI"

A sixth house project—*Wohngebäude mit grossem Hof*—was not featured in the *Sammlung* but was published in great detail in plates 29-33 of the *Grundlage* immediately preceding the other type organized around a large courtyard, House II. For a lot 115 by 180 feet, Schinkel designed a quasi-Palladian structure arranged around a 22-meter square courtyard, the side elevations of which are tautly defined by an expressive grid of slender columns and windows [Figure 27]. The overall structure of the plan is asymmetrical with a deep front wing to house the formal rooms of the two large apartments which each occupy an entire floor. The main living rooms are placed on the central axis with one facing the street and the other the courtyard. For the latter, Schinkel creates a visual tour-de-force by framing views to the garden through the glazed loggia on the far side of the courtyard. The side wings contain children's bedrooms and other domestic spaces; they are narrow in order to keep the courtyard square. As the ground floor contains offices facing the street with two smaller apartments behind, the route to the main apartments is quite complex and spatially innovative requiring residents to take a passageway from the open entry porch to reach the staircase that rises on the outside edge of the left-hand wing.

The street façade with its emphatic ten-bay arcade framing eight tall windows and a pair of gated openings is of great interest. Curiously, even though the house is shown in plan as a traditional party-wall type

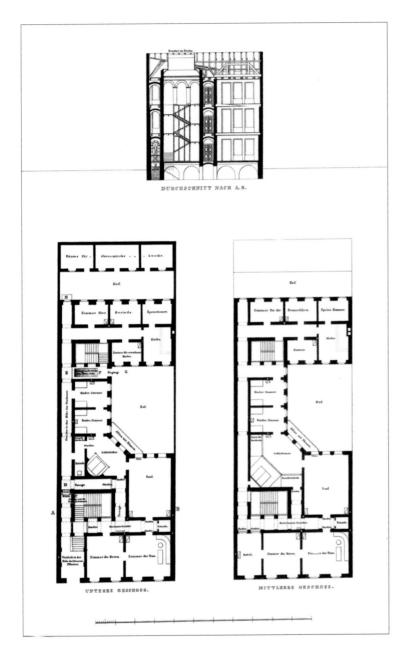

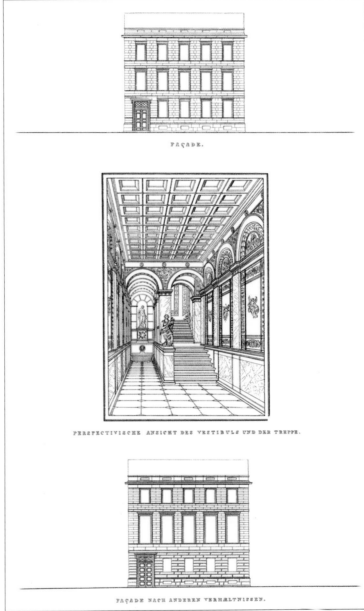

with no outside openings along its side wings, Schinkel's street elevation shows low garden walls with gates on either side of the house.[64]

THE FEILNER HOUSE

Schinkel eventually had a single opportunity to apply his ideas about the modern bourgeois residence: the house that he designed and built in 1828-29 for the stove manufacturer Tobias Christoph Feilner (plates 113-114) [FIGURE 28].[65] The project was originally designed by the master builders Hahnemann und Glatz (February 1828); it formed a double house on both sides of a central corridor linking the street to a courtyard with a single stucco façade of low windows unifying the whole. Two projecting wings enclosed the court, and their articulation

Figure 23 (opposite left): House II, plate 64 of the *Sammlung.*

Figure 24 (opposite right): House II, plate 65 of the *Sammlung.*

Figure 25 (left): House IV, plate 69 of the *Sammlung.*

Figure 26 (right): House IV, plate 70 of the *Sammlung.*

with the main volume created the usual, poorly lit "Berlin room." Soon after, Schinkel got involved with the design. He solved the "Berlin room" dilemma by cutting the angle of the back façade at forty-five degrees and drawing up a couple of well-lighted room arrangements, some of which included a half-circular niche containing the bed as seen in House IV. Schinkel's final plan (plates 113-114 in the *Sammlung*) was eventually not implemented even though the built house displayed the cut corner on the courtyard. Although beautiful and skillfully arranged to maximize all the light available, Schinkel's plans seem oddly old-fashioned with their traces of mannerist poché that dominate the subtle yet dated articulations—such unusual presence of poché space did not appear in the other house types.

Although the Feilner house was transformed repeatedly until its destruction in 1945, the main legacy of his intervention was the full brick street façade—a stunning example of "architecture parlante" as applied to a manufacturer of clay-based products [FIGURE 29].[66] The façade, organized on nine axes, follows the gridded pattern proposed by Schinkel for House IV [FIGURES 30-31]. More specifically, it was composed horizontally with terracotta bands dividing it in three equal levels, thus breaking emphatically with the tradition of the piano nobile (the first floor was somewhat higher to allow light into the basement floor). Likewise, by inserting one row of glazed violet bricks every four rows, which divided each floor into nine equal bands, Schinkel accentuated the horizontality of the elegantly proportioned façade [FIGURE 32]. The thin window frames with their decorative terracotta panels—each depicting two young men flanking a female mask—strengthened the horizontal expression while also permitting a vertical reading of the windows' axes and creating the impression of a grid. The modernity of the house was also evident in the large, quasi-industrial tripartite windows, which Schinkel designed for the obliquely cut corners of the courtyard. Beneath them he placed long terracotta panels, here describing a genius with a music instrument, perhaps, as the Berlin historian Hans Mackowsky wrote, "an obvious allusion to the musical hobbies of various family members."[67]

Overall, House IV—and the Feilner house as a built example—were the most influential of Schinkel's projects. Their impact on future practice in the emerging industrial city was large but paradoxical. On the one hand, Schinkel's hope that brick would become the material of choice in the future residential Berlin—"this sturdy, permanent, beautiful and true architecture, using burnt clay without any white-wash, will be imitated by many for the construction both of public and private buildings"—was a poignant failure.[68] As Eric Forsman has

rightly pointed out, he himself was not quite ready, nor was the Berlin society at large, for a full use of the material and the aesthetics it suggested.[69] Not brick, but thick and quality stucco became the symbol of bourgeois status and pretension. Mackowsky mentions but one instance of its residential use and one had to wait to the beginning of the twentieth century to see it resurface, in full or in part, in the architecture of Hermann Muthesius, Paul Mebes, Alfred Messel, and Bruno Taut. On the other hand, the sobriety of Schinkel's gridded façade design provided the city with a rational and efficient model for the hundreds of builders who would eventually build the new quarters of the city. Eventually what Schinkel had envisioned as an instrument of individuality and self-expression in reaction against repetitive Baroque façades was transformed into a new type of urban "neutralization," which would overwhelm Berlin as the so-called Schinkelschule (Schinkel school) of strict façades became the rule of quasi-anonymous neighborhood construction in Hobrecht's Plan, in Luisenstadt and Kreuzberg, and Prenzlauer Berg. Linked to the progressive class structuring of the city, the Schinkelschule became well suited to "the ennobling of poverty."[70] Houses everywhere followed Schinkel's sober classicism, but they were now five-stories high at least, not three. Likewise, the courtyards were often reduced in size compared to Schinkel's proposals and the quality of light which he sought was neglected in favor of increasing density. As a result, the building type became a symbol of what Werner Hegemann called "Mietskazernenstadt" (city of rental barracks) and which he would lament and vituperate against in *Das steinerne Berlin*.[71] At the same time, the long anonymous streets became the paradigm of the "street corridor" decried by Le Corbusier in the 1920s.

In conclusion, Schinkel's approach to the house in the city can be understood within the context of a reciprocity between the romantic interest for self-expression within the city and the necessary subordination of the individual to a collective vision. As Buddensieg wrote in relation to Schinkel's defense of his project for the Redern Palace, and which could easily apply to the residential projects discussed in this essay: "Schinkel expressed one of the conflicts between the individual and the collective which, on several levels, has defined the architectural history of the nineteenth and twentieth centuries."[72]

Jean-François Lejeune is a Professor in the School of Architecture at the University of Miami.

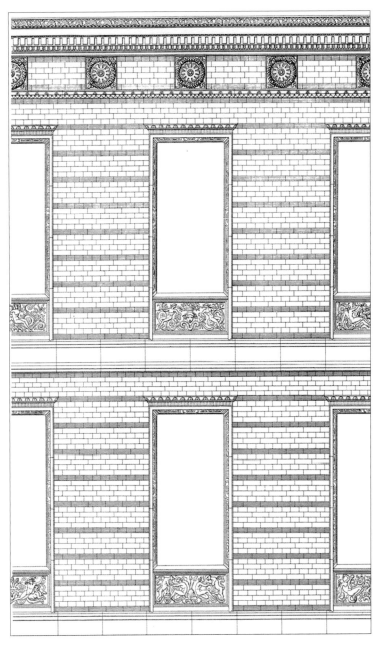

Figure 27 (opposite): House VI, plate 32 of the *Grundlage.*

Figure 28 (top left): Feilner House, detail of plate 113 of the *Sammlung.*

Figure 29 (above): Examples of the ceramic stoves produced by the Ofenfabrik Feilner.

Figure 30 (top middle): Feilner House, Berlin.

Figure 31 (top right): Detail of façade, Feilner House, Berlin.

Figure 32 (right): Feilner House, plate 114 of the *Sammlung.*

Notes

1. This essay was first presented at the international conference *Schinkel 2006* held at the Humboldt-Universität zu Berlin, July 21-24, 2006; the conference was co-organized by Humboldt-Universität zu Berlin, Vereinigung Deutscher Schinkelpreisträger e. V., and the Friends of Schinkel. The author thanks Susan Peik, Rand Carter, and Barry Bergdoll for their valuable feedback on his presentation.

2. The *Sammlung architektonischer Entwürfe* (Collection of Architectural Designs) were first published as individual issues (Hefte) from 1819 to 1840. The residential projects discussed here first appeared in Hefte # 9 and # 10 in 1826. On the history of the Sammlung, see Rand Carter, Hermann G. Pundt, et al., *Collection of Architectural Designs* (Chicago: Baluster Books Inc., 1985), pp. 10-21.

3. Paul Ortwin Rave, *Berlin: 3. Teil, Bauten für Wissenschaft, Verwaltung, Heer, Wohnbau und Denkmäler*, (Berlin: Deutscher Kunstverlag, 1962), p. 196. The only extensive treatment of Schinkel's residential projects discussed here is in Rave, *op. cit.*, pp. 196-269. In the Oberbaudeputation, Schinkel was charged with the supervision of the design of civic, royal, and religious buildings in Prussia. He was also responsible for the control of architectural preservation throughout the kingdom.

4. In the original *Hefte* of the *Sammlung*, the numbering of the houses is inconsistent, therefore the numbering of the house projects used in this essay is as set out here by the author by reference to the plate numbers in the 1866 edition of the *Sammlung*.

5. Goerd Peschken, "The Berlin 'Miethaus' and Renovation," in Doug Clelland, ed., *Berlin: An Architectural History*, AD Profile, 50 (London: AD Publ., 1983), p. 51.

6. The author thanks Katherine Pasternack for her assistance in locating the *Vorlegeblätter für Maurer*.

7. The author hopes to have an opportunity in the future to investigate further the distribution of this volume and its impact on vernacular practice.

8. Gerd Albers, "Schinkel und der Städtebau des neunzehnten Jahrhunderts" in Julius Posener, ed., *Festreden: Schinkel zu Ehren 1846-1980* (Berlin: Frölich & Kaufmann, 1981), p. 347: "In der Regel ist jeder Eigentümer seinen Grund und Boden mit Gebäuden zu besetzen oder seine Gebäude zu verändern wohl befugt."

9. Rave, *op.cit.*, pp. 240-41: "Die Entwürfe sind also keineswegs für Schul- oder Lehrzwecke erdachte und in die Luft geplante Vorbilder, sondern gehen von ganz bestimmten Wünschen aus und beruhen auf stets verschiedenen Gegebenheiten der Grundstücke."

10. Wolfgang Büchel, "Die *'Sammlung architektonischer Entwürfe'. Paradigma selten genutzter Werkkategorie,*" in his *Schinkels sieben Einmaligkeiten: Essays zu Leben, Zeit, Werk* (Hildeheim, Olms: 2010), and also published online at www.tc.umn.edu/~peikx001/B%FCchel.htm: "[als] Schinkels Podium, ein Fachpublikum und überhaupt ein kritisches zu erreichen und das Mögliche zu jedem Projekt mitzuteilen."

11. According to Kurt Forster in his presentation at the Collins/Kaufmann Forum for Modern Architectural History at Columbia University, "Architecture in Print: How Karl Friedrich Schinkel Invented the Oeuvre Complète," on Thursday, March 24, 2011.

12. Goerd Peschken, *Das architektonische Lehrbuch* (München: Deutscher Kunstverlag, 2001).

13. Büchel, *Ibid.*,: "Diese Art der graphischen Wiedergabe verfolgt auch ein didaktisches Ziel, nämlich die Körperhaftigkeit der Architektur als eine Summe der zeichnerischen Details mitzuteilen und sie eigentlich der Wirklichkeit des Gebäudes an seinem Ort zu überlassen."

14. See Helen Dorey, "12-14 Lincoln's Inn Fields," in Margaret Richardson and Mary Anne Stevens, eds., *John Soane Architect: Master of Space and Light* (Milano: Skira, 1999), p. 163.

15. Quoted by Rave, *op. cit.*, p. 229.

16. Rave, *op. cit.*, p. 230: "Die Einförmigkeit im Stil der Wohnhäuser ist ohnehin in moderner Zeit sehr allgemein geworden, und auch Berlin leidet daran; sie hat sogar [dann] etwas Unangenehmes, wenn eine vollkommen regelmäßige Anlage mit guter Architektur dabei Anwendung gefunden hat, weil jedermann sogleich das Gezwungene empfindet, den Besitzern von sehr verschiedenen Vermögens- und Berufsverhältnissen und überhaupt von verschiedener individueller Ansicht des Lebens eine so gleichartige Form der Wohnungen aufzuzwingen."

17. Rave, *op. cit.*, p. 230: "Auch bemerken wir noch gehorsamst, dass unter den hier stattfindenden Verhältnissen auch eine vortretende Architektur nach dem im Plan angenommenen Maße sehr wohl zu gestalten ist, ja dass es für Verschönerung einer Stadt zu wünschen wäre, öfter dergleichen zu sehen, weil die zu glatt in gerader Flucht fortge-
führten Häuserlinien einer Straße etwas höchst Ermüdendes erhalten und das Charakteristische und Wirksame in der Architektur der Straßen am meisten durch vortretende Teile der Gebäude, welche eine interessante Form haben, erreicht werden kann."

18. Buddensieg, *op. cit.*, p. 33. "Dem barocken Einheits- und Ordnungsbegriff setzt Schinkel die architektonische Selbstdarstellung des Individuums entgegen, die sich im privat abgesonderten Eingriff in den öffentlichen Straßenraum der Stadt zu verwirklichen sucht."

19. For an important example of this approach of presenting the city from the point of view of the ordinary spectator, see the detail of Eduard Gaertner's *Panorama* on the page immediately preceding this essay.

20. Ralf F. Hartmann, *Von königlicher Weltflucht zu bürgerlicher Staatsutopie: Karl Friedrich Schinkels Entwurf zur "Residenz eines Fürsten"* (1835). Dissertation Philipps-Universität Marburg ([s.l.], 1997), p. 291: "als politisch motivierten Stadtplaner… der nicht nur um das ästhetische Erscheinungsbild der Stadt besorgt ist, sondern ebenso die gesellschaftlichen Verhältnisse Berlins im Blick hat."

21. See Jean-François Lejeune, "Schinkel and Lenné in Berlin: From the Biedermeier Flâneur to Beuth's Großstadt," in Susan Peik, ed., *Karl Friedrich Schinkel: Aspects of his Works* (Stuttgart: Axel Menges, 2001), pp. 82-99.

22. Clelland, *op. cit.*, p. 11. From James Hobrecht, "Über die öffentliche Gesundheitspflege" (Stettin, 1868) (in English: "Concerning Public Health"), quoted from Werner Hegemann, *Das steinerne Berlin: Geschichte der größten Mietskasernenstadt*, (Berlin: Ullstein Bauwelt Fundamente, 1963; reprint of the 1930 edition), pp. 232-233.

23. Hobrecht, *ibid.* Vilified through the twentieth century for describing Berlin as a "city of barracks," the work of James Hobrecht has recently been revisited and is now discussed with less prejudice. See for instance Claus Bernet, "The 'Hobrecht Plan' (1862) and Berlin's Urban Structure," *Urban History*, 31, 3 (Cambridge: Cambridge University Press, 2004), pp. 401-419; Hans Stimman, "Hegemann's *Das steinerne Berlin: A Misunderstanding,*" in Chuck Bohl and Jean-François Lejeune, eds., *Sitte, Hegemann and the Metropolis: Modern Civic Art and International Exchanges* (London/New York: Routledge, 2009), pp. 295-305.

24. Another interesting example was Schinkel's redevelopment of Wilhelmstraße between Unter den Linden and the Schiffbauerdamm (*Sammlung*, plate 19).

25. As Hans Mackowsky writes in "Das Feilner Haus," *Häuser und Menschen im alten Berlin* (Berlin: Cassirer, 1923), p. 175: "Paradoxically, if somebody wants to gain an accurate insight into the old Berlin, he or she must start his studies in Potsdam. There, almost everything that once made the royal Prussian residence town of Berlin so attractive, but that was gradually devoured by the metropolis, is still visible together. Above all, Potsdam is the commentary on the long forgotten bourgeois existence of the erstwhile Berlin generations."

26. Mackowsky, *op. cit.*, p. 176; Peschken, *op. cit.*, p. 50.

27. For this section of the essay, the author is indebted to Tilman Buddensieg, "Straßenraum und Stadtbild in Berlin. Etappe ihrer Geschichte," in *Festschrift Wolfgang Braunfels: zum 65. Geburtstag*, (Tübingen: Wasmuth, 1977) pp. 31-44. Quote: p. 31.

28. Marc Antoine Laugier, *An Essay on Architecture*, translated by Wolfgang and Anni Herrmann, (Los Angeles: Hennessey & Ingalls, 1977), p. 130. In Germany, the practice flourished in the urban reconstruction following the Thirty Years' War (1618-48).

29. David Leatherbarrow, "Friedrichstadt—A Symbol of Toleration," in Clelland, *op. cit.*, p. 30.

30. Peschken, *op. cit.*, p. 50.

31. Leatherbarrow, *idem.*

32. Buddensieg, *op. cit.*, p. 31.

33. Buddensieg, *op. cit.*, p. 32. Quote from Alfred Freiherr von Wolzogen, *Aus Schinkels Nachlaß*, II (Berlin: Decker, 1862-4), p. 211.

34. Quoted from Goethe in Buddensieg, *op. cit.*, p. 32.

35. Buddensieg, *op. cit.*, p. 33. See Karl Friedrich Schinkel, *The English Journey: Journal of a Visit to France and Britain in 1826*, David Bindman and Gottfried Riemann, eds. (New Haven: Yale University Press, 1993), p. 199: "Zehntausend Häuser werden jährlich in London gebaut, lauter Spekulation, die durch die sonderbarsten Gestaltungen reizbar gemacht werden soll. Oft sieht man lange Reihen von Palästen, welche nichts anderes als viele, drei und vier Fenster breite, aneinander geschobene Privatwohnungen sind, denen man gemeinschaftliche Architektur gegeben hat."

36. Laugier, *op. cit.*, p. 131.

37. Likewise, the French theorist Quatremère de Quincy praised diversity in his *Dictionnaire historique d'architecture* published in Paris in 1832: "Still let us say that, as a product of architecture, the most beautiful city, for the man of taste, will be that which contain the most beautiful productions of the genius of this art. However, the beauties which the art can produce comprise the most numerous differences." A. Ch. Quatremère de Quincy, *Dictionnaire historique d'architecture* (Paris: Librairie d'Adrien le Clere et Cie, 1832), p. 674.

38. See Klaus Jan Philip, *Karl Friedrich Schinkel: späte Projekte* (Stuttgart: Axel Menges, 2000); Jean-François Lejeune, "The City at the Foot of the 'Residenz eines Fürsten': Schinkel's Vision of the Modern City set in the Mediterranean Landscape," in Maria Giuffrè, et al., eds., *The Time of Schinkel and the Age of Neoclassicism between Palermo and Berlin* (Reggio di Calabria: Biblioteca del Cenide, 2006), pp. 93-108.

39. Buddensieg, *op. cit.*, p. 32. See Hans Mackowsky, *Karl Friedrich Schinkel: Briefe, Tagebücher, Gedanken* (Berlin: Im Propyläen Verlag, 1922), p. 197.

40. Jean-François Lejeune, "Schinkel and Lenné in Berlin: From the Biedermeier Flâneur to Beuth's *Großstadt*," in Susan Peik, ed., *Karl Friedrich Schinkel: Aspects of his Works* (Stuttgart: Axel Menges, 2001).

41. The expression "first bourgeois city" comes from Jean Castex, Philippe Panerai, and Jean-Charles Depaule, *Formes urbaines de l'îlot à la barre* (Paris: Dunod, 1977).

42. See Tilman Harlander with Harald Bodenschatz, et al., *Villa und Eigenheim: suburbaner Städtebau in Deutschland* (Stuttgart: Deutsche Verlags-Anstalt, 2001).

43. Philippe Gresset, "The Picturesque Bourgeois House at the Edge of the Neoclassical city," in Andrew Ballantyne, ed., *Rural and Urban: Architecture between Two Cultures* (London/New York: Routledge, 2010), p. 89.

44. Gresset, *op. cit.*, p. 94.

45. See Lejeune, "Schinkel and Lenné" cited above in note 40.

46. Paraphrasing the title of Christoph Frommel's essay "Living *all'antica*: Palaces and Villas from Brunelleschi to Bramante," in Henry Mellon and Vittorio Magnago Lampugnani, eds., *The Renaissance from Brunelleschi to Michelangelo: the Representation of Architecture* (London: Thames & Hudson, 1996).

47. Karl Friedrich Schinkel, *Sammlung architektonischer Entwürfe* (Berlin: Ernst & Korn, 1866), p. 6: "Entwurf für das Wohnhaus eines begüterten Mannes in Berlin, der dasselbe mit seiner Familie ganz allein bewohnt, und dazu einen Gartenplatz von 200 Fuß Länge an der Straße gelegen, 490 Fuß Tiefe zwischen nachbarlichen Grundstücken gewählt hat." [author's translation].

48. Frank Lloyd Wright adapted a similar system in his early Prairie style projects in Chicago.

49. Schinkel, *op. cit.*, p. 7: "Ein wohlhabender Mann, der durch sein Geschäft so an die Stadt gefesselt ist, dass es ihm den Sommeraufenthalt auf dem Lande nicht gestattet, hat in einem lebhaften Theile der Stadt einen Platz, 238 Fuss längs der Straße breit, 462 Fuß tief, angekauft, auf welchem er ein bequemes Wohnhaus für sich in der Art zu bauen, daß die ganze Anlage ihm in gewissem Sinne die Wohnung auf dem Lande ersetzt."

50. Interestingly, this solution recalls typologically the largest Renaissance palace along the Strada Nuova in Genova, the Palazzo Doria-Tursi (1565 with additional loggias in 1597).

51. Rave, *op. cit.*, p. 252, mentions how the 1830 publication of the house differed significantly. The lot was shortened from 239 to 198 feet wide. As a result, the main house remained the same but the two side pavilions were cut in half and lost their economic functions. Schinkel also set them back about 25 feet from the street.

52. Schinkel, *op. cit.*, p. 6: "In großen Städten finden sich häufig Aufgaben für Wohnhäuser… wo die Beengung des Bauplatzes und die durch sehr hohe nachbarliche Gebäude auf demselben erzeugte Dunkelheit dem Architekten, wenn er freundliche Wohnungen bauen will, viele Schwierigkeiten in den Weg legt, und zu Anordnungen zwingt, welche von den gewöhnlichen durchaus abweichen müssen."

53. See Michael Dennis, *Court and Garden: From the French Hotel to the City of Modern Architecture* (Cambridge: The MIT Press, 1986). The Pompeian type appears unchanged when republished as plates 40-42 in the *Grundlage der praktischen Baukunst.*

54. Schinkel, *op. cit.*, p. 6: "durch Anlegung von Waarenmagazinen einträglich gemacht, und dem Ganzen ein möglichst freundlicher Charakter gegeben werden."

55. Schinkel, *op. cit.*, p. 6: "Der Hof ist durch diese Anordnung unterhalb rings umschlossen und mit Säulenlauben umgeben, so daß er dem Eintretenden als eine Vorhalle, wie das alte Atrium, dienen kann."

56. Schinkel, *op. cit.*, p. 6. See for instance *K.F. Schinkel: Möbel und Interieur* (München: Deutscher Kunstverlag, 2002), p. 122.

57. See Richard Röhrbein, "Ländliche Wohnung in Sizilien," *From the Italian Vernacular Villa to Schinkel to the Modern House*, Emanuele Fidone, ed. (Siracusa: Biblioteca del Cenide, 2003), pp. 211-227.

58. *Berlin und die Antike: Architektur, Kunstgewerbe, Malerei, Skulptur, Theater und Wissenschaft vom 16. Jahrhundert bis heute* (Berlin: Deutsches Archäologisches Institut, 1979), p. 329.

59. See for instance Wolfgang Sonne, "Dwelling in the Metropolis: Sitte, Hegemann, and the International Dissemination of the Reformed Urban Blocks, 1890-1940," in Chuck Bohl and Jean-François Lejeune, eds., *Sitte, Hegemann and the Metropolis* (London/New York: Routledge, 2009), pp. 249-273.

60. Wolfram Hoepfher, "The Wiegand house in Berlin-Dahlem," in *Composición arquitectonica, Art & Architecture*, No. 1 (Oct. 1988), pp. 59-68. Also see Stanford Anderson, "Schinkel, Behrens, an Elemental Tectonic, and a New Classicism," *Karl Friedrich Schinkel: Aspects of His Work*, pp. 119ff.

61. Schinkel, *op. cit.*, pp. 6-7: "Die Laube an der Decke ist auf kräftig blauem Grunde in frischen Farben gemalt, das Gitterwerk in Goldgelb. In gleicher Art sind die Kinder mit den Blumengehängen über der Glastür farbig auf blauem Grunde ausgeführt. Die Architektur der Wände ist in einer hellen Steinfarbe gehalten, die Füllungen zwischen den Pilastern sind von Friesen eingefasst, welche bunte Arabesken auf rotbraunem Grunde zeigen, die schwebenden Figuren in den Feldern sind in leuchtenden Farben auf weißem Grunde gemalt. Die Seite des Vestibüls ahmt eine grünliche Marmorart nach. Der Fußboden ist mit glasürten Fliesen von dunkel rotbrauner und lichtgelber Farbe ausgelegt." The type is shown unchanged on plates 34-36 of the *Grundlage der praktischen Baukunst.*

62. Kurt Forster, "'Eine gewisse rastlose Thätigkeit…' – Beobachtungen an Schinkels Interieurs," *Karl Friedrich Schinkel: Möbel und Interieur* (München: Deutscher Kunstverlag, 2002), p. 15. "Schinkel's Entwürfe bürgerlicher Wohnungen für den Fabrikanten Feilner und für eine Gruppe von 'Stadt-Gebäuden' belegen seinen Wunsch, den Wohnungen ein eigentliches 'Innenleben' zu verleihen: Mit Vorliebe erschließt er jedes Stockwerk direct vom Vestibül und gliedert die Wohnungen durch Korridore, deren Licht durch Glastüren aus den angrenzenden Zimmern dringt." Forster mentions Jefferson's house in Monticello for the use of glass doors.

63. It is here important to notice Schinkel's alternative and more traditional, more aristocratic alternative presented at the bottom of the same plate 69, which reintroduced a strong vertical hierarchy.

64. For this type, see also Rave, *op. cit.*, pp. 254-256.

65. Schinkel, *op. cit.*, p. 9.

66. Eric Forssman, *Karl Friedrich Schinkel: Seine Bauten heute* (Dortmund: Harenberg, 1991), p. 198.

67. Mackowsky, *op. cit.*, pp. 183-85: "eine Anspielung auf die Musikliebhaberei der weiblichen Familienmitglieder bedeuten sollte."

68. Schinkel, *op. cit.*, p. 6.

69. Forssman, *idem.*

70. Buddensieg, *op. cit.*, p. 35.

71. Werner Hegemann, *op. cit.* Also see Hans Stimmann, *op. cit.*

72. Buddensieg, *op. cit.*, p. 33: "Damit formuliert Schinkel einen der Konflikte zwischen Individuum und Allgemeinheit, der auf verschiedenen geschichtlichen Ebenen die Architekturgeschichte des 19. und 20. Jahrhunderts bestimmt hat." For a further discussion, see Kurt Walter Behrendt, *Die einheitliche Blockfront als Raumelement im Stadtbau: Ein Beitrag zur Stadtbaukunst der gegenwart* (Berlin: Bruno Cassirer Verlag, 1911).

From the Offices

Ferguson & Shamamian Architects

New York, New York

A New Residence
Malibu, California

Project Team:
Oscar Shamamian, *Partner in Charge*; Stephen Chrisman;
Joseph Singer; Bogdan Borgovan; Benjamin Hatherell;
Matthew Enquist; David Eastman; Julio Gavilanes;
Michael Okonkwo; M. Damian Samora;
Andre Mellone, *renderer.*

This residence on a six-acre oceanfront site in Malibu, California, is an alteration of an existing house, but it is radically different from the original structure. The clients, a couple who planned to use the home for weekends and entertaining, found the existing house grandiose and overly ornamental and thus requested a design that would be more subtle and humane in scale. In order to maintain the spectacular ocean views and proximity to the coastline of the existing house, zoning rules required that the alteration maintain the existing footprint and at least 51 percent of the existing frame. Within these parameters the overall size of the house was reduced and the exteriors were recast with restraint and more authentically concerned details.

The main house is now composed of a central two-story main block with two flanking single-story wings, which help to diminish the mass. The wooden structural shell was removed or altered in some places to suit the new floor plan, and the roof structure was entirely refashioned to fit new wall heights and slopes.

The first floor has a casual, open plan with adjoining rooms opening onto the exterior terraces and pergolas. Axial relationships, including a clear line of sight from the front entry through the house to the ocean, guide the view in several directions and out to the landscape. *Pietra serena* stone floors, used throughout, unify the interior and exterior. Tall ceilings, a minimum of interior trim and ornament, and large paned steel doors and windows focus the interest on the view of the ocean. Interiors feature plaster walls and cornices, limestone door casings, and walnut doors. The more private second floor, containing the bedrooms and master suite, is similarly detailed.

The exterior of the house has a stucco façade with monolithic cast-stone columns in an engaged portico, steel French doors and windows, and antique roof tiles. The site has been developed with new and renovated outbuildings and recreation areas, including a guesthouse, exercise pavilion, tennis court and pavilion, pool and spa, caretaker's house and garage, pergolas, fountains, and a gatehouse.

A New Residence
Chagrin Falls, Ohio

PROJECT TEAM:
Mark Ferguson, *Partner in charge;* Tod Elliot;
Scott Reinthaler; Frank Bostelmann; Brian Covington,
Interior Design. Associate Architect of Record:
Thomas Woodman, Thomas Woodman and
Associates, Ohio.

Located in a rural township with pockets of suburban development several miles from the historic town of Chagrin Falls, Ohio, this house is on a dead-end road that serves a dozen developed house sites. Neighboring homes are secluded behind stands of trees and are not generally visible. The owners had lived in an existing house on this site, but wished to build a larger home for themselves and their two teenage children. The existing house was removed to allow for new construction.

The two-and-a-half-acre site is long and narrow, and features a large pond along the road on its front boundary that extends beyond the side yard onto the adjoining property. The land was cleared prior to the construction of the original house to provide a gently rising grade from the pond to the house site, with woods beyond. In order to maintain this bucolic vista, uninterrupted by driveway or parking, a new driveway was cut close to the side-yard boundary line and a new motor court placed behind the site of the new house. The house commands the view up from the road to a very open garden façade. In keeping with the inverted nature of the site layout, the garden façade of the house faces the pond and street front. The closed, formal façade on the motor court faces the rear of the site. Glazed side entrance doors in each wing align with garden elements on the front and rear façades.

The street view of the house across the pond recalls the aesthetic predilections of English landscape design, complementary to the Federal style of architecture, which is the model for this house.

In colonial times, this area of northern Ohio was part of land holdings known as the western reserve of Connecticut. The owners have an affinity for the Federal style of early New England and New York town and

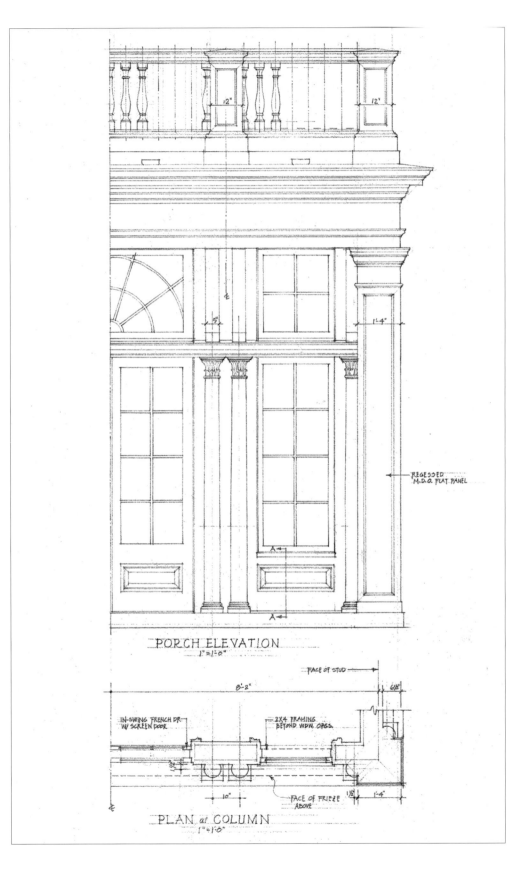

PORCH ELEVATION
1"=1'-0"

PLAN at COLUMN
1"=1'-0"

farmstead houses, and they found that it was coincident with this historical fact. The scale, styling, and materials of houses such as Boscobel became the inspiration for the design. The exterior is wood clapboard with applied detailing and ornament designed to bring dignity to the composition and appropriate scale to this 8,000-square-foot house. The first story is wood rustication, the upper story and porches are trabeated, and the roof is capped by a balustraded widow's walk. The core is a two-story square block, which has symmetrical hyphens and wings. The hyphens afford offsets of massing, and the alignment of interior axes of doors and windows provide multiple exposures in all interior spaces and views out into the landscape in multiple directions. Tall ceilings on the first floor further enhance the infiltration of natural light and access to the landscape views.

The first floor has the major entertaining and family gathering rooms. On the second floor, the center bay of the main block is occupied by two semiprivate sitting rooms, each with a shaped ceiling. The rooms are axially linked, and the main axis extends through window openings overlooking the front and rear façades.

All images are used by permission of Ferguson & Shamamian Architects. Photography by Scott Frances.

Thomas Gordon Smith Architects

South Bend, Indiana

CHAPEL OF SAINTS PETER AND PAUL, OUR LADY OF GUADALUPE SEMINARY
Denton, Nebraska

PROJECT TEAM:
Thomas Gordon Smith, *Principal;* John P. Haigh and William C. Heyer, *Project Managers;* John Mead, *Designer;* Donald D'Angelo, *Draftsman.*

In February 2010, the Chapel of Saints Peter and Paul was consecrated at Our Lady of Guadalupe Seminary. The seminary was built for the Priestly Fraternity of St. Peter in the small town of Denton, near Lincoln, Nebraska. The seminary accommodates the residential, educational, and religious needs of one hundred seminarians in a structure of nearly 70,000 square feet. The Priestly Fraternity was formed to teach and serve the old Latin rite in conformance with Vatican norms.

The program for the seminary was ambitious even as the budget was austere. The first phase of construction was completed in 2000. The educational and administrative functions face west. The north wing is a residence for priests and seminarians and the refectory and kitchen are at the southeast. The east residential wing, which completes the cloister, was constructed in 2005.

The distribution of functional wings around the cloister follows the model of a traditional monastery. Romanesque prototypes are reflected in the disposition of the plan and the building's appearance. Requirements of durability and economy demanded straightforward simplicity of form and a solid concrete structure faced with weather-resistant brick. Hierarchically important areas, such as the Aula Magna at the northwest corner, the pedimented entry to the administrative offices, and the vaulted refectory, are emphasized by the articulation of special doors, windows, and interior volumes. On the other hand, the dormitory rooms, offices, and classrooms follow repetitive modules. The major building components were further distinguished with brick color.

The building was carefully sited to minimize grading and to take advantage of the beautiful setting. The local climate and geology allowed for a ground loop heating and cooling system utilizing economical heat pumps.

The 9,300-square-foot chapel is a free-standing structure of basilical type. A choir for seminarians is located in the nave, focused on the sanctuary. The chapel's volume and details have been designed to support chant and to reflect traditional architectural models.

All images are used by permission of Thomas Gordon Smith Architects. Photography by Alan McIntyre Smith.

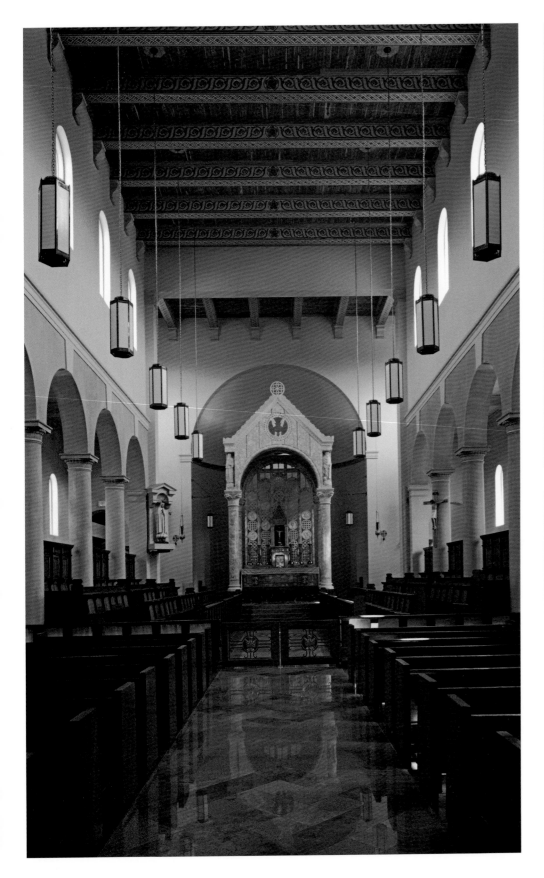

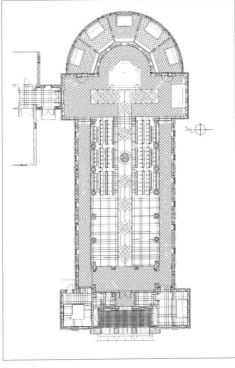

John Simpson & Partners

London, United Kingdom

Pipe Partridge Building and New Masterplan for Lady Margaret Hall
Oxford, United Kingdom

Project Team:
John Simpson, *Principal;* Joanna Wachowiak, *Associate Director and Project Architect;* Michael Simpson, *Director of Building Implementation;* Bart Gloger, *Associate and Project Coordinator.*

Lady Margaret Hall was Oxford's first women's college. It developed from a single Victorian villa in 1878, and by 1964 came to encompass a collection of early- and mid-twentieth-century classical buildings by Reginald Blomfield, Giles Gilbert Scott, and Raymond Erith. In the 1970s two unsympathetic blocks were built to provide additional student accommodation. All of the buildings, with the exception of the 1970s blocks, enjoy statutory protection as they are listed by English Heritage with a Grade II status. The practice was commissioned to create a masterplan that would incorporate new teaching facilities and accommodation for both undergraduates and graduates within the existing College grounds, while retaining all existing structures. These new spaces would also need to function as conference facilities outside of term time. The College required that the masterplan complete the unfinished 1964 Raymond Erith-designed entrance approach.

In the design that evolved, three new blocks were arranged amongst the existing buildings to create a number of new quadrangles. This unites the 1970s blocks and new buildings with the historic heart of the college, continuing the traditional typology of Oxford. The implementation of the masterplan was split into two phases. In the first phase, an L-shaped building provides new undergraduate accommodation, teaching

MASTERPLAN OF THE COLLEGE

and seminar rooms, a multi-purpose lecture theater, dining room, and student common rooms. Phase II incorporates two new buildings: a new building for graduate students, providing accommodation and teaching facilities, as well as a new Porter's Lodge.

These buildings complete Raymond Erith's sequence of spaces at the entrance of Lady Margaret Hall, creating a quadrangle open on one side to give the College a new public face. The proposed entrance quad includes two new gatehouses, which formalize the approach to the College. The gatehouses draw from the architectural symbolism of Erith's façade, which was inspired by the Porta Maggiore in Rome, and from Blomfield's Tempietto-inspired portico of the Talbot Building beyond.

The Oxford City Council Planning Authority granted permission for the masterplan in 2006 and in January 2010, the new undergraduate building was completed. The

buildings at Lady Margaret Hall, like all Oxford colleges, incorporate teaching space with halls of residence for students and fellows. Called the Pipe Partridge Building, the undergraduate building provides a total of sixty-six individual student rooms that occupy the first and second floors. Continuing the historic layout for women's colleges, each student room is accessible from a central corridor. The rooms' ensuite bathrooms make them useful for conferences outside of term time. A 134-seat lecture theater on the ground floor incorporates classical interiors and uses acoustic technology that allows it to be used for lectures and musical events, as well as small theatrical productions.

Keeping alternative energy sources in mind, solar collectors are incorporated within the design of the Pipe Partridge Building. By placing the solar collectors between the two pitched sides of the roof, the panels are integrated into the design and provide an easily maintained service space at roof level. The Phase II buildings will also address environmental concerns through the use of ground source heat extraction technology.

All images are used by permission of John Simpson & Partners. Photograph of snow-bound Pipe Partridge building by Ed Simpson; other photographs by Andreas Von Einsiedel.

G. P. Schafer Architect, PLLC

New York, New York

A New Greek Revival Residence
Millbrook, NY

PROJECT TEAM:
Gil Schafer III, *Principal;* Kevin Buccellato, *Project Manager;*
Diana Reising, *Job Captain.*

A couple commissioned this 7,500-square-foot new Greek Revival residence on a dramatic hillside site two hours north of New York City. Initially intended as a weekend house, it will ultimately become the couple's full-time residence.

The clients were drawn to the Palladian classicism of Jefferson's country villas in Virginia, and this design idea guided the development of a symmetrically balanced house with a Greek Revival character. The plan is designed around the lifestyle of a sophisticated couple who enjoy entertaining and whose grown children will have use of a separate carriage house apartment connected to the main house through a mudroom breezeway. The large central drawing room with commanding views of the Hudson River Valley and the Catskill Mountains beyond is to be used as both a living room and dining room. A matched pair of scagliola fireplaces were designed for each end of the room.

The master suite with an intimately-scaled paneled library, bedroom, and "his and hers" bathrooms and dressing rooms lies at one

of the house, which is in turn balanced by an informal paneled family room and open kitchen wing at the other end. Two guest suites and an office for the husband are located on the second floor, approached by a curving staircase. The New York designer Miles Redd has decorated the interior of the house.

The landscape surrounding the house, developed by Warren Byrd of Charlottesville, Virginia, terraces various hedged garden rooms around the house and includes an elegantly proportioned swimming pool between the family room wing of the main house and the carriage house.

All images are used by permission of G. P. Schafer Architect, PLLC. Photography by Paul Costello.

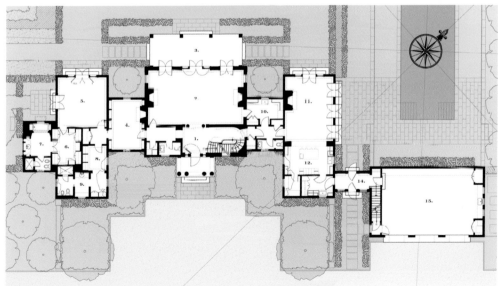

David D. Harlan Architects, LLC

New Haven, Connecticut

EXTOWN FARM "GUEST COTTAGE"
New Canaan, Connecticut

PROJECT TEAM:
David Harlan, *Architect/Principal Design*; Edward Barros, *Project Captain/Draftsperson*; Ben Northrup.

The 17-acre Extown Farm is all that remains of an estate of several hundred acres, which was first established in 1778. In 1852, the property was acquired by the town of New Canaan to serve as the municipality's "poor farm." The town sold it in 1929 (hence the name Extown) to a private family who renovated and transformed the main house in a Georgian style, while retaining and adding to the colonial interiors. The farm was sold again in the 1940s to the Findlay family who secured a "Deed of Conservation" in 1998 with Historic New England (HNE). This deed protects the main house, principal barn, pastures, fields, meadows, and trees so that their combined character is protected in perpetuity from subdivision and demolition. Modifications and improvements to these protected elements require the approval of HNE. A public roadway bisects the property; the main house, garage, and meadow are to the north and the cottage, barns, pasture, and outbuildings are to the south.

The current owner acquired Extown Farm in 2006 and initially renovated the 1930s caretaker's cottage so that it could be lived in during the longer process of restoring the main house. The foundations and some of the original framing of the cottage were incorporated into a new design, which maintained the character of the farm by modelling the form, materials, and details after existing buildings on the property. Exterior porches were added and the roofline was restructured to accommodate a central Great Room lit by clerestory windows and heated by a new fireplace and chimney. The East Porch was enclosed with windows to create a sunroom and to suggest a sense of gradual changes in the building over time. The addition of porches to add functionality and enhance identity is also a characteristic of the renovations of the main house and the garage.

All images are used by permission of David D. Harlan Architects, LLC.

Quinlan and Francis Terry, LLP

Dedham, Essex, UK

264-267 TOTTENHAM COURT ROAD
London, UK

PROJECT TEAM:
Martyn Winney

The new development at 264-267 Tottenham Court Road was commissioned by London & Regional Properties for a site on St Giles Circus, London. It replaces a nineteenth-century building in the French chateau style. Many schemes had been proposed for the site, and at the suggestion of the planners it was decided that classical detailing would be appropriate, following the example of many fine twentieth-century classical buildings on Oxford Street. Quinlan and Francis Terry worked in conjunction with the London-based planning and design firm ESA who carried out the interior. The contractor was Kier; Ketton Architectural Stone and Masonry provided the stonework; and the windows were manufactured by Stewart Fraser Limited. The building was completed in 2009.

The elevation facing Tottenham Court Road is a nine-bay classical building 100 feet wide in natural limestone, bronze, and glass in keeping with the buildings on either side, which are also constructed in Portland stone, glass, and bronze. This composition starts at ground level with a rusticated arcade supporting a giant Palladian Ionic order. Above, a giant Corinthian order complete with entablature and balustrade is superimposed, with an attic at the top and slate roof behind the parapet. At the two ends of the colonnade are plain and rusticated "book ends" to frame the composition and make a clean break with the neighbouring classical buildings.

The development is mixed use: The ground floor is used for retail, the next four floors are offices, and there are residential units at roof level. In this way the architecture of the façade reflects the different functions of the building. The rusticated arches work well as shop fronts allowing signage to be positioned in a controlled and respectful manner. The office floors have columns that mark these floors as the most prestigious and the large windows allow light deep into the office interior. The residential units within the roof are lit by dormer windows, which impart an appropriate domestic character.

The superimposition of orders was commonly used in Roman architecture, of which the earliest examples were theatres and amphitheatres. The most famous of these is the Colosseum using three orders: Doric, Ionic, and Corinthian. The Theatre of Marcellus is a well-preserved example, which uses only Doric and Ionic. Both structures were a great influence on Palladio who used superimposed orders for his palace designs in Venice and the Veneto. Palladio's Basilica and Palazzo Chiericati superimposed Ionic on Doric. The Palazzo Antonini uses Ionic and Corinthian and the Carità in Venice uses all three.

The detailing of the column capitals, bases, and cornices are all derived from Palladio's *Quattro Libri* with the Corinthian order being a simplified version that follows the one with uncut leaves used at San Giorgio Maggiore.

All images are used by permission of Quinlan and Francis Terry, LLP. Photography by Nick Carter and David Grandorge.

Hanover Lodge
Regent's Park, London, UK

PROJECT TEAM:
Francis Terry

The original part of Hanover Lodge was designed by Decimus Burton in 1827 to Nash's master plan of Regent's Park. It was a modest villa that was extensively remodelled by Sir Edwin Lutyens in 1910. Lutyens added a second floor with incongruously high roofs and a wing on the west side. Much of Lutyens' work was removed after 1947 when the building became a Hall of Residence for Bedford College. When the College left in 1995, unsightly additions, which the college had made in the 1960s, were removed and the Crown Estate offered a lease of the building for use as a private dwelling.

In 2002 Quinlan Terry prepared a design to make the house a symmetrical and substantial residence. His proposal included a large reception room with a centrally placed bow,

echoing those in Decimus Burton's two nearby villas, The Holme and Nuffield Lodge. The design also balanced the Lutyens wing with a similar block on the east side. The interior is centred around a huge entrance hall, inspired by the one designed by Inigo Jones at the Queen's House in Greenwich (1616-35). The decoration is the most rich and imposing of any of the firm's portfolio to date. During the construction process Francis Terry also designed a portico for the front façade based on the Erechtheum.

This major house is a more demanding commission than Terry's previous six villas in Regent's Park as it is on a far larger scale, involves the retention of work by two previous architects, and has an extremely ornate interior. Its completion in 2009 brings to an end twenty years of work on the Regent's Park villas, and serves as the final example of seven possible ways in which the classical repertoire can be employed today.

Photography by June Buck. Drawing by Francis Terry.

HOWARD THEATRE, DOWNING COLLEGE
Cambridge, UK

PROJECT TEAM:
Francis Terry; Roger Barrell

The new Howard Theatre is the latest addition to the late-Georgian classical campus at Downing College, Cambridge. It is situated in the newly formed Howard Court behind William Wilkins' west range, which is made up of two other Quinlan Terry buildings. The new building creates the missing side of the court and in so doing encloses an "outside room" with architectural elements repeated on all three sides. Like the other Terry buildings, it has three stories and a pitched roof. The walls are constructed from Ketton stone with a baseless Doric colonnade.

The architecture of the theatre is focused on the auditorium which is on the first and second floor. It is a small theatre with 128 seats downstairs—including a single row of chairs down either side beneath a gallery—and upstairs there are 32 more seats. The inspiration came from the Wilkins-designed Theatre Royal in Bury St Edmunds. Wilkins has great significance for this project as he not only designed many theatres in East Anglia but he also was the first architect of Downing College.

The back drop is painted with a capriccio based on the Acropolis with buildings by Wilkins and Terry's college buildings blended into the scene. On a roundel above the stage is a painting of Apollo and the Muses, after Meng's *Parnassus*. Three pairs of griffins—the college's crest—are rendered on the remaining three sides of the gallery cove.

Despite the theatre's classical appearance, the servicing is very much state-of-the-art in terms of sustainability. The grass court conceals three kilometres of ground source heat pump pipes that produce five kilowatts of heat for every kilowatt of electricity expended. As a result, the theatre has no need for a boiler. Solar heating provides hot water, and the naturally ventilated theatre uses gray water flushing.

Photography by Nick Carter. Drawing by Francis Terry.

Back drop for the Howard Theatre, Downing   Francis Terry '09

A The Parthenon
B The West Range at Downing
C The Propylaea
D The Maitland Robinson Library
E Govt. Bury St Eds by Wilkins

Peter Pennoyer Architects

New York, New York

DRUMLIN HALL
Pine Plains, New York

PROJECT TEAM:
Peter Pennoyer and Thomas P. R. Nugent,
Architects-in-Charge; Gregory Gilmartin, *Design Director;*
Nebojsa Savic, Anton Glikin, Sean Blackwell,
Timothy P. Kelly, F. Patrick Mohan, Eero Schultz,
Andrew Davis, and James Taylor, *Associates.*

Drumlin Hall, a 7,500-square-foot house in
Pine Plains, New York, was built to house a
collection of Federal style furniture and
Hudson River School paintings. Constructed
from 2006 to 2009, this four bedroom classical
stone house is conceived as a square Palladian
villa, which also reflects the client's interest in
Robert Adam and Duncan Phyfe.

    Above the granite base, the house is faced
in warm buff sandstone and capped with a
natural slate roof. The pedimented south
façade commands the long approach from the
south, and bas-relief cornucopias enrich the
lunettes above the French doors. The south
façade is marked by the tall terrace doors of
the central rooms, carved panels, and massive
chimney stacks. The entrance to the west is
centered on an arched porte-cochere. The
north elevation is more heroic in scale; severe
wings contrast with the columned bay of the
breakfast room, and a massive chimney rises
up through the roofs. The chimney masses
join into a flat extension of the inner wall of
the stair hall, expressing the important central
vaulted volume within.

    The plan of the house revolves around
two central axes and succinctly absorbs all
of the requisite rooms into a contained
rectangle with windows that express themselves
symmetrically on the façades. Inside, the front
door leads from the porte-cochere, through a
groined foyer and vaulted hall, past the library
and spiral stair, and into the drawing room.
The public rooms are arranged around the
groin-vaulted hall, which frames the cylindrical

stair, and the tall walls serve as a gallery for the client's art collection. The drawing room is the most heavily ornamented room in the house, with Greek Revival door casings and Aeolic pilasters. The grained library boasts small, domed book recesses on either side of the fireplace; between them is a bar concealed behind the chimney breast. Details such as the repeated star motif, which purposely hints at the client's Texan heritage, the intricate and ornate ironwork of the stair balusters, the cornice in the library with carved anthemia, and the gold leafed bead molding within the miniature vaults of the bar, prove the challenge of designing a house both singular to the client, and also firmly grounded in historical accuracy.

One of the most notable design features of this project is the central axis of the house that runs from the east to the west, and connects the entry gallery and the drawing room with the semi-cylindrical stair. In turn, the axis of the stair is equally powerful with its exposure north towards the library, and its southern facing views over the Hudson Valley. In addition, the large open space of the vaulted second floor gallery, which is lit by a lay light at the center of a handkerchief dome, echoes the fluid movement of public rooms as they radiate from the central first floor hallway. Every space within the house was designed to relate to the vault on the first floor and the dome on the second floor that mark the center of the building.

All images are used by permission of Peter Pennoyer Architects. Photography by Jonathan Wallen. Wireframe rendering by Timothy Kelly.

Harrison Design Associates

Atlanta, Georgia

POLAND RESIDENCE
Atlanta, Georgia

PROJECT TEAM:
Gregory L. Palmer, AIA; William H. Harrison, AIA

The guiding factors in the design of this historically-based Georgian home include classical detailing, proportion, and scale. The five-part brick structure comprises a main block connected to symmetrical wings with short hyphens. Limestone quoins, jack arches and sills, and carved limestone plaques are apparent on the central block of the home. The detailing is intentionally less intricate on the wings and hyphens. These differences impart a feeling of age, suggesting expansion by successive generations. This house received the 2009 Shutze Award for Excellence in Residential Design (Over 10,000 Square Feet) from the Southeast Chapter of the Institute of Classical Architecture & Art.

Oakley Residence
Atlanta, Georgia

Project Team:
Gregory L. Palmer, AIA; William H. Harrison, AIA; Derek Hopkins, *Architectural Design*; Karen Ferguson, ASID, *Interior Design.*

This 1920s Tudor cottage was designed by the New York firm of C. C. Wendehack and executed in Atlanta by Ivey and Crook for Joel Chandler Harris, Jr., son of the well-known writer and folklorist Joel Chandler Harris. Viewing themselves as stewards of the property, the current owners wanted to carefully restore and expand the home in order to accommodate their growing family. By approaching the project with a shared philosophy of respect, understanding, and restraint, the collaborative efforts of the owners and Harrison Design Associates resulted in a house that provides modern functionality while celebrating the essence of its original character.

Less formal than many of the surrounding homes, the cottage employs a rich vernacular that evokes a sense of nostalgic charm. These sentiments are expressed in the form of intimate spaces, warm materials, and imaginative detailing. The clients' vision not only included retaining as many original elements as possible in the existing spaces, but also incorporating these elements into the planned expansion. The team accomplished this goal in part by ordering new windows from a small manufacturer

in Great Britain to precisely match the home's 1920s windows. Additionally, oversized custom carved mouldings were designed to complement the originals and the unique texture and application methods of the plaster walls were replicated. This house received the 2009 Shutze Award for Excellence in Renovation or Addition to a Private Residence from the Southeast Chapter of the Institute of Classical Architecture & Art.

Before and After (at top): Exterior of the Oakley Residence before the renovation and addition by Harrison Design Associates.

All images are used by permission of Harrison Design Associates. Photography by John Umberger.

Paul Cret and Louis Kahn

BEAUX-ARTS PLANNING AT THE YALE CENTER FOR BRITISH ART

By Sam Roche

Most scholars and admirers of Louis Kahn's architecture recognize that it does not fit neatly into a single stylistic category. Many of those who argue that his stark, monumental buildings revived a flagging modernist movement also acknowledge that they reflect influences from outside that movement, specifically the classical architecture Kahn knew from his education and travels.

Most of us do not yet recognize, however, the clear and concise relationship that exists between two seemingly opposing aspects of his architecture, which has been obscured by the kind of misconception that often surrounds great artistic achievements. This situation owes something to Kahn himself, who cultivated a mystique by describing his work with abstract, poetic language. His interpreters subsequently added new layers when, without distinguishing between creative license and critical responsibility, they indulged in the same habit.[1] In so doing, they established critical terms that being both vague and absolute at the same time are obstacles to clear analysis, and which persist despite attempts at clarification.

The relationship between modernism and classicism in Kahn's architecture has been further obscured by writers who either don't want to acknowledge it or whose assumptions prevent them from recognizing it. Without failing to mention Kahn's classical Beaux-Arts education, these writers invariably consider his later fellowship at the American Academy in Rome to be the stronger influence on his subsequent style. The fellowship, which came to Kahn mid-career after he had designed some characteristically modernist buildings, allowed him to document the remains of ancient buildings not only in Rome but also in Egypt and Greece. Thereafter his architecture began to incorporate traditional monumental qualities and to achieve its celebrated resonance. There is more than timing, however, to recommend antique ruins to modernist writers as sources for the traditional qualities in Kahn's later work. For romantically inclined minds, historical processes reinforce ideological priorities, and the current reduced state of ancient classical buildings suggests to them that time has stripped away all inessentials until only

a proto-modernist architecture of construction is left [FIGURE 1]. Such imagined, retroactive characterization overlooks the fact that through his early education Kahn was already familiar with most of what he later observed firsthand in Rome, Greece, and Egypt. It is of interest to note that Kahn's sojourn at the American Academy in Rome was his second trip to study architecture in Europe.[2] This fact alone is sufficient to challenge a critical narrative that has come to be taken for granted.

Even the critics and scholars who have tried to be fairer have for the most part underestimated the influence of Kahn's early education on his mature style. They acknowledge and sometimes explore its Beaux-Arts sources but also argue that in combining them with an abstract architectural language Kahn somehow distilled or transformed them. The remade elements are no longer identified with specifically Beaux-Arts concerns but rather with an altogether new phenomenon.[3] This argument invests a process of reductive abstraction with a power to make new which overwhelms all previous associations.

Vague characterizations and faith-based arguments have so far prevented us from recognizing that Kahn's architecture is a straightforward synthesis of modernist language and Beaux-Arts planning. Resonant as the results of this synthesis may be, these are its primary elements. They represent the two major, disparate strands of Kahn's personal experience: his Beaux-Arts education at the University of Pennsylvania and his conversion to modernism early in his professional career. In his later buildings he combined the hierarchical, axial planning of the one with the other's architectural language of industrialized construction. It was not until his later stay in Rome that Kahn observed these qualities together in classical ruins, and thus it was not until after that experience that they appeared together in his buildings. The Roman use of a common module of structure and design supplied a further point of overlap with Beaux-Arts and modernist traditions. Roman ruins thus presented

---

Opposite: Detail of façade, Pan American Union Building by Paul Cret and Albert Kelsey. Photograph by John Collier (Prints and Photographs Division, Library of Congress). Bas-relief depicting Washington's farewell to his generals by Gutzon Borglum.

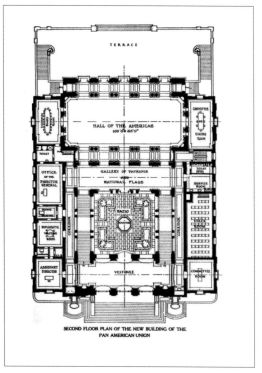

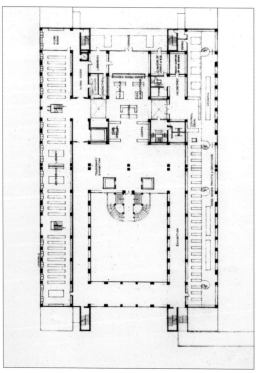

Figure 1 (above): The Basilica of Maxentius, Rome. Photograph by tomfs.

Figure 2 (far left): Second floor plan, Pan American Union Building by Paul Cret and Albert Kelsey.

Figure 3 (left): Second floor plan, Intermediate scheme for British Art Center (March 1971), by Louis I. Kahn.

Figure 4 (opposite): Façade, Pan American Union Building by Paul Cret and Albert Kelsey. Photograph by John Collier (Prints and Photographs Division, Library of Congress).

Kahn with a metaphor and a catalyst for reconciliation, which he pursued in the service of ideals that stressed architecture as a public art that communicates institutional values. These ideals pertain to all kinds of monumental building, but Kahn would have first understood them as the central axioms of his early education.

This thesis shifts the emphasis on facts we already know, giving (at least) equal weight to conventional and innovative aspects of Kahn's architecture. Understood in these terms his achievement is more than a personal one, for by engaging preexisting conventions Kahn also advanced a collective cultural enterprise. His achievement is also more than historical, for the classical and modernist strains in his work are also the primary antagonists of modern architecture, which remains riven by their seemingly irreconcilable conflict. In showing how this conflict can be resolved Kahn opened a new path of inquiry not only to scholars but also, even primarily, to practicing architects. To follow that path we must reconnect the conventional aspects of Kahn's architecture to their original sources.

Reviewing some neglected priorities and strategies of Beaux-Arts planning and pointing them out in Kahn's architecture can help recover an understanding of their influence on his architecture, and for this purpose broad descriptions and limited examples will suffice. Compare two plans for public buildings by Kahn and his teacher at the University of Pennsylvania, Paul Philippe Cret. The first is Cret's plan for the Pan American Union in Washington, D.C. [FIGURE 2]; the second is an intermediate scheme by Kahn for the Yale Center for British Art, in New Haven, Connecticut [FIGURE 3]. Both plans show the same sequence of clearly defined spaces arranged from beginning to end of a central axis that is defined by symmetrically disposed secondary rooms. In both cases this consciously monumental arrangement reflects a complex public program that simultaneously invites and restricts access. As realized, the Yale Center for British Art refines and simplifies Kahn's intermediate scheme while improving some of the shortcomings evident in Cret's plan, an evolution which we can trace through the stages of Kahn's design process once we understand the goals and strategies of Beaux-Arts planning.

These goals and strategies were determined by the movement's official origins as a national academy of design sponsored by the French state. The École Nationale Supérieure des Beaux-Arts in Paris was charged by the government to create an enduring official style through the education of young architects [FIGURE 5]. Having established itself during the nineteenth century as the leading international model of architectural education and practice, the Beaux-Arts system was adopted by the leading schools in the United States around 1890, at a time when the country's post-Civil War economic and political consolidation demanded a new scale of public building. Kahn studied architecture at the University of Pennsylvania near the end of this era,

from 1920 to 1924, when, under the direction of Cret, a French émigré and graduate of the Paris Ecole, it was regarded as the country's leading Beaux-Arts design program.

The official origins of the Beaux-Arts curriculum were evident in its emphasis on architecture as a public art with a symbolic role, in which buildings represented and reinforced an existing social structure dominated by institutions. In communicating the purpose and relative status of these institutions, Beaux-Arts design dealt with larger relationships as well as individual buildings and relied on familiar conventions and associations. Thus it recognized an established hierarchy of building types, employed a standard classical vocabulary that could be enriched or simplified as needed, and looked to historical examples as precedents for new designs. Most of these priorities and assumptions are reflected in Kahn's evident belief in the power of institutions and in his related preference for designing public buildings.

In individual buildings the Beaux-Arts focus on abstract, hierarchical relationships was naturally evident in an emphasis on planning and arrangement The characteristic Beaux-Arts plan was organized around a central axis defined by a building's most important rooms, arranged as a clear path with a beginning, middle, and end. This path gradually revealed a particular purpose, beginning with an entry hall or vestibule and proceeding through transitional lobbies or stair halls to a specialized room such as a courtroom or council chamber. This narrative, axial sequence distilled abstract concerns of use, hierarchy, and social relationships into a clear and simple composition. It could be extended

Figure 5 (top): The newly renovated atrium of the École Nationale Supérieure des Beaux-Arts, Paris. Photograph by Johnny Bananapeel.

Figure 6 (left): Patio, Pan American Union Building by Paul Cret and Albert Kelsey. Photograph by John Collier (Prints and Photographs Division, Library of Congress).

Figure 7 (opposite): Section, **Pan American Union Building** by Paul Cret **and Albert** Kelsey.

beyond the building to organize the site and negotiate urban relationships, or expanded laterally around courtyards or plazas. As a line of bilateral symmetry the central axis arranged the secondary program elements to either side, which themselves were often grouped around smaller perpendicular or parallel axes. These secondary spaces created a background against which the central axis could be read, and the distinction between shaped and shaping elements typically coincided with the division between public and private spaces. Beyond these reciprocal relationships, the Beaux-Arts plan was unified by a common module of planning and structure and a single system of progressive embellishment that climaxed at the termination of the central axis.

Beaux-Arts planning strategies were above all practical design guidelines that are best illustrated through specific examples. It is not just his role as Kahn's teacher that suggests we look to Cret's architecture when discussing Kahn's use of the Beaux-Arts approach.[4] Cret's interests and opportunities—his equal emphasis on teaching and designing, the public character and prestige of his commissions, even the types of buildings he designed—prefigured Kahn's own.[5] It should come as no surprise that throughout his career Kahn regarded Cret as his master,[6] or that amidst the bad habits of Kahn scholarship this tribute is consistently overlooked.

The Pan American Union Building, awarded to Paul Cret and Albert Kelsey through competition in 1907 and completed in 1910, was Cret's first major commission [FIGURE 4].[7] Its Beaux-Arts planning, and the institutional program and values which it serves, are characteristic. The client was an international organization of North- and South-American republics, who required a headquarters building that would provide a significant assembly space, a repository for an existing library of Pan-Americana, and, in the words of the architect, "a home which should be the visual expression of the ideals of unity, solidarity, and amity to which the Union is dedicated."[8] The site was a large, prominent corner lot adjacent to the Mall, large enough to surround the building with lawns and gardens.

Cret's plan shows how a standard repertoire could convey complex uses and associations through hierarchical, axial planning. He imagined the Union as a Latin-American palace built around a square courtyard or patio, a metaphor that reflected institutional purpose and character and presented the right balance of public and domestic associations. Cret arranged this patio and the other major spaces on a central axis that one moves around as well as along [FIGURE 6]. At the end he placed the major program elements, a large assembly hall and a smaller library, one over the other, with their long sides facing the patio, through which they could be reached via lobbies and, in the case of the raised assembly hall, flanking stairs. Cret surrounded this central sequence with secondary rooms running in two long rows from front to back, set off by halls that terminated in stairs and elevators.

The clarity and unity of this arrangement owe something to Cret's skills as a planner, but are also inherent in the planning strategies themselves. In relating qualities that are typically understood as opposites —hierarchy and uniformity, stability and movement—Cret promoted the same synthesis in application. Throughout the Union Building accentuated elements thus coexist and coincide with repeated ones—

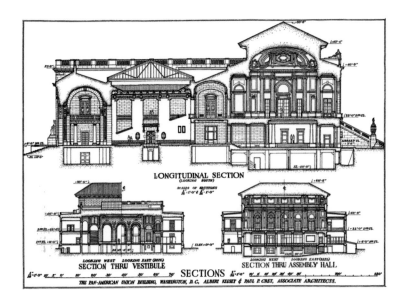

LONGITUDINAL SECTION
(LOOKING SOUTH)

SCALES OF SECTIONS

SECTION THRU VESTIBULE
LOOKING WEST   LOOKING EAST (RIGHT)

SECTION THRU ASSEMBLY HALL
LOOKING WEST   LOOKING EAST (RIGHT)

SECTIONS

THE PAN-AMERICAN UNION BUILDING, WASHINGTON, D.C., ALBERT KELSEY & PAUL P. CRET, ASSOCIATE ARCHITECTS.

as in the common module that runs through the central axis and is evident in the arches that pass through the entire building from front to garden façade. Simply by placing rooms in sequence, the technique of narrative planning reconciles individual character and connective roles. The central patio, for example, is both a clearly defined space with its own evocative character and a transitional space between generalized and specific public spaces. Cret identified this economy with a rational approach to design as problem-solving, in which the best solution "solves [the given problem] simply and directly without apparent effort or wasted motion."[9]

This rational emphasis may also explain the one limitation of Beaux-Arts planning. Cret's central sequence, enriched as it is by circulation around the patio, can be grasped and in some cases seen in its entirety from any point along it. At some level then it is too legible; it lacks the mystery or sense of surprise that might enhance the desired monumental effect. This may also arise from the consistent emphasis on planning over other aspects of the design process. The Beaux-Arts exterior typically projects the plan's hierarchical arrangement into three dimensions through its overall massing and through changes in scale and embellishment to distinguish primary and secondary elements. Sectional considerations can often seem overlooked; the Union's section, where the assembly hall and library are variations on a single axial theme, is hardly more than two stacked plans [FIGURE 7].

These, therefore, are the compositional strategies and limitations inherited by Kahn. In addition to combining them with a modernist language he also reworked and improved upon the conventions themselves, not by distilling them but through their elaboration. This can be seen in the design process of the Yale Center for British Art, in New Haven, Connecticut, which emerged from multiple schemes in two major phases. The publication of some of these preliminary schemes shows how Kahn relied on Beaux-Arts planning throughout the design process, first to identify basic challenges of site and program and then to bring these in line with Beaux-Arts compositional ideals.[10]

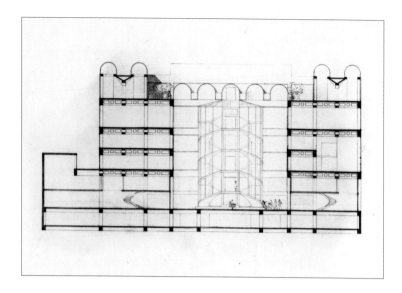

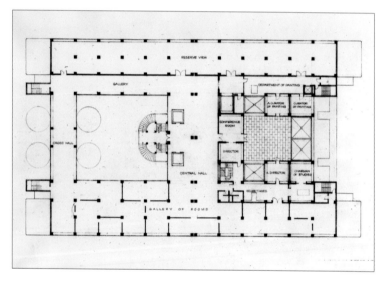

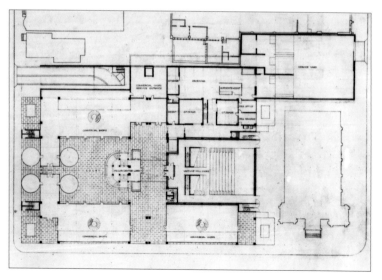

Funded by the banking heir Paul Mellon to house his art collection and a research center for scholars, the Yale Center for British Art was given a complex program that, like the Pan American Union, had both public and private associations. The donor, the university representative, and the architect all agreed that Mellon's paintings, primarily landscapes and sporting scenes of the kind found in English country houses, would be shown to best advantage in a context that recalled their original domestic setting. The site was on a prominent corner in central New Haven, across Chapel Street from the university campus and Kahn's earlier Yale University Art Gallery of 1953 (his first completed public building after his fellowship in Rome). This site was more urban than Cret's in Washington, and as a concession to New Haven, which expected to receive tax revenue from any building on the site, the ground floor of the new building facing Chapel Street was to be given over to retail shops, adding another element to its multi-use program.

From the beginning Kahn focused on basic planning questions, a conclusion supported by the design documentation and by his collaborators on the project.[11] The initial proposal shows a building organized by axial, hierarchical relationships around a central sequence of major spaces, which is comprised of two multi-story courtyards, or courts as Kahn called them, on either side of a central stair hall on the building's short axis. These courts divide the plan into two equal parts—one devoted to research and the other to exhibition spaces—which are raised on a single-story podium housing an auditorium and shops facing Chapel Street.

This early scheme takes a first step to reconcile compositional ideals with the demands of a particular problem. Beaux-Arts strategies are present—the hierarchical separation of public and institutional program, the identification of the latter with dedicated spaces at the end of a ceremonial path—but they are kept from coalescing into a coherent sequence by Kahn's larger site strategy. In an effort to orient this long building to Chapel Street Kahn established its major axis between the institutional courts rather than through the two of them; thus making them equivalent, adjacent spaces rather than complementary, sequential ones.[12] The first-floor plan arranged around perpendicular axes suggests that Kahn realized that his desired internal sequence conflicted with his desired external orientation. Both desires reflect Beaux-Arts priorities—for an interior path with beginning, middle, and end on the one hand and for a bilaterally symmetrical elevation on the other.[13]

That Kahn sought to resolve these conflicting priorities without compromising either is evident in the intermediate scheme represented in a set of office drawings dating from March 1971 that recalls Cret's plan for the Pan American Union. Kahn re-planned the upper floors on the long axis to make a sequence of the two courts, which are now no longer interchangeable but, as points of departure and arrival, have taken on complementary characters with complex associations [FIGURE 3]. The gallery court has incorporated the covered square below and assumed its public character to become a grand vestibule that runs through the whole building [FIGURE 8], while the library court, still raised over the auditorium, retains its privileged, institutional character and incorporates a two-story, skylit reading room beneath a ring of administrative offices [FIGURE 9].

Figure 8 (opposite top): Transverse section, Intermediate scheme for British Art Center (March 1971), by Louis I. Kahn.

Figure 9 (opposite middle): Third floor plan, Intermediate scheme for British Art Center (March 1971), by Louis I. Kahn.

Figure 10 (opposite bottom): First floor plan, Intermediate scheme for British Art Center (March 1971), by Louis I. Kahn.

Figure 11 (left): Exterior, British Art Center by Louis I. Kahn.

Figure 12 (above): Library court, British Art Center by Louis I. Kahn. Photograph by KAALpurush.

In this resolution, Kahn moved toward a proper Beaux-Arts sequence. Unlike Cret, however, he cannot conceal the fact that there are elements that, while their arrangement suggests they are equivalent, are in fact of different sizes. As the gallery court has grown larger, the library court has been subdivided into multiple uses; the two have lost their original parity. The reading rooms that run the full length of the building along its outside edges also undermine the original programmatic distinctions between the two courts.

Kahn continued to emphasize the cross-axis that separates the two courts with the placement of the building's main entrance on Chapel Street, and he sought to relate this to the longitudinal axis by means of a monumental stair that acts as a sort of three-dimensional, reorienting hinge [FIGURE 8]. Its placement at the intersection of these axes, however, allows the visitor entering from Chapel Street to bypass the public court and also the formal beginning of the longitudinal Beaux-Arts sequence. The severity of this compromise is only partly mitigated by the stair's projection into the public courtyard, which at least establishes a visual connection with the bypassed starting point [FIGURE 10].[14]

In the final scheme Kahn resolved the choice between a proper Beaux-Arts sequence and a symmetrical orientation to Chapel Street. On the outside of the building he allowed his original common module of planning and structure to come to the fore and establish the exterior as a neutral container without any particular emphasis, its regular divisions more-or-less freely filled in with metal panels and windows [FIGURE 11].[15] He left the modules open at one end of the first floor to give the building the corner entrance suited to its location on an intersection.[16] In so doing, he brought together the previously separate entries on perpendicular axes in a single square covered porch on their diagonal. From here the visitor enters directly into the public gallery court, now placed at the end of the building's long axis at the beginning of its central narrative sequence.

This sequence Kahn rendered secret and unknowable from the point of arrival. He pushed the connecting stair back into the library court, encased it in a concrete silo [FIGURE 12], and turned it around to face the public court through a simple double door, so that it intimates a way forward without revealing a destination. On the second floor the enclosed stair brings the visitor not into the library court but rather deposits him after a full turn in a vestibule facing away from it [FIGURES 13 AND 14]. He must turn around and negotiate the silo—space into object!—to enter the institution's protected heart. The entire sequence, including a full revolution, has occurred on the building's long axis.

Without ever abandoning Beaux-Arts planning strategies—in fact by adopting them ever more faithfully—Kahn overcame in this way their characteristic deliberateness at the Yale Center for British Art. By encasing the organizing sequence of spaces in a regular, neutral

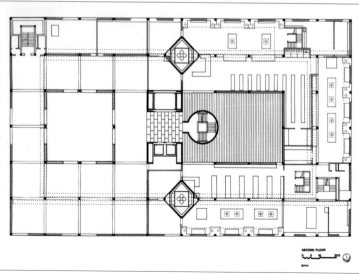

Figure 13 (top left): Staircase, British Art Center by Louis I. Kahn. Photograph by Ani Od Chai.

Figure 14 (left): Second Floor Plan, British Art Center by Louis I. Kahn.

container he detached the building's interior from its exterior, giving the latter a life of its own and allowing the former to become only gradually apparent. This process of discovery was further dramatized when Kahn hid the end of this sequence from the beginning. The full revolution effected by the staircase, and its transformation from a space that draws one in and establishes a clear path to an object that obstructs or deflects it, are strategies that embroider rather than simplify Beaux-Arts conventions. Both inside and outside Kahn concealed an organizing axial sequence behind added elements and layers, and by incorporating the element of surprise added drama to monumentality and recast a deliberate path as a revelatory journey.

With an understanding of Kahn's Beaux-Arts planning we might now return to the question of his modernist language. The monumentality of the Yale Center for British Art surely owes something also to its architectural language, which identifies the stages of the central sequence of spaces not with particular uses but with elemental relationships. Although the visitor may not immediately understand that he has arrived in the library court, which is surrounded on three sides by reading rooms, he will immediately recognize that he has reached his destination at the center of the institution. This potency is achieved at the cost of indicating particular uses. Kahn's language also obscures the purpose and meaning of the path, emphasizing a general rather than a particular institutional character. In an architectural language of construction, only material choices and finishes and changes in scale can distinguish between spaces that are built in the same way. The options for expressing either a hierarchy of purpose or associations with specific uses are consequently limited when compared with an architectural language that is premised on the embellishment of recognized forms. For this reason there is little beyond fittings, furniture, and proportions to identify Kahn's courts with research and exhibition, or his façade with an art museum. Muteness with regard to purpose and status is the cost of a language that emphasizes how a building is made over how it is used. When these aspects of use are elevated and special the cost is high. ✤

Samuel Roche graduated with an M.Arch. from Yale University in 2007, participated in the ICAA's Winterim in 2011, and is currently a Lecturer at the University of Miami.

NOTES

1. The critical tendency to abstraction is evident in a representative list of titles: *Louis I. Kahn: In the Realm of Architecture; What Will Be Has Always Been: The Words of Louis I. Kahn; Louis I. Kahn: The Idea of Order; Louis I. Kahn: Beyond Time and Style: A Life in Architecture.* There are also plenty of titles and books that do not emphasize this aspect of Kahn's architecture. For Kahn's own words about his work, see Richard Saul Wurman, *What Will Be Has Always Been: The Words of Louis I. Kahn* (New York: Access, 1986) and *Louis Kahn and Robert Twombly, Louis Kahn Essential Texts* (New York: Norton, 2003).

2. Kahn's first trip to Europe occurred in 1928, after his recent graduation from college.

3. For example see the discussion of Kahn's architecture in William Curtis's *Modern Architecture Since 1900*, (Englewood Cliffs, NJ: Prentice-Hall, 1983) which though more specific than most consistently mischaracterizes the classical aspects of Kahn's architecture either as mysterious and ineffable qualities of space and light or as the simplistic points of departure from which Kahn achieved these qualities. Specifically see the discussion of the Salk Institute, which addresses classical precedent primarily as it relates to literal formal quotation, which it denigrates as 'source hunting' (Curtis's quotation marks). Where Kahn's axial planning is recognized, it must be filtered through "intentions and experience…that are not so simple" to achieve an "air of ritual" and the "character of a philosopher's stage where ideas may be exchanged and the mysteries of nature studied." Thus are the elevated character and enriching effects produced by axial planning detached from their cause.

4. Richard Etlin discusses Kahn's architecture and his debt to Cret in *Symbolic Space: French Enlightenment Architecture and Its Legacy* (Chicago: University of Chicago Press, 1994), p. 86.

5. For Cret's employment of Kahn in his office from 1928 to 1930, where among other projects the young architect worked on the drawings for the Folger Library in Washington, D.C., see Vincent Scully *Louis I. Kahn* (New York: George Braziller, 1962) p. 14.

6. Scully, *op. cit.*, p. 12.

7. For a thorough account of the building, including a full bibliography, see Robert Alexander González, *Designing Pan-America: U.S. Architectural Visions for the Western Hemisphere*, (Austin: University of Texas Press, 2011), pp. 66-96.

8. Paul P. Cret, "The Pan-American Union Building," in Edward Warren Hoak and Willis Humphry Church, Masterpieces of Architecture in the United States (New York: C. Scribner's Sons, 1930), p. 127.

9. *Ibid.*

10. See Patricia Loud, *The Art Museums of Louis I. Kahn* (Durham: Duke University Press, 1989), pp. 176 ff.

11. The design process is traced in Loud, *op. cit.*, pp. 173-243. David Brownlee and David De Long, *Louis I. Kahn: In the Realm of Architecture*, (New York: Rizzoli, 1991), p. 411, cites Kahn's early emphasis on planning.

12. Kahn's first scheme is thus an elaboration on his Yale Art Gallery across the street (where the main entrance, however, is separated from the central spine of circulation). It also recalls Cret's plan for the Detroit Institute of the Arts from 1927, the central hall of which terminates in a covered garden court rather than a monumental stair.

13. The addition of an extra bay at one end of the building, presumably to achieve a double-loaded corridor around the gallery court, both undermines and calls attention to the overall bilateral symmetry. The plan also suggests that a proposed tunnel between the Center for British Art and the Yale Art Gallery might also account for the slight asymmetry.

14. The tension between these axes is also reflected in the elevation for this scheme (rendered in Beaux-Arts fashion to show cast shadows), which stresses all at once the dual nature of the program, the cross axial line of symmetry, and a uniform structural module. See Loud, *op. cit.*, figure 4.41, p. 195.

15. The sizes and positions of windows varied with the use of the rooms beyond; one could therefore "read" the façade in the Beaux-Arts manner as an arrangement of uses.

16. Reflecting the realities of frame construction rather than subverting the Beaux-Arts convention of a solid base; another instance in which the building could be "read."

Education and the Practice of Architecture

By Michael Lykoudis

With a traditional and classical approach to the city and its architecture, the University of Notre Dame School of Architecture strives to educate leaders who will build a future that is at once more humane, functional, and beautiful. The program's approach is predicated on the idea that architecture and urbanism shape both the public and private realms, and through them impact the ways in which we inhabit our planet. Using the latest technology and those time-tested techniques that were a necessary part of sustainable building before the Industrial Revolution, the School of Architecture has established itself as a leading voice in the contemporary Green Movement.

Almost by definition classical architecture embodies the principle of sustainability. The lessons learned from tradition must be relevant in resolving tomorrow's problems. We are told that certain Native American tribes never made any decisions without considering the consequences for the next seven generations. Today we barely think in terms of the next financial quarter.

Tradition can be thought of as the projection of society's highest aspirations into the future, thus ensuring that the best and most sustainable aspects of a culture endure. It is the inventive quality of tradition that allows each generation to shape its future. It is tradition's "memory" that provides the sense of stewardship required for sustainability.

One of the strengths of Notre Dame's School of Architecture is reflected in the diversity of the architectural practices who hire our graduates. In addition to the usual traditional and classical firms, offices that are not necessarily traditional in orientation have sought our classically trained alumni. The students of the school are attractive to firms regardless of their philosophical direction because they have three important characteristics:

First, they can draw and sketch. Possessing this skill is much like having a fluency of language that assists the architect in maintaining his or her clarity of thought. If students can draw well, they can more effectively identify the issues and express solutions more clearly.

Second, they understand the relationship between principles of construction and architectural form. During the course of their education, students study traditional methods of ventilation, heating, and earthquake readiness, among other topics, along with contemporary tenets of sustainability and durability. Therefore they are able to conceive buildings that surpass technological novelty and contribute to environmentally sound streets, blocks, neighborhoods, and cities.

Third, with their background in the study of urbanism they appreciate the complexity of the problems that they are asked to solve. They look for connections and relationships from environmental and cultural perspectives. Our students are equipped to meet the modern demands of urban planning by drawing upon the methods used to build and preserve the best cities in the world.

In the third-year Rome Studies Program, students work in varied European locations with local professionals. In the last two years alone, students have contributed to reconstructing the village of San Gregorio after the L'Aquila earthquake in Italy; furnishing a plan for development in Bath, England; and preserving historical sites in Romania.

The collaborative and interdisciplinary skills students develop are then put to use when re-introducing them into the American professional culture through a series of regional studios in the fourth-year curriculum. Students have designed new mixed-used residential neighborhoods on a brownfield site in Albuquerque, New Mexico; improved circulation conditions in Ventura, California; and proposed a revitalization of Los Angeles' Chinatown through studying zoning typologies and vernacular building types.

Operating under the assumption that the world doesn't need more suburbs—it instead needs to fix the eroding, suburbanizing cities—the school's Center for Building Communities coordinates viable solutions for locations throughout the United States. Students and faculty collaborate with real-estate developers and civic leaders to propose affordable housing, walkable communities, and regionally appropriate and sustainable building that is cohesive and loved.

The Notre Dame School of Architecture's approach to contemporary practice is not limited to theory and design. The curriculum covers many pragmatic and business issues as well, such as contracts and accessibility. Issues

TOP OF CUPOLA
56'
TOP OF CEILING
33' 6"
F.F.
15'4"
TOP OF CEILING
12'9"
F.F. LEVEL
COVE LIGHTING
STEEL JOIST
SUSPENDED PLASTER CEILING
1" RIGID INSULATION ON METAL C-SHAPED FURRING
2 WYTHE CMU WALL
1" AIRSPACE
CMU LINTEL
YELLOW BRICK VENEER

of the environment, high-quality construction, and better conditions for society to flourish are the cornerstone principles that all studios uphold. The school's philosophy places building at the center of a city with a global understanding of the implications that building has on the environment. Assessments of buildings based on their social, cultural, environmental, and intellectual worth reflect the idea that they are part of something larger than their clients or their designers. Whether the site is a plot at the edge of a village in India, or in the center of a large European city, the basic issues of how the building responds to and revitalizes the quality of life for its citizens and the preservation of the environment remain the same.

The practice of architecture will change even more dramatically than it already has. Architects will become more and more involved with the concept of design-build and large-scale development in order to survive as a profession. The boundaries between architecture and urban design are also becoming more and more blurred as the practice of architecture deals with the significant shift in the scale and diversity of work. The faculty's challenges with respect to preparing the students for this new world are to preserve a balance between the practical and business realities they will face with the ethical judgment of placing the needs of communities and the environment first.

Michael Lykoudis is the Francis and Kathleen Rooney Dean of the School of Architecture at the University of Notre Dame.

Figure 1 (Pages 58-59): Nicole Bernal-Cisneros, Redevelopment, Chelsea Barracks, London, UK, Aerial perspective.

Figure 2 (above): Nicole Bernal-Cisneros, Redevelopment, Chelsea Barracks, London, UK, Elevation and section.

UNIVERSITY OF NOTRE DAME

Fifth Year Undergraduate Studio
Spring 2010

INSTRUCTOR:
Samir Younés

PROJECT: Redevelopment, Chelsea Barracks, United Kingdom

In 2009, celebrated architect Richard Rogers proposed a master plan for a site known as the Chelsea Barracks in London. With her counter-proposal, fifth-year student Nicole Bernal-Cisneros reflected the Chelsea residents' sense of identity while creating a more environmentally friendly design. The site is in a rich historical context and its proximity to London's transit systems gives it great development potential. "By looking at traditional neighborhood models in London," Bernal-Ciseros says, "I proposed for the site a series of smaller blocks and squares to bring an appropriate density and visual scale to the area."

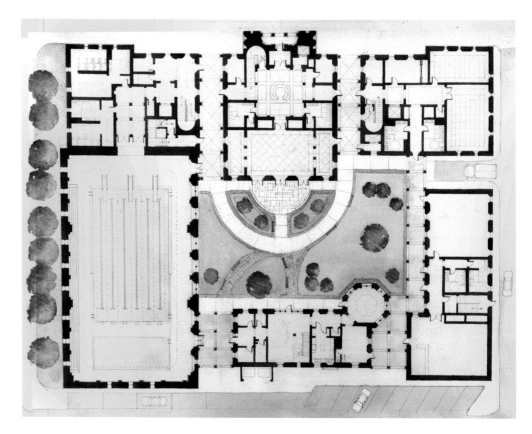

C I T Y   C L U B   O F   C H E L S E A ,   U. K.

Figures 3 and 4 (above): Nicole Bernal-Cisneros, Redevelopment, Chelsea Barracks, London, UK, Floor Plan and Elevation.

UNIVERSITY OF NOTRE DAME

Fifth Year Undergraduate Studio
Spring 2010

INSTRUCTOR:
Stella Papadopoulos

PROJECT: Steel City Development

Fifth-year student Kevin Sommers used his thesis to design an expansion of Pittsburgh's Station Square on the South Shore of the Monongahela River. Sommers focused on a mixed-use, condominium mid-rise located in the center of the redevelopment, combining residential units for an influx of people moving to the heart of the city, and entertainment venues to attract visitors. Steel framed with a stone veneer, Sommers pays homage to "The Steel City," blending the new structure into its historic setting.

Figures 1, 2, and 3 (below): Kevin Sommers, Station Square, Pittsburgh, Pennsylvania, Perspective, Site Plan and Elevation.

UNIVERSITY OF NOTRE DAME

Fourth Year Undergraduate Studio
Spring 2010

INSTRUCTOR:
Gilbert Gorski

PROJECT: Eco Retreat
Fourth-year student James Paul Hayes designed an Eco Retreat in Oman on the southeast coast of the Arabian Peninsula, which allows guests to live as locals—wearing local fashions, eating local fare, using local transportation (camels, caravans), and practicing local meditation and spa techniques. The site was a hypothetical bluff backed by mountains overlooking a vast stretch of sand dunes. The retreat's design is a contemporary take on classical Islamic architecture, including shops, spas, a dining area, and a mosque, in addition to the guest rooms, which are all on the bluff's exterior to allow for uninhibited views of the dunes.

Figures 1 and 2 (top and bottom): James Paul Hayes, Eco Retreat, Nizwa, Oman, Plans and Perspectives.

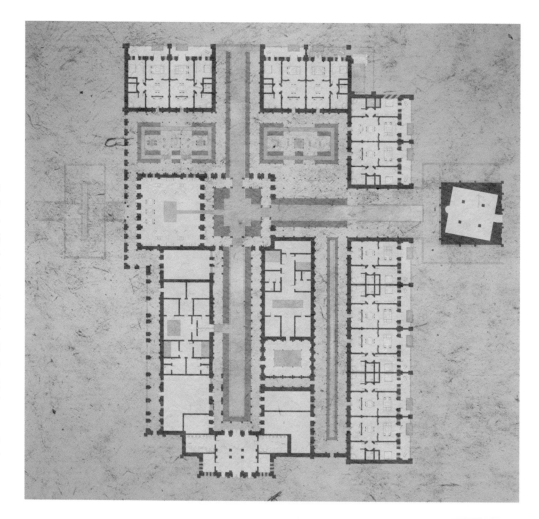

UNIVERSITY OF NOTRE DAME
Fifth Year Undergraduate Studio
Spring 2010

INSTRUCTOR:
Samir Younés

PROJECT: A Muslim Community Center
Fifth-year student Dennis Varvaro designed a mosque to serve the Muslim community in Tampa, Florida. A monumental courtyard, bordered on its inner side by a colonnaded peristyle, precedes the mosque itself, which features a dome and two minarets. Intended to serve both religious and cultural needs, the complex includes a religious school, library, a cultural center, a food kitchen for the poor, dining halls, shops, and offices for community outreach.

Figures 1 and 2 (left and below): Dennis Varvaro, Muslim Community Center, Tampa, FL, analytique and section detail.

GEORGIA INSTITUTE OF TECHNOLOGY

Master of Science in
Classical Architectural Design
Spring 2010

INSTRUCTORS:
Michael Mesko
Jeremy Sommer
Clay Rokicki

PROJECT: New stations for the Belt Line
The studio assignment proposed six neighborhood transit hub stations for the future Belt Line, a light rail line and greenway, which will eventually combine parkland, trails, transit, and new development along 22 miles of historic rail segments that encircle the urban core of Atlanta. Each student was charged with designing one station for a unique Atlanta neighborhood.

While satisfying the functional requirements of the proposed transit line, the stations were designed to also serve as identifiable civic landmarks for each community. In locations where an infrastructure of traditional streets and blocks had not been established or had degenerated, modifications were proposed to encourage pedestrian oriented redevelopment.

Each station design includes waiting areas and ticketing services as well as commercial space, community meeting rooms, and areas for public gathering.

Figures: Peachtree Station by Syl Bartos *(top).*

Piedmont Park Station by Cameron Bishop *(middle left).*

Glenwood Station by Race Alexander *(middle right).*

Highland Avenue Station by Ryan Moss *(bottom right).*

West End Station by Glenn Larrimore *(opposite top).*

Metropolitan Station by Darius Stewart *(opposite bottom).*

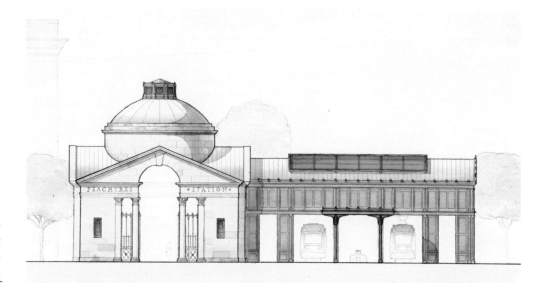

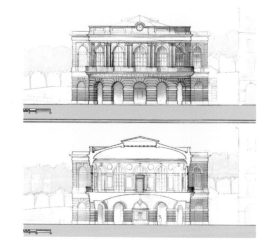

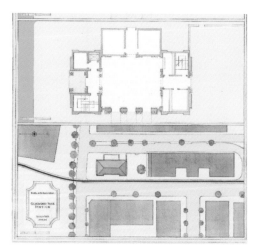

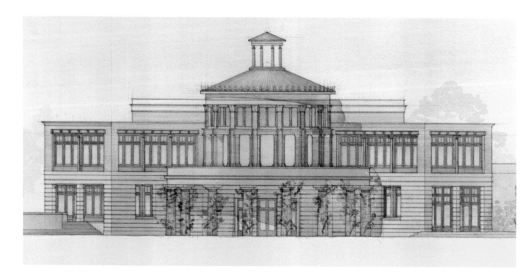

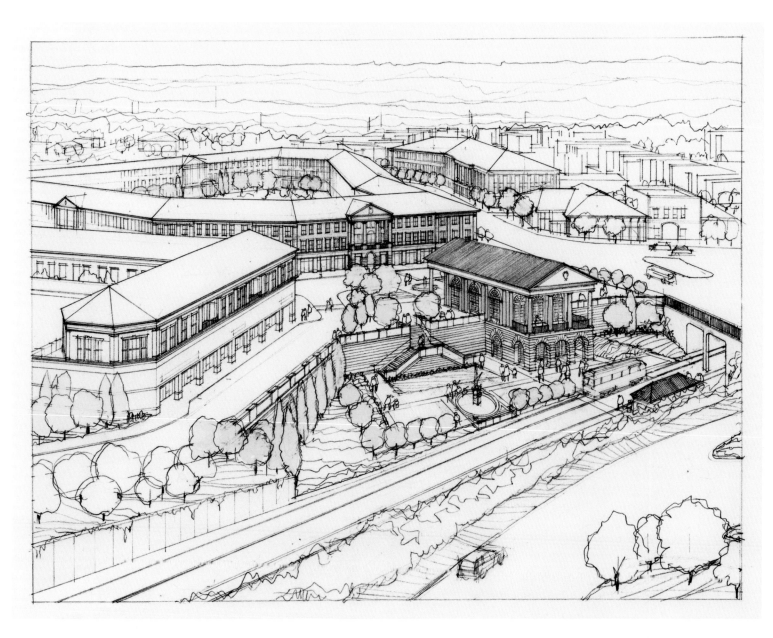

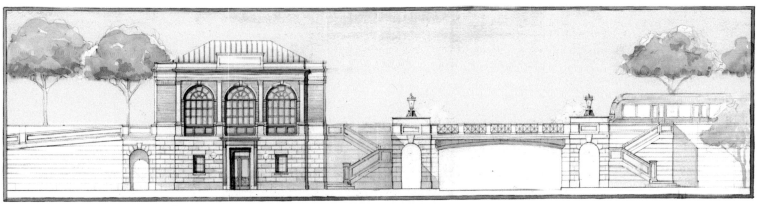

GEORGIA INSTITUTE OF TECHNOLOGY

M.Arch. Thesis: David Pearson
Spring 2011

THESIS COMMITTEE:
Douglas C. Allen
Jude Le Blanc
Russell Gentry

PROJECT: A New Museum and Entrance for the Palatine Hill in Rome

The Palatine Hill, with over one thousand years of archaeological evidence, represents one of the most signifcant sites in the history of Western Civilization. The present museum rests on top of the seam where the Domus Flavia and the Domus Augustana meet. It presently inhibits a coherent narrative display, rendering the Palatine an enigma to the majority of its visitors.

To provide the visitor a more intelligible entrance sequence to the Palatine Hill, this proposal demolishes the existing structure and offers a design for a new pedagogical museum on a different site. A secondary aim is to design in such a way as to be sympathetic to and cognizant of the building traditions present on the Palatine.

To acknowledge the significance of the Palatine, not only in the formation and life of ancient Rome, but as the origin of the most signifcant city in the history of western civilization, the design treats the site so as not to disturb the material record and allow the visitor to experience the Palatine as a complex historical artifact.

A study of the site using maps and personal observation concluded that the project should be related to the physical remains of the structures that are on the hill. An investigation into Roman domestic architecture and a course on the Roman City helped formulate the opinion that the new museum should resemble these structures. The Domus Flavia and Domus Augustana are based on the plan of a typical Roman House; their spatial organization therefore guides the design of the new museum. The site for the new entrance and museum is the southeast corner of the Palatine on the former location of the now destroyed Septizodium, the giant fountain complex glorifying the Severan emperors. The Septizodium was located at the terminus of the Via Appia and to this day the site is one of the chief entrances into the city from the airport.

Figures 1, 2, and 3 (below): David Pearson, A New Museum and Entrance for the Palatine Hill, perspectival views from the model show shadows cast on the morning and afternoon of Rome's birthday, April 21, 2011.

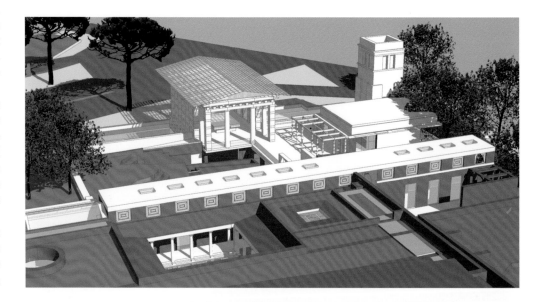

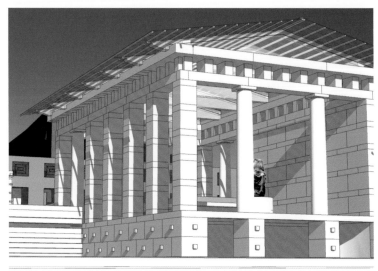

UNIVERSITY OF MIAMI
New(est) New Urbanism Studio
Spring 2010

INSTRUCTORS:
Jaime Correa
Andrew Cogar
Christopher Carrigan
Josh Martin

PROJECT: The Repair of Suburbia: A case for the retrofit of sprawling areas

In the spring semester of 2010, the South Carolina Coastal Conservation League and the Atlanta-based firm Historical Concepts sponsored a studio in the University of Miami School of Architecture. The studio, led by Prof. Jaime Correa, was dedicated to the exploration of traditional American urbanism and architecture in three stages: Documentation, Master Plan, and Architecture.

The studio examined four neighborhoods along a proposed light rail line in the Charleston, South Carolina, region in order to demonstrate the principle of repairing suburbia through Transit Oriented Development. One group of students focused on a station in historic Summerville, which exemplified the revitalization of the delicate downtown fabric. Two other groups of students studied two stations in North Charleston (Ashley Phosphate Road and Dorchester Road), which consisted of suburban neighborhoods with monotype housing subdivisions and car oriented offices and retail. Finally, a group of students studied a station in the Upper Peninsula of Charleston in which the historic urban fabric had been bisected by a conventional suburban highway.

Figure 1 (top). Master Plan with perspectives by the Ashley Phosphate Road team: Aaron Aeschliman, Katherine Guyon, and Damir Islamovic.

Figures 2 and 3 (middle and bottom). Master Plan with Street Sections and Figure Ground Comparison by the Summerville team: Oscar Carlson, Lindsay Hardy, and Lucia Perez.

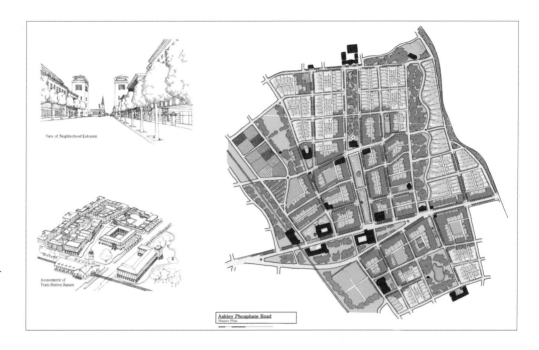

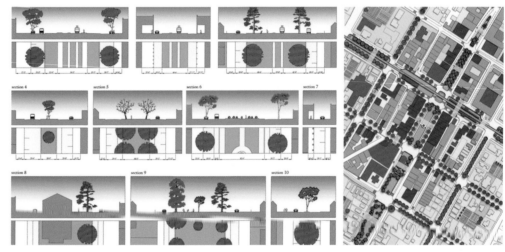

UNIVERSITY OF MIAMI
Upper Level Elective Studio
Spring 2011

INSTRUCTORS:
Joanna Lombard with adjunct faculty and visiting consultants including Michael Swartz and Sean Nohelty.

PROJECT: Healthcare Studio
This studio focuses on the design of a health care campus, streetscape, and related facilities in collaboration with teams from the Masters in Real Estate + Urbanism Program. Projects include a new children's hospital, medical office buildings and specialty clinics, as well as related buildings—hospitality house, retail, and work-force housing. Two sites—the Miami Health District and Richmond's West End—provide opportunities to explore evidence–based design, sustainability, and community building.

Figures 1 and 2 (above and right): Abigail Bricker, Jeffrey Oxsalida, and Melissa Walton, Proposal for a new Bon Secours Children's Hospital for Richmond, Virginia.

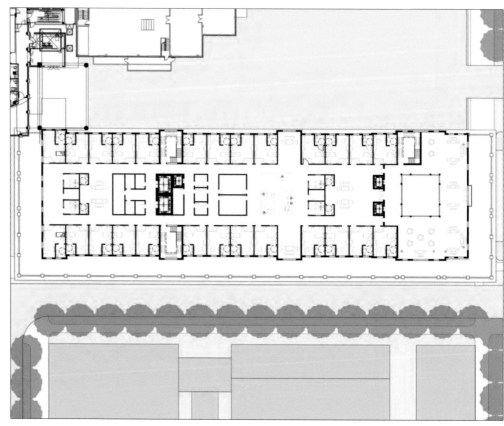

UNIVERSITY OF MIAMI
First Year Graduate Studio
Fall 2010

INSTRUCTOR:
Carie Penabad

PROJECT: Composing a new façade for San Lorenzo

As part of their introductory studio, students were asked to complete the unfinished façade for the church of San Lorenzo in Florence, Italy. The existing building, located on the site of a pre-existing Romanesque church, was designed in the 1420s by Filippo Brunelleschi, who died before the work was completed. In 1517, Pope Leo X commissioned Michelangelo to design a façade for San Lorenzo. It would have been the artist's first architectural project. Michelangelo worked on the design until 1520, when the Pope lost interest in the project. Nearly five centuries later, the façade remains unfinished.

To carry out the design, students were required to engage in a dialogue with the rich history of the period and to acquire an understanding of the immediate physical setting (i.e. San Lorenzo and its surrounding buildings) as well as the broader urban, architectural, historical, and cultural contexts of Florence. Graduate student Christopher Stoddard made a study model of Raphael's facade design based on a drawing preserved in the Gabinetto Disegni e Stampe of the Uffizi.

Figure 1 (below): Christopher Stoddard, Model of Manfredo Tafuri's reconstruction of Raphael's design for the façade of San Lorenzo based on Uffizi drawing UA 2048.

YALE UNIVERSITY SCHOOL OF ARCHITECTURE
Advanced Design Studio
Spring 2009

INSTRUCTORS:
Demetri Porphyrios
George Knight

PROJECT: A Spa Center
The studio studied the tradition of Hellenistic, Roman, and Muslim baths from a typological and morphological point of view. Students visited Marrakech to study relevant architectural and urban design examples and were then asked to design a present-day spa center, informed by historical precedent, on a site of their own choice.

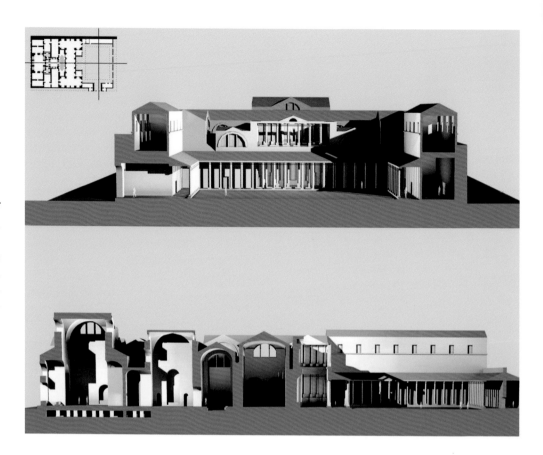

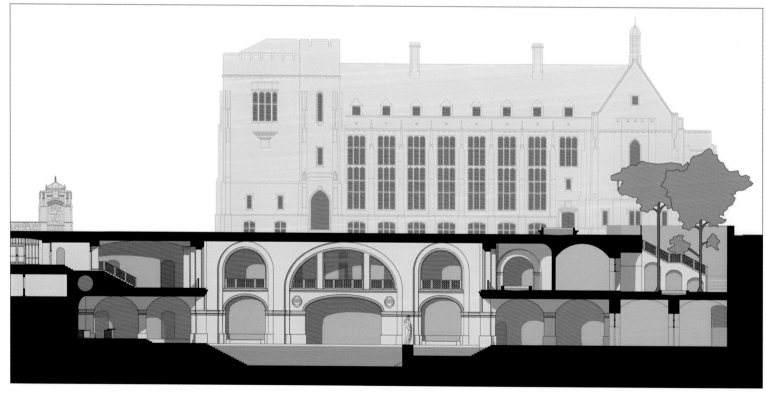

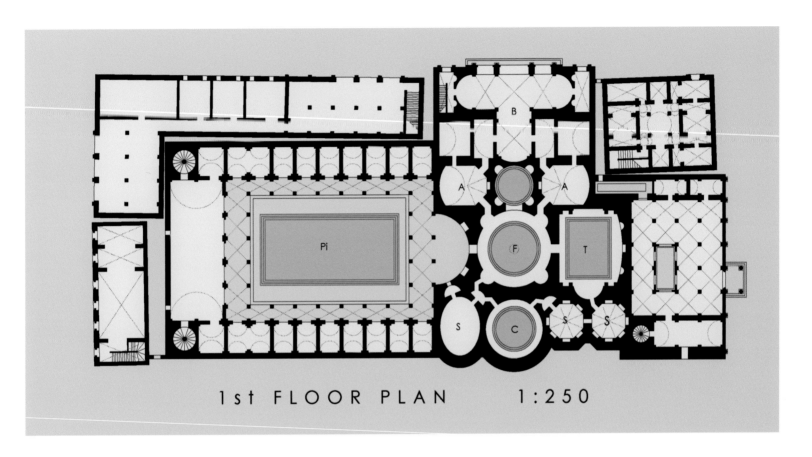

1st FLOOR PLAN   1:250

Figure 1 (opposite top): Scott O'Daniel, Baths of Vedius, Ephesus, study model.

Figure 2 (opposite bottom): Scott O'Daniel, Proposed Thermae (Baths) for Yale University, section.

Figures 3, 4, and 5 (this page): Angel Beale, Proposed Spa Complex, Old San Juan, Puerto Rico, plan, section, and 3-D plaster print model.

JUDSON UNIVERSITY
Advanced Design Studios

INSTRUCTOR:
Christopher Miller

Judson University's liberal arts character and the rich student interest in ethical service shape Judson's architecture program. The curriculum works to integrate the diverse approaches of its faculty (including a value in the history of architecture in contemporary practice) and the importance of cultivating the tradition of urban environments. At present, opportunities for students to explore classical architecture and traditional urbanism are found in summer European study, in a civic architecture studio, in watercolor instruction, in a substantial history and theory curriculum at the undergraduate and graduate levels, and in independent and thesis projects.

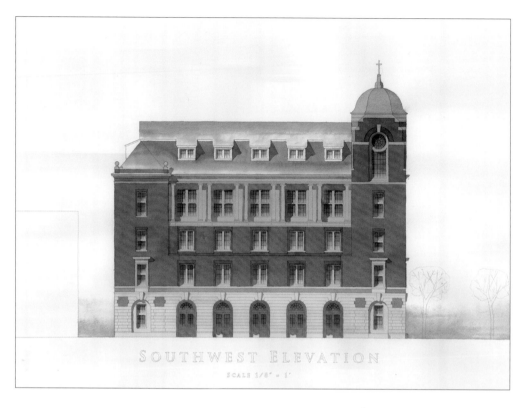

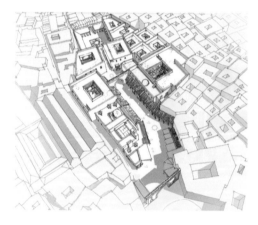

Figure 1 (above): Jessica Otte, Urban design proposal for brownfield site in Fez, Morocco, aerial perspective.

Figure 2 (top right): Samuel J. Lima, Mixed use building for Chelsea Barracks site, London, UK, elevation.

Figure 3 (bottom right): Jared Natalino, New City Hall for Boston, MA, side elevation.

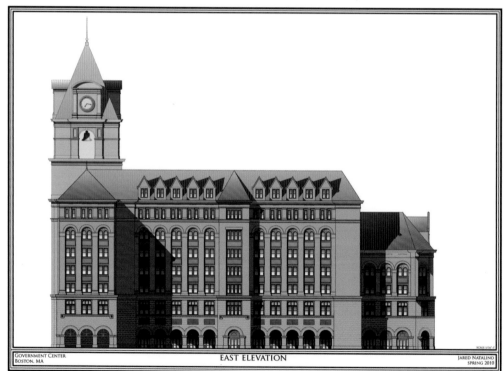

COLLEGE OF CHARLESTON
Architectural Design Studio

INSTRUCTOR:
Ralph Muldrow

PROJECT: Doodads and Whatchama-columns
The College of Charleston is a venerable liberal arts institution that dates back to 1770. Surrounded by the tightly woven urban fabric of the city of Charleston, with all its glorious and idiosyncratic architecture, it is a beguiling place for architecture buffs.

For fifteen years, Ralph Muldrow has taught the only Architectural Design Studio course at the college, successfully encouraging students in the study of historic buildings. Although students are permitted to pursue a variety of approaches, most want to learn to design in the traditional Charleston classical and vernacular modes.

This project assignment inspires the creativity of the students by asking: "What kind of orders of architecture, and especially column capitals, would you use of your own accord?" The students find this broad invitation an eye-opener to the many kinds of column capitals found in Charleston. Student Michelle Manning decided to make the order her own by reflecting on the emblems on the state flag: palmetto trees and a crescent. The Palmetto tree harkens back to the Revolutionary War when General Moultrie built a fort on Sullivan's Island so that the bombardment of British cannon balls would be stymied: The resistant palmetto logs of the fort caused the cannonballs to bounce away into the water. The crescent, strangely enough, does not represent the moon, but rather the protective collar worn by soldiers, called a gorget.

The capital on Jacob Hinton's design features a compass in the center with swags made from local foliage. Randi Stevens's project features sunflower volutes reminiscent of the sunflower metope enrichments at Drayton Hall, the early-eighteenth-century house near Charleston.

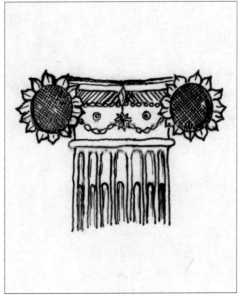

Figure 1 (top): Capital by Michelle Manning.

Figure 2 (bottom left): Capital by Jacob Hinton.

Figure 3 (bottom right): Capital by Randi Stevens.

INSTITUTE OF CLASSICAL ARCHITECTURE & ART
Rome Drawing Tour
June 2010

INSTRUCTORS:
John Woodrow Kelley
Michael Mesko
John Varriano

The annual ICAA Rome Drawing Tour has attracted students, professionals, and lay people over the years. Instructors are selected for their individual talents and collective knowledge. Each has a proven ability to teach effectively and, most importantly, their combined disciplines—history, fine art, and architecture—serve to foster a meaningful appreciation for the enduring aesthetic achievements in Roman art and architecture from Antiquity to the Baroque. 2010 tour highlights included the Villa Lante at Bagnaia, the Palazzo Farnese at Caprarola, and the work of Bramante, Michelangelo, and Borromini.

Figure 1 (below): Greg Shue, Courtyard of the Sapienza, Rome.

Figure 2 (right): Ryan Moss, Courtyard of the Sapienza, Rome.

INSTITUTE OF CLASSICAL ARCHITECTURE & ART

Elements of Classical Architecture
Winterim 2010

INSTRUCTOR:
Martin Brandwein

The ICAA Professional Intensive programs are designed to provide current and future design professionals with the unique chance to receive in-depth training in the principles of classical design, in both its technical and artistic dimensions. Elements of Classical Architecture, a key course in the program, provides an introduction to the vocabulary of classical architecture through free-hand drawing. Students learn to draw the fundamental classical orders and frequent sketch problems allow students to understand the compositional principles by which the orders and other classical elements are used to create a classical building. Issues of proportion, history, traditional construction techniques, interior planning, and ornamentation are also reviewed. Course instruction includes lectures and studio sessions.

Figure 1 (below): Construction of the Corinthian capital by Jeff Dicicco, recipient of the I-Grace Scholarship, Winterim 2010.

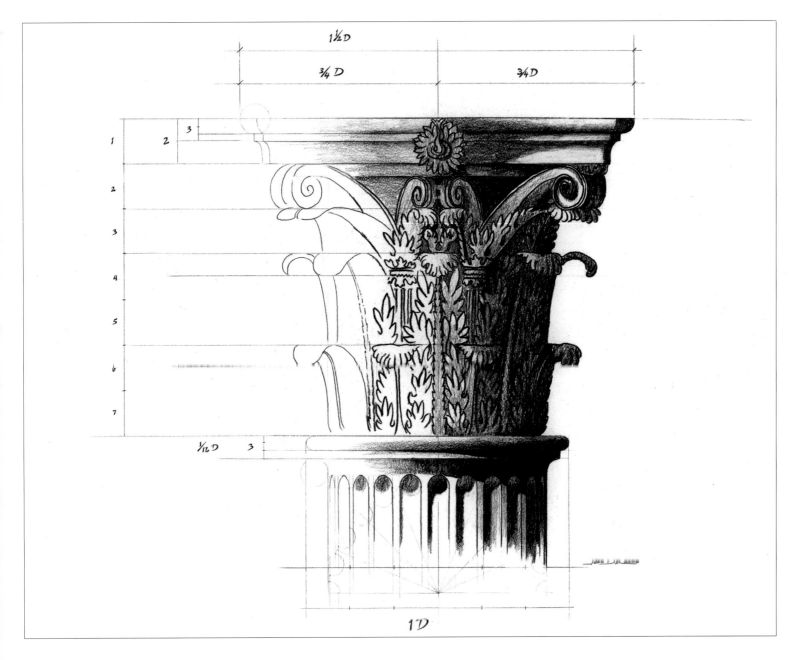

DEMETRI PORPHYRIOS
REFUTATIONS AND CONJECTURES

By Kyle Dugdale

Few would deny that Demetri Porphyrios is among the more academic of today's practitioners of traditional and classical architecture. An uncompromising presence in the studio at Yale, he can argue ontology and linguistics with the best of them; he is not only familiar with Hegel and Heidegger, but he is prepared to disagree with both.[1] The practice of architecture, he argues, is a serious scholarly enterprise, an enterprise in which ignorance is inexcusable; and for an architect who builds, Porphyrios has published extensively, even if it is possible to detect the traces of an inverse relationship between his publishing output and the success of his practice. In this regard, no doubt, he is in good company.

It must be said that the style of his early writing can prove obscure and frustrating to the reader.[2] Yet it succeeds in conveying an impression of immense erudition. The nadir of textual complexity seems to have been passed shortly after he earned his Ph.D. at Princeton, and his writing has grown more transparent over the years. In his speech, as in his suiting, he is impeccably presented; if, in the inflections of the former, one is perhaps reminded of his native Greek origins, his powers of articulation are nonetheless unchallenged. And yet some would argue that he is broadly misunderstood today, not least because his architecture seems, on the face of it, so straightforward, so readily categorised as an exercise in unrepentant historicism. If, on this interpretation, the more obviously complex work of an architect like Daniel Libeskind or Peter Eisenman might be considered (if the reader will forgive the expression) a "known unknown"[3]—that is, one can acknowledge the difficulty of immediately articulating the thesis behind the architecture—Porphyrios' work might instead be characterised as an unknown unknown masquerading as a known known. What follows here aims to explore that characterisation and to begin to unravel a few of the influences behind Porphyrios' practice.[4]

CRITIC AND CRITICISM

It is clear to all that Porphyrios is not a modernist—and this despite a considerable expertise on the subject. He turned his doctoral thesis into a book that is still held by many to be a definitive point of reference for the critical analysis of Alvar Aalto: *Sources of Modern Eclecticism*, published in 1982 by Andreas Papadakis' Academy Editions and structured around the work of Foucault and Althusser [FIGURE 1].[5] In fact, Porphyrios takes a strong position on the integrity of the modernist project, as this paper will suggest.

What may be less obvious is that he would not call himself a postmodernist. Postmodernism, he explains, is "just wallpaper" [FIGURE 2]. He condemns, as he puts it, both "Post-Modern Classicism and Post-Modern Modernism," arguing that "a few pilasters or some riveted joints thrown in as . . . signs of a constructional order are not enough to give a building a tectonic presence."[6] Nor is he interested in what he calls "the self-indulgent antiquarianism of the 'Heritage' industry," or in "the sentimentalities of historicism."[7] He is equally dismissive of "revivalism," which "promises the restitution of past life and, ultimately, . . . reduces history into cosy and pacifying fetishes."[8]

And yet this is exactly how many other architects think of him: as an "antiquarian" (to use the term proposed in George Kubler's *Shape of Time*)—an antiquarian of the more pedantic sort, who "only re-creates" while "the historian composes."[9] In other words, he is considered a mere imitator, and as such (setting aside, for the moment, Aristotle's arguments to the contrary) he is deemed not only fundamentally uninteresting but possibly even dangerous.

Opposite: Demetri Porphyrios, Interamerican Headquarters, Athens, Greece, 2000-02.

All images of the work of Dr. Porphyrios are Copyright ©D. Porphyrios.

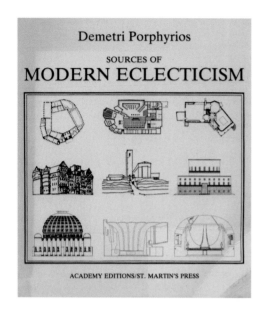

This latter allegation is reminiscent of the position taken by Peter Eisenman in 2003, when it was announced that Porphyrios would be building a new Gothic college for his alma mater [FIGURES 3-4]. Eisenman, quoted in *Metropolis*, "objects to building collegiate Gothic anywhere today but is particularly troubled by the decision to do it at Princeton."[10] The reason for the objection is that Princeton's Gothic architecture (in this case the work of Ralph Adams Cram) is for Eisenman indelibly tainted by association with the sins of our fathers—our prejudiced, elitist, perhaps even racist fathers;[11] and building in such a vocabulary today runs the risk of condoning, or even exacerbating, those sins.

This is a serious allegation, and not one that can simply be shrugged off. Indeed, it can be directed not only towards Gothic architecture at Princeton, but to other architectural languages and to other sites further afield.[12] It represents, in effect, the thin edge of a wedge to be driven between traditional architecture and contemporary practice; and at the further end of that same wedge is the darker memory, often unspoken, of an association between the language of classical architecture and the purposes of Nazi Germany. If it is impossible to do justice to such questions in an essay as short as this, it also seems disingenuous to avoid them altogether.

The linguistic parallels to this allegation have, perhaps, been more rigorously explored than their architectural counterparts. It is clear that language often bears the traces of past abuse; the history of racial epithets might provide a ready example. It is also clear, if perhaps less obvious, that the peculiarities of a language and the idiosyncrasies of its application can obstruct or facilitate particular patterns of thought in ways that may tie that language in a more than casual manner to error or to violence. Not only are there many for whom it remains impossible entirely to disassociate the German language from the rhetoric of National Socialism; some might argue that the German language lent itself with peculiar facility to the purposes of that rhetoric—just as

Martin Heidegger's distinctive use of language not only communicated but in some regards made possible the direction of his thinking.

But what are the implications for contemporary communication? And do those lessons hold when translated into architectural terms? Indeed, architecture in general (and classical architecture in particular) is in some significant ways *not* a language, and it is perhaps important to be wary of assuming too close a parallel. While Porphyrios himself invites examination of the analogy between architecture and language,[13] he too advises caution: he is unwilling to condone "the historicist fallacy of Modernism,"[14] the assumption of too close an association between form and cultural or political ideology. Language, in his view, is not irredeemably corrupted by the history of its own abuse; and in the specific case of Princeton, avoidance of a Gothic vocabulary would do little to address the concerns expressed by Eisenman.

Taken to extremes, the logic of avoidance can lead to absurd conclusions. Barring the possibility of identifying an age of historical innocence—the possibility of rediscovering Adam's house in Paradise—each generation would have to invent a new vocabulary of forms in which to express itself in hopes of disassociating itself from the faults of its forebears.[15] To pursue the linguistic analogy, each new generation, troubled by the violence done by its fathers through language, would be obliged to invent a new language with which to communicate. Instead, the

Figure 1 (top left): Cover of *Sources of Modern Eclecticism.*

Figure 2 (top center): Wimberly Allison Tong & Goo, The Venetian, Las Vegas, NV, 1999.

Figures 3 and 4 (opposite): Demetri Porphyrios, Whitman College, Princeton University, NJ, 2002-07.

Figure 5 (top right): Cover of *Oppositions.*

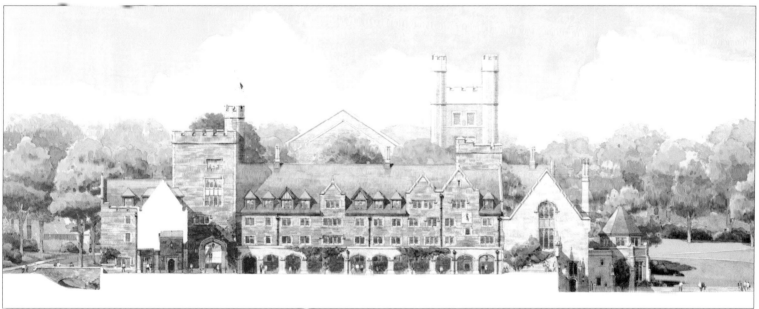

Figure 6 (top): Ralph Adams Cram, Old Graduate College, Princeton University, NJ, 1913. Photograph by Marissa Smith.

Figure 7 (bottom): Hibben-Magie Apartments, Princeton University, NJ.

Figure 8 (opposite left): Michael Graves, Hanselman House, Fort Wayne, IN, 1967-71.

Figure 9 (opposite right): Michael Graves, Clos Pegase, Calistoga, CA, 1984-7. Photograph by Wally Gobetz.

traditionalist might argue that one should no more reject *tout court* the idiom (in this case) of collegiate Gothic than one should forbid the use of German. Indeed, it is not German alone, nor, for that matter, Gothic or classical architecture alone, that would stand condemned by a strict application of such standards: no language is spared. It rapidly becomes apparent that the most contemporary of languages are themselves tainted by their own sins both of commission and of omission. Not only is the past irredeemable; there is little in the way of hope for the present. What remains is despair.[16]

The alternative, for the traditionalist, is to insist that in architecture linguistic content should not be subordinated to form, even if the two can never be fully separated—or to insist on the primacy of content and the relative autonomy of form, arguing that disuse of a particular language cannot substitute for active critique of prior misuse. This points, perhaps, towards a denial of the assumption that avoidance absolves the speaker from further responsibility. The rejection of Gothic architecture at Princeton, in other words, would do little to combat the dangers of prejudice, elitism, or racism; one might even argue that construction of a new collegiate Gothic building at Princeton, if accompanied by debate over the dangers involved, is ultimately more valuable (in these terms at least) than construction of a more contemporary structure, which might never provoke that debate. That, of course, assumes the existence of such a debate.

Much also depends upon the character of historical awareness in a given situation. On one level, perception will always trump reality. If the building of new Gothic architecture is indeed interpreted by Princeton's constituencies as an assertion of prejudice, then that is a real problem with which the architect must contend, whatever the merits of the case. Happily for Porphyrios, it is not clear that Eisenman's sensitivities in the context of Princeton were shared by many others— at least, not consciously. That said, each case must, by the same token, be assessed separately; the pursuit of traditional architecture at Princeton is unlikely to provoke the same reactions as the pursuit of traditional architecture at Oxford, in Germany, or in the Middle East.

This sort of specificity clearly has broad implications; indeed, the difficulties of assessing linguistic impact across culture might argue against the sort of international practice so frequently courted today. Further, such challenges cut across all boundaries of architectural allegiance. There are many for whom any architecture that smacks of modernism bears with it a host of poisonous associations, for reasons that may prove remarkably similar to those attributed to irresponsible traditionalism. In all cases, it seems, the architect must proceed with caution.

But there is an additional strand to the noose of Eisenman's accusation. Eisenman argued that Porphyrios' architecture was simply not a good fit for a university that in 2003 was "a very radical institution."[17] The implication was that Porphyrios' architecture was *not* radical, but rather fundamentally conservative. This too is a not uncommon assessment today. But if conservatism is, at least in part, marked by an unwillingness to challenge the prevailing orthodoxy of one's own generation, the labelling of Porphyrios as "conservative" would at the least need to be qualified quite carefully. To judge by the speed with which Porphyrios was dropped by the mainline architectural establishment once he started building according to his supposed non-radical theory, he rather quickly became something of a pariah among his peers. As a young architect and academic he consorted with the likes of Rem Koolhaas (five years older) and Zaha Hadid (one year younger); the rumour is that it was he who arranged for Hadid her position in Koolhaas' office. There was a time when he was invited to contribute to *Oppositions* magazine, his texts featured alongside submissions by Anthony Vidler, Kurt Forster, and Kenneth Frampton [FIGURE 5]. But that did not last. Until quite recently the list of schools at which he has been invited to teach has remained short, and attitudes within the academy towards his work have been unsympathetic. Eisenman in 2003 compared Porphyrios' approach at Princeton to creationism: "I mean, they don't teach creationism here, right? This is akin to teaching creationism."[18]

EDUCATION

If the work of Porphyrios has been exposed to conflicting evaluations, a review of his biographical background might encourage a more careful assessment. He was born in Athens in 1949, his parents having left Constantinople during the anti-Orthodox purges of the 1920s. This was the decade of the so-called "population exchange" between Greece and Turkey, an agreed mutual expulsion, based on religion, of about two million people, most of whom were forcibly made refugees from their homelands. The Greek population of Constantinople was technically exempt from this expulsion, but in reality 70,000 of them fled around the same time. And so for Porphyrios, growing up in Athens, "life was always about loss, about trying to regain what we'd had."[19] One might argue that this experience rendered him unusually qualified to speak with a clear perspective on the rootless nature both of the human condition in general and of modern existence in particular, with a peculiar sensitivity, born of the experience of diaspora, to culture, history, and place. On the other hand, it is not as clear whether this experience would make him a good spokesman for the architectural profession more broadly—although one might want to compare the influence of Léon Krier's childhood in Luxembourg,[20] of wartime loss "made good" by reconstruction.

Porphyrios' father, a Homeric scholar, was of the opinion that architecture was too much of a trade, unsuitable for his academically brilliant son. So Demetri studied art history at the University of Athens for a while, before leaving for Princeton to study architecture against the wishes of the elder Porphyrios.[21]

His experience of post-war architecture in Athens had been unrewarding: most of it was poorly built, utilitarian, and insubstantial. But at Princeton, where he earned his M.Arch. (1974) and his Ph.D. in history and theory (1980), he not only found an intellectual home (in his own words, he "learned that architecture could be about ideas"),[22] but he also found in the buildings of Cram the architectural solidity that he longed for [FIGURE 6]. "When I was in the Graduate College, it was a fantastic experience—the rooms, the spaces, the courtyard and its relation to the great hall. All of those things were really memorable. Then in my third year I got married." This proved an architectural disaster, as Porphyrios was obliged to move "into one of those towers down by the lake (the 1960s Hibben-Magie Apartments [FIGURE 7]). It was devastating. I was stuck in a fifth- or sixth-floor apartment. Every time I looked at the nature outside—which was so beautiful—when I reached to touch it I had to go through the mediation of an elevator."[23]

Porphyrios' disillusionment with the state of contemporary architecture put him in good company. Already in 1961 Alvar Aalto, who would become the subject of his Ph.D. thesis, had set the scene: "the architectural revolution is still going on but it is like all revolutions: it starts with enthusiasm and it stops with some sort of dictatorship."[24] Porphyrios' generation was faced, right out of school, with the collapse of that dictatorship, the loss of the comfort of modernist certainty. If 1920s modernism had promised that "the old chaos was to be superseded by a New Order replete with its own laws,"[25] then that new order seemed to have been overcome in turn by a new chaos. What would take its place? A return to the old laws?[26]

To frame the context: In 1966 Robert Venturi had published *Complexity and Contradiction;* in 1972, while Porphyrios was at Princeton, Venturi published *Learning from Las Vegas;* and on July 15th of that same year, "at 3:32 P.M. (or thereabouts),"[27] the demolition of Minoru Yamasaki's award-winning Pruitt Igoe housing after fewer than twenty years of occupancy marked for many the definitive disintegration, quite literally, of modernist certainty. In 1975, just as Porphyrios had

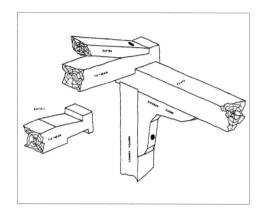 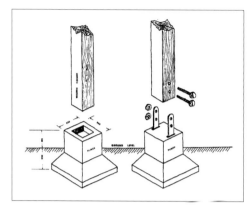 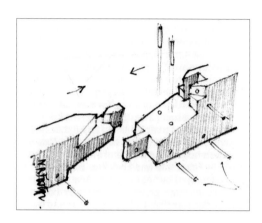

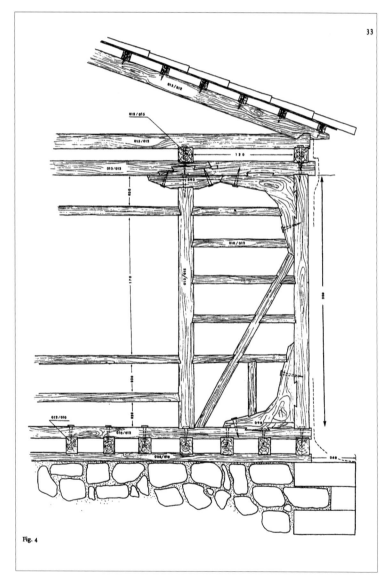

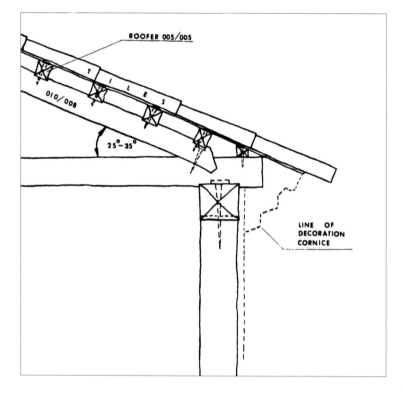

Figures 10 and 11 (top left and center): Demetri Porphyrios, drawings of traditional earthquake-resistant construction, 1971.

Figures 12 and 13 (left and above): Demetri Porphyrios, drawings of traditional earthquake-resistant construction, 1971.

Figure 14 (top right): Norman Foster, detail of a study drawing of sixteenth-century oak-pegged roof, student work at Manchester University, 1959.

completed his M.Arch., MoMA opened its Beaux-Arts exhibition. In 1977, in a special issue of *Oppositions* edited by Vidler, Porphyrios wrote of "our already aging modernity; a modernity which only a decade ago was still alive, but which, unfortunately or fortunately, is now slowly disintegrating before our eyes."[28] The landscape of architectural discourse was in the throes of radical reassessment.

That said, Porphyrios' teacher at Princeton in the early 1970s, a young Michael Graves, was still very much a Corbusian, not a postmodernist—one can observe clearly the later shift, under the influence of Krier, around 1975-76 [FIGURES 8-9].[29] Graves ruled the roost at Princeton, and Porphyrios acted as his teaching assistant;[30] Porphyrios himself produced neo-Corbusian work, in the manner, perhaps, of Richard Meier.[31] Only his final M.Arch. studio thesis project, under Diana Agrest, was atypical in its debt to the work of Aalto. But he remembers what he describes as "fantastic" lectures by Louis Kahn and by Colin Rowe, who, at the time, were both reinterpreting classical architecture in new ways.[32]

Porphyrios went on to pursue his dissertation on Aalto, advised by Vidler. His interest, it seems, was piqued by a recognition that the taste-makers of recent architectural history had been highly selective in their telling of the modernist myth:

> The name of Alvar Aalto was seldom brought up in any discussions, and when it was, it was put under the carpet, so to speak. So I decided to go and meet the man. It was a great experience for me on two counts. Aalto stressed the importance of how you make things, whether handmade or machine-made. He also spoke about a wide range of precedents for his ideas in the design of a building. At Princeton, the only precedents were the Corbusian villas. Otherwise, "precedent" was not a word to be used.[33]

Porphyrios accordingly applied for a Graham Foundation fellowship to pursue research in Finland during 1975-76, and spent eight months in Aalto's office.[34] Aalto himself had an extraordinary classical education and was fluent on the subject of the monuments of Greek antiquity, with a particular interest in their siting within the landscape. The great man embarrassed Porphyrios by asking about urban and architectural precedents of which he, a proud Greek, knew nothing:[35]

> Discussions on precedent came up almost immediately in our acquaintance. Aalto used to say to me, "Oh, you're Greek, what do you think about such-and-such a temple?" And I knew nothing. I had no clue at all about any classical buildings in Greece. . . . I had never heard anything about classical antiquity. And so it was Aalto who encouraged me to study those buildings. And in that sense he influenced me enormously. If I were to identify the point when my interests moved closer to the European traditional city and to classical architecture I would have to say it was the time that I spent with him[36]

Thus Porphyrios suggests that it was Aalto who planted the germ of his interest in classical and traditional architecture, an interest which he then nurtured *after* his formal education.

But this cannot have been entirely true. For one, it ignores the role of other contemporary voices, even if these are sometimes difficult to assess. Accounts differ, for example, as to the influence of Léon Krier, who may already be credited with corrupting the modernist purity of James Stirling, Colin Rowe, and Michael Graves. In the years after 1976 both Porphyrios and Krier spent time in London; and Krier, three years

Porphyrios' elder, remembers a series of private in-progress slide presentations of Porphyrios' doctoral thesis,[37] which, in lieu of offering a hagiography, as might perhaps have been expected, instead developed a critical evaluation that presented Aalto's work as a case study in the contradictions, prejudices, and myths of the middle years of twentieth-century industrialized society[38]—a provocation, as it were, to those who would succeed him in shaping the environment of modernity.

On the other hand, an exclusive focus on Aalto fails also to acknowledge Porphyrios' own pre-existing interests. His earliest indexed publication dates to 1971, based on research done two years earlier, *before* he began his studies at Princeton. In the summer of 1969, while America's youth descended upon Woodstock, the twenty-year-old Porphyrios was researching traditional earthquake-resistant construction on a somewhat barren Greek island.[39] The resulting article was published in the *Journal of the Society of Architectural Historians* under the name "Demetrius Thomas Georgia Porphyrios, Colgate University," apparently under the sponsorship of Prof. John Fitchen, a Yale graduate who was interested in the history of construction techniques [FIGURES 10-13].[40] Here, albeit under the functionalist cloak of an analysis of seismic performance, one may already observe an interest in vernacular architecture (and note that Bernard Rudofsky had published *Architecture Without Architects* just five years earlier),[41] accompanied by a certain ambivalence towards the profession of architecture and, for that matter, of engineering; Porphyrios writes about "the practices and techniques, evolved by the local builders from on-the-spot experience rather than from imported architects or engineers and their theoretical knowledge."[42]

One can also identify an interest in themes that will prove important for Porphyrios' later work: first, the validity of fairly simple forms and structures, with a corresponding lack of interest in structural acrobatics, or in what he calls technological "gadgetry;"[43] secondly, the possibility of building well in very basic materials—wood, clay, brick, stone, lead; and third, clarity of *tectonics*, here expressed in the articulated assembly of vernacular buildings and particularly in wood structure. These concerns encompass the relationship of structure to ornament, and, in turn, the role of ornament in articulating the legibility of a building. Later Porphyrios will write about all of these issues as defining characteristics of both classical and vernacular architecture, understood as opposite ends of the same spectrum.

For Porphyrios, wood construction is of particular didactic value: more valuable, in a tectonic sense, than brick or stone or metal (and here he will point to the origins of the word *tectonics* in the ancient Greek τεκτων, "builder," or more specifically, "carpenter").[44] Wood, he argues, by its nature invokes "a potential order which is defined by the form-giving capacity of the material. . . . Thus in carpentry, timber [as a material] is not shapeless but is suggestive of form. At the same time timber has a finite length and width and therefore invites the artisan to treat construction in a dimensional and scalar sense. In addition, timber is discontinuous and so it begs the skill and knowledge of jointing."[45]

One might note that this is counter-intuitive to many design tendencies today, which are more likely to demand complete freedom of form-making, with material limits understood not as boundaries to be respected as bearers of meaning, but as constraints to be overcome

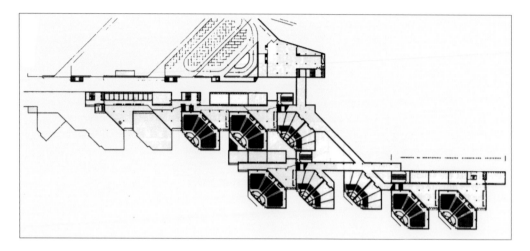

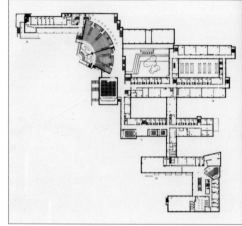

through technological refinement. One might also compare Porphyrios' early interest in timber jointing with the work of Norman Foster and Richard Rogers (both M.Arch. Yale 1962, twelve years ahead of Porphyrios' sojourn at Princeton), leading in a very different direction, that of "high-tech," a celebration of that very technological refinement which aims to overcome material limits [FIGURE 14].

Even before completing his Ph.D., Porphyrios was already teaching at the Architectural Association in London (between 1977 and 1979) as master of "Unit 9" together with Elia Zenghelis, Rem Koolhaas, and Zaha Hadid. Other colleagues at the time included Peter Cook, Terry Farrell, Charles Jencks, Léon Krier, Daniel Libeskind, Mohsen Mostafavi, Bernard Tschumi and Dalibor Vesely. He still speaks warmly of those years as "a wonderful time. . . . There were so many great people . . . around. . . . We were all questioning many of the same things and were all of the same opinion that functional Modernism was dead and we all really wanted to get rid of it. What happened later was that it became clear [that] . . . we had the same agendas but were on completely divergent paths."[46]

Between 1976 and 1977 Porphyrios had also spent a year working as Chief Designer for the Greek architect Alexandros Tombazis. His winning 1977 competition entry for the Athens Law School, under-taken jointly with Tombazis, is not a project that would later be included in his monograph; but the influence of his interest in Aalto is very evident [FIGURES 15-16].

This project was published in *Architectural Design (AD)*, the child of Andreas Papadakis, a Greek Cypriot-born, London-based nuclear physi-cist and publisher. Now something of a legend, Papadakis had changed career by mistake, got off to a strong start by publishing loosely-bound prints by Aubrey Beardsley, moved into architecture, and by the time he began working with Porphyrios, had already published the English editions of Rudofsky's *Architecture Without Architects*, Rudolf Wittkower's *Architectural Principles in the Age of Humanism*, and, in 1977, Jencks' *The Language of Post-Modern Architecture*. Despite his success, he was always viewed with suspicion by the English architectural establishment, not least because of his promiscuous pluralism; but he was the first to publish architects as diverse as Krier, Libeskind, and Hadid, with strong links to, among

others, Eisenman. Between 1977 and 1993 Porphyrios was a regular feature in *AD*, first for his theory and later for his practice, with the same projects sometimes published several times in successive issues.

Porphyrios' second published project comes, perhaps, as something of a surprise, and has also been omitted from later monographs of his work. Dating to 1979 and located in Virginia Water, Surrey, a rather nice village near Windsor, and published in an edition of *AD* entitled "Aalto and After," the project is essentially a renovation and addition to an existing house, mainly involving a new pool and what Porphyrios calls a *nymphaeum*—a typical commission, no doubt, early in an architectural career [FIGURES 17-18]. Here one can identify, perhaps, something of Richard Meier; an unmistakable hint of Aalto; a touch of Miesian classicism (early Mies, that is—note the very minimal articulation of the pillars); and the influence of the Greek vernacular, particularly in the archetypal forms of the gatehouse. In his project description Porphyrios explained that by generally avoiding "the tedious, costly and incomprehensibly fractured notations known as working drawings" he was able to encourage "personal character of execution" among the builders.[47]

DIDACTIC IMITATION

Porphyrios was not invited to take part in the 1980 *Strada Novissima* exhibition at the Venice Biennale. But the following year, in much the same vein, he published a project for a series of three "garden pavilions"[48] in the leafy north London suburb of Highgate.

Porphyrios had by this point published much but built little; this commission, offered by a friend, a Greek shipping owner, provided an opportunity and a challenge to put his words into practice. So the approach was intentionally didactic, leading the visitor (and, perhaps, himself) through an exercise in the basics of the classical vocabulary. The so-called "Tea Pavilion," in particular, has the makings of a case study [FIGURES 19-20]. The elements are carefully defined: plinth, col-umn, architrave, roof, the wall behind (very self-consciously extending past the limits of the roof on its point supports), articulating an open pavilion that stands in contrast to the closed volumes of the other pavilions; and all is executed in simple, solid materials. The drawing

style is reminiscent of Aalto and especially of Meier, in stark black and white with cast shadows. The section drawing, meanwhile, is a good illustration of Porphyrios' interest in the careful articulation of structure, and bears close comparison to the drawings of Lefkas ten years earlier.

This sort of didacticism, which is never entirely absent from Porphyrios' work, tends to irritate critics today;[49] but it was very much a part of the architectural discourse of the time—as is evident from the *Strada Novissima* projects [FIGURE 22]. Porphyrios himself acknowledges this didactic element, which was sustained in later projects also; for example, he has described his 1989 pavilion for Battery Park City [FIGURE 28] as "a didactic piece with which I tried to explain what I thought was relevant in architecture. I tried to demonstrate the significance of technique, of craft, of typological reference and symbolic meaning. For me, that little pavilion was a commentary about the plan of the house, the idea of the atrium, but also about materiality and construction."[50]

At this point one might touch on another of the criticisms typically directed at Porphyrios: that his architecture is unoriginal, imitative; or, to return to Kubler's terms, that he merely re-creates, while others compose.[51]

This turns out to be something of a trap. Not only will Porphyrios readily plead guilty to imitation; he will argue that imitation, the Aristotelian *mimesis*, is the true basis of art. What is more, he will suggest that it is through imitation that architecture can begin to fulfil its highest calling: to help us "come to terms with the world" (and here we should doubtless be thinking quite soberly of our world and our culture as a place that is in some profound ways inhospitable to us); to show us "the way by which the world is true for us;" and, since imitation presupposes recognition (with reference to game theory and to Huizinga's *Homo Ludens*),[52] "to begin to elicit that which is lasting and true for us from the transient."[53]

So upon opening his book *Classical Architecture* (which is in effect a manifesto for his own architecture as much as it is anything else), one finds that the very first chapter is entitled "Imitation in Architecture." Classical architecture is, in this sense, imitative by intent, by design. And what does it imitate? "Any classical building," the reader is told, "may be studied not only as an imitation of the world and of construction, but as an imitation of other buildings as well."[54]

This statement deserves closer attention—it ties back to the issue of tectonics, for one—but it is also clear that it puts a great deal of pressure on the issue of precedent in Porphyrios' own work. After all, he insists that "any serious study of architecture (and art in general) soon shows that the real difference between the great and the lesser architect is that the former imitates the principles of a great heritage, unlike the latter who copies the mannerisms of his predecessors or of his contemporaries" (and note the vocabulary here: the "principles" of a great heritage compared to the "mannerisms" of contemporaries).[55]

It is therefore perhaps unsurprising that the reader who turns the pages of the book will find images of Porphyrios' own work alongside precedents that are typically not from the recent but rather from the more distant past [FIGURE 24]. Porphyrios is in good company here, in a tradition stretching from Palladio to Le Corbusier; he is placing his work very explicitly within a continuum that draws not from the surface of the twentieth century, but from altogether older, presumably deeper wells.[56] As might be expected, he is heavy on the Greek, both classical and vernacular, including, to his credit, examples that are often overlooked; but his sympathies also extend more broadly, revealing, for example, a strong familiarity with Islamic architecture. All of the photographs, furthermore, are taken by Porphyrios himself, which would suggest that he is exceedingly well-travelled.

There is a conspicuous lacuna in published work between 1981 and 1985, when Porphyrios succeeded Alan Colquhoun as Director of History and Theory at the Polytechnic of Central London (now the University of Westminster). Precise biographical details during this period are elusive, but it seems that he made an attempt at establishing a practice in Greece; he had married well, as they say, and was able to draw on family resources; he entered a number of competitions, even willing to explore the possibilities of prefabricated construction, if that would generate opportunities to build; and he teamed up briefly with Léon Krier, who was at the time living on a Greek island, on a project for a highway interchange at Piraeus—a venture that marked the end of their collaboration for several years. But in the end these efforts were unsuccessful, and he returned to London, where he established Porphyrios Associates in 1985.

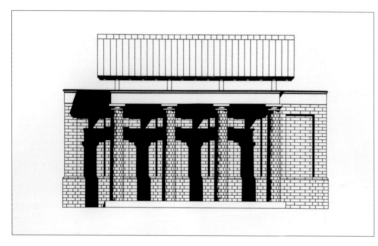

Figures 19 and 20 (top and middle): Demetri Porphyrios, Tea Pavilion in Highgate, London, UK, 1981.

Figure 21 (bottom): Raymond Erith, gates, lodges and cottages for King George VI, Royal Lodge, Windsor Great Park, England, 1938 *(see note 48, page 95)*. Photograph by Sirpecangum.

The firm has recently celebrated its 25th anniversary, and has a rather larger portfolio of built and unbuilt projects than many critics are aware, ranging from hotels in Frankfurt to island resorts in the Caribbean, additions to colleges in Oxford and Cambridge and palaces in the Middle East, along with a good number of private homes in pleasant places.

PLACE

In addition to designing individual buildings, Porphyrios has also tackled the planning of larger communities. This is important to his polemic, as it tests the paradigmatic claims of his approach. That is, if an architect intends to propose an architecture that is not a series of one-off "signature buildings," his approach should be capable of broader application; and it should be capable of adoption by other architects, a good number of whom will by definition be of below-average ability. This is in a sense the converse of the imitation theory; and some might point out that it disqualifies a fair proportion of alternative architectures from this particular competition: one might for example enjoy a singular Libeskind masterpiece within an otherwise conventional context, but one might be less enthusiastic about a neighbourhood of Libeskind knock-offs; whereas cities of fairly unexceptional classical/vernacular buildings may prove to be exceedingly agreeable places—there are parts of New Haven, or, for that matter, New York, which could illustrate this quite forcefully.[57]

On a more rustic note, one might turn to a project dating to 1990: Belvedere Farm, near Ascot, very close to Virginia Water and in the general area of Windsor [FIGURE 23 and 25]. This is not a part of England known for farms of purely agricultural distinction. The property to the west of the project site, for instance, belonged to John Lennon and Yoko Ono, then to Ringo Starr, and then to the Sheik of Abu Dhabi; not one of them a farmer as such. Belvedere Farm (which has gone through a series of name changes in the last few years) was designed for Canadian billionaire Galen Weston, one of the world's richest individuals, owner of Selfridges and of Fortnum & Mason, keen collector of avant-garde art, and one of the original funders of the Congress for the New Urbanism. Weston also owned a polo team, for which Prince Charles was known to play (Porphyrios had likewise developed a good relationship with the Prince, and served on the board of the Prince's Institute of Architecture in the mid 1990s); and Weston thus had a need for stables.

Often referred to by Porphyrios as "Belvedere Village," the project was intended as something like an exercise in the creation of an English village: intended to be a *place*, not just a building or series of buildings; and it was mainly built of brick fired locally of good English clay. Although the client was Canadian, the project was intended as a specific response to its uniquely English context—more about the *genius loci*, the spirit of the place, than about the *Zeitgeist*, the spirit of the time.[58]

This was, it seems, Porphyrios' first attempt at vernacular architecture on a large scale. At the time he discussed the design with Krier;[59] and certainly one can identify parallels with Krier's own sketches. More fundamentally, perhaps, one can compare Porphyrios' "menu" of farm buildings to the kind of drawing that Krier had been producing a few years earlier [FIGURE 26], reminiscent of Jean-Nicolas-Louis Durand's

Figure 22 (far left): Strada Novissima, Venice Biennale, 1980 (showing facades by Thomas Gordon Smith and Studio G.R.A.U.).

Figure 23 (above): Demetri Porphyrios, Belvedere Farm, Ascot, UK, 1990.

Figure 24 (left): Pages from Demetri Porphyrios, Classical Architecture (London: Academy Editions, 1991).

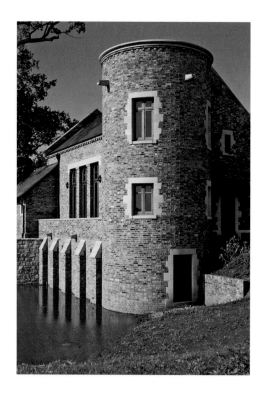
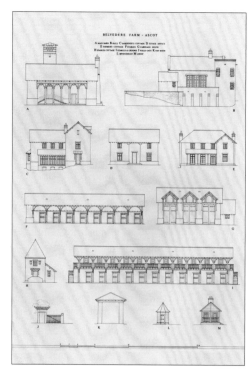
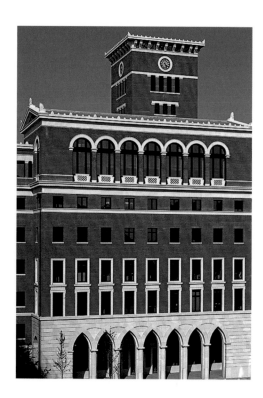

Recueil et parallèle des édifices de tout genre, anciens et modernes (1799-1801), and offering a kit of parts, of building types to be applied judiciously according to specific need. These in turn were a critique of the undifferentiated universality of modernism in the wake of Mies van der Rohe, who went on record in 1960 as stating "I am, in fact, completely opposed to the idea that a specific building should have an individual character—rather, a universal character which has been determined by the total problem which architecture must strive to solve."[60]

That said, it is not always clear that Belvedere Village is quite as specific to its own geography as one might want to believe. Even if there are, indeed, close references to the English Picturesque tradition,[61] it sometimes feels more continental than English, and if one compares, again, Krier's earlier sketch for a project in France (the "belvedere," for example, or the "wooden portico"), one begins to feel a general sense of kinship with the Gallic and Mediterranean world, perhaps even with Greece. At the least, the Village betrays a cosmopolitanism in sympathy with the world of its owners.

Nevertheless, if it is fair to think of Porphyrios' architecture as being *critical*, one might think of it as a critique of modernism as characterised by St John Wilson: that is, a critique of modernism as "an architecture of extreme abstraction of form, the appearance of levitation and dematerialization of substance," to achieve which "structure was reduced to a series of subterfuges," of "lying façades and false trickeries."[62] In fact, one could make an argument for Porphyrios as a sort of anti-Mies: both share a keen sense of loss, a longing for a past authenticity; both propose a very clear remedy to the ailments of modernity, with a somewhat totalising application; both lean towards a basic austerity of form; both are obses-

sive in their attention to construction detail; and both were, in a sense, self-taught; but Mies converted from classicism to modernism, whereas Porphyrios' conversion, if one could name it such, was of a different sort.

Belvedere Farm gave Porphyrios the opportunity to experiment in a variety of building types, all very carefully executed, with impeccable craftsmanship, solid materials, and a general simplicity, even austerity, that is typical of almost all his work.[63] The absence of cars from the published images, combined with the architect's studious attention to the vernacular, render the images curiously difficult to date, at least at first glance; Porphyrios could surely appeal to his aspiration to an architecture that is not overly obsessed with its own modernity. But closer study of the elements of the kit of parts could provoke speculation about other influences, not all of them English; one might look, for example, to the work of Heinrich Tessenow or of Gunnar Asplund.

At this point the story of this particular project takes something of a curious twist. In due course the farm was sold to Prince Jefri of Brunei, a man with a reputation as a wealthy playboy capable of spending vast sums of money—on polo teams and on properties, for example.

Figure 25 (top left): Demetri Porphyrios, Belvedere Farm, Ascot, UK, 1990.

Figure 26 (top center): Demetri Porphyrios, comparative plate of elevations of the buildings of Belvedere Farm.

Figure 27 (top right): Demetri Porphyrios, Three Brindleyplace, Birmingham, UK, 1996-98.

Figure 28 (opposite): Demetri Porphyrios, Pavilion, Battery Park City, New York, NY, 1989.

He was eventually accused by the Government of Brunei of embezzling 16 billion dollars; and so, along with the country house to which it was attached, the farm passed into the hands of the Brunei government's investment holding arm, which handed it over to one of its subsidiaries, the Dorchester hotels.

In September of 2010, after a few adjustments, the property opened for business as Coworth Park Hotel. Contrary to the expectations of critics,[64] the forms of Porphyrios' *parallèle* proved remarkably flexible: the barn is now a dining space, with a conference room in the tower; and, for a price, one may lodge in the head groom's cottage. By all accounts the hotel is proving exceedingly successful, and Porphyrios' buildings have quietly been absorbed into the fabric of their re-imagined context.

BUILDER'S METHOD

One might close with a glance at Porphyrios' commercial work. Over the last fifteen years he has executed a series of well-received office projects both in England and beyond [FIGURE 27]. Between 1996 and 1998 he masterplanned the redevelopment of the previously rather down-at-heels Brindleyplace district in Birmingham, to which he also contributed two buildings. These projects seem to have turned profits that are not at all old-fashioned; the satisfied developer has become a repeat client for the firm.

However, in order to render these projects viable, Porphyrios does something which some have portrayed as a betrayal of principle: that is, he separates the exterior masonry from the internal steel structure of the buildings, so that construction can proceed on the interior while the masons take their time about the composite stone detailing of the façade.[65] Some have argued that this is façadism at its worst; indeed, Porphyrios himself has criticized modernism's tendency to dissociate a building's external envelope from its structure on the grounds that this "limits architectural expression to a kind of applied rain-screen wallpaper" and tends towards an architecture that is inherently ephemeral—not to mention unsustainable.

Although this technique is most evident in his commercial work, similar methods are employed in other projects, including Whitman College, which is structured in concrete block with reinforced slab flooring. Porphyrios notes that the exterior wythe of masonry bears its own weight; but to his critics this seems a compromise at best, a concession to the "lying façades and false trickeries" of modernism, in which structure is "reduced to a series of subterfuges."[66] In an appraisal of Whitman's construction, Fred Bernstein has argued:

> The resemblance to true gothic buildings will be only skin deep. Although Porphyrios calls the walls load-bearing, they will support only their own weight. . . . The building's true structure, concrete blocks supporting concrete slab floors, will be in place before the first piece of argillite is installed nearly a year into the construction process. For that first year, Whitman will look pretty much like any other new building.[67]

Porphyrios, on the other hand, is prepared to defend his approach with vigor, noting that the critique is itself based on a modernist fallacy, which not only employs a double standard but also misrepresents the breadth of the Gothic tradition and fails to acknowledge the frequent separation within traditional architecture of masonry wall from wood or iron roof and floor structure.[68] Indeed, it would be difficult to describe Porphyrios' work as an architecture of "applied rain-screen wallpaper"—the construction of Whitman College, for example, required the quarrying of over 6,000 tons of bluestone alone, and the thickness of wall section permits deep articulation of the façade. Certainly it is not ephemeral; nor is it—in comparison to standard practice—unsustainable: the masonry offers high thermal mass and extraordinary longevity, and the familiarity of language improves further the odds that the building will be loved and preserved. What is more, far from aiming at deception, Porphyrios notes that this "hybrid construction" is typically not hidden but clearly expressed, another opportunity for didactic clarity; and if this clarity may be absent at Princeton, it is certainly present in much of his commercial work, occasionally to a fault.[69]

More essentially, however—and more pragmatically—this is also the means that Porphyrios employs in order to get such projects built. Léon Krier has argued that "criticism without a project is merely a

Figure 29 (above): Ed Venn, Portrait of Demetri Porphyrios.

higher form of surrender" that "reveals our wounds but does not show the way to recovery."[70] In this respect Porphyrios must be judged by the standards of his realism: his theory can only be valid if it can be translated into practice. He notes that he has "spent years searching for an authentic, robust constructional system that would be compatible with present-day building."[71] Ironically, his position proves to be fundamentally different from that of Krier's, who, because he is an architect, famously cannot build.[72] Demetri Porphyrios, in contrast, is a builder, a τεκτων [FIGURE 29].

ENIGMATIC CONCLUSIONS

Porphyrios' work remains, for many, something of an enigma. This account attempts to unravel a few strands of that enigma; and yet it remains true that none of the threads of influence examined above, if considered in isolation, can fully account for the fabric of Porphyrios' underlying premise, his commitment to a traditional language of architecture. Others, after all, have questioned modernist dogma, and have echoed his condemnation of postmodernism, of antiquarianism, and of revivalism, without sharing his subsequent response. Others have pursued an interest in vernacular traditions while drawing very different conclusions. Others have elaborated a commitment to tectonic clarity, to constructive integrity, or to specificity of place, while articulating that commitment in very different vocabularies. Indeed, one might find similar preoccupations at the root of modernism itself, or in the work of Alvar Aalto, or in the practice of architects whose careers have overlapped with that of Porphyrios—Luis Barragán, Glenn Murcutt, Peter Zumthor, Mark Mack. Even Peter Eisenman, after all, is not disinterested in the question of tectonics. But very few of Porphyrios' contemporaries have pursued the practice of architecture within the same theoretical framework, and he remains an exception to the rule established by the judgment of his peers. If the question of influence can rarely be met with an easy answer, there may also exist in this case, perhaps, other unexplored influences on Porphyrios' work, and one might speculate further as to what those might be. His turn to an explicitly traditional vocabulary, for example, seems generally to have coincided with the launching of his career in England; and one might examine more closely the opportunities that nurtured his interests in what, in other regards, could still be considered inhospitable terrain. And there must be, no doubt, still other, more fundamental, motivations —more personal and less readily articulated, perhaps, but no less influential for that. There remains opportunity, in other words, for further refutation and conjecture—and, by the same token, for misunderstanding. ❧

Kyle Dugdale is a Ph.D. candidate in architecture at Yale University.

SELECTED BIBLIOGRAPHY

Barksdale Maynard, W. "Something Old, Something New." *Princeton Alumni Weekly,* February 13, 2008.

Bernstein, Fred. "Building Whitman College." *Princeton Alumni Weekly,* December 18, 2002.

Bernstein, Fred. "One Campus, Different Faces." *Princeton Alumni Weekly,* December 18, 2002.

Bernstein, Mark F. "Demetri Porphyrios *80." *Princeton Alumni Weekly,* October 24, 2007.

Bicknell, Julian. "Classical Roles." Review of *Classical Architecture,* by Demetri Porphyrios. *Country Life* 186, no. 31 (July 30, 1992), p. 72.

Brook, Daniel. "Old School: Princeton Visiting Professor Peter Eisenman Throws Down the Gauntlet over a Gothic-Style Dorm." *Metropolis* 22, no. 10 (June 2003), pp. 52, 76.

Cram, Ralph Adams. "The Work of Messrs. Cope and Stewardson." *Architectural Record* 16, no. 5 (November 1904), pp. 409-438.

Dorrell, Ed. "Hooked on Classics." *The Architects' Journal* 219, no. 23 (June 10, 2004), pp. 22-23.

Harries, Karsten. *The Ethical Function of Architecture* (Cambridge, MA: MIT Press, 1997).

Krier, Léon. *Drawings 1967-1980* (Brussels: Archives d'Architecture Moderne, 1980).

Krier, Léon. "Architectura Patriae; or The Destruction of Germany's Architectural Heritage." *Architectural Design* 54, no. 7/8 (1984), pp. 101-102.

Kubler, George. *The Shape of Time: Remarks on the History of Things* (New Haven: Yale University Press, 1962).

Penny, Nicholas. *Review of Demetri Porphyrios: Selected Buildings and Writings. AA Files* 26 (Autumn 1993), pp. 103-107.

Porphyrios, Demetrius Thomas Georgia. "Traditional Earthquake-Resistant Construction on a Greek Island." *Journal of the Society of Architectural Historians* 30, no. 1 (March 1971), pp. 31-39.

Porphyrios, Demetrius. "The 'End' of Styles." *Oppositions* 8 (Spring 1977), pp. 119-133.

Porphyrios, Demetri. "National Competition for the Athens Law School." *Architectural Design* 49, no. 3-4 (1979), p. 98.

Porphyrios, Demetri. "House at Virginia Water." *Architectural Design* 49, no. 12 (1979), pp. 338-341.

Porphyrios, Demetri. "Pavilions in Highgate, London." *Architectural Design* 52, no. 5-6 (1982), pp. 76-79.

Porphyrios, Demetri. *Sources of Modern Eclecticism: Studies on Alvar Aalto* (London: Academy Editions, 1982).

Porphyrios, Demetri. *Classical Architecture* (London: Academy Editions, 1991).

Porphyrios, Demetri. *Selected Buildings and Writings* (London: Academy Editions, 1993).

Porphyrios, Demetri. *Porphyrios Associates: Recent Work* (London: Papadakis, 1999).

Porphyrios, Demetri. "From Techne to Tectonics." In Andrew Ballantyne, ed., *What is Architecture?* (London: Routledge, 2002), pp. 129-37.

Ray, Nicholas. *Alvar Aalto* (New Haven: Yale University Press, 2005).

Sammons, Richard. "Leaving the Dark Ages." *Traditional Building* 21, no. 1 (February 2008), p 20-22, 24.

Stein, Jeff. "A Traditional Revolution: Demetri Porphyrios Talks with Jeff Stein, AIA." *Architecture Boston* 7, no. 5 (September/October 2004), pp. 46-51.

St John Wilson, Colin. "Open and Closed." *Perspecta* 7 (1961), pp. 97-102.

University of Notre Dame School of Architecture. *The Richard H. Driehaus Prize: Demetri Porphyrios* (South Bend, IN: University of Notre Dame, 2004).

Notes

This paper began as the product of a 2009-2010 graduate seminar at Yale School of Architecture, "Parallel Moderns: Toward a New Synthesis?", directed by Dean Robert A. M. Stern with the assistance of Matthew Persinger. The seminar sought, in part, to explore historical influences on the architectural expression of the 1970s and 1980s. The author is grateful to Dean Stern and to Kurt W. Forster, George Knight, Léon Krier, and Anthony Vidler for their willingness to discuss the subject of this paper as he is, of course, to Demetri Porphyrios himself.

1. See, for example, Demetri Porphyrios, *Classical Architecture* (London: Academy Editions, 1991), pp. 33 and 94.

2. Commenting in a review of Porphyrios' *Classical Architecture* on the author's "opacity of prose, peppered with specialist terms"—a trait that he attributes to the American academic influence—Julian Bicknell has noted that "one longs for a ruthless editor to cut out the jargon, for the ideas are interesting and important" (Julian Bicknell, "Classical Roles," review of *Classical Architecture* by Demetri Porphyrios, *Country Life* 186, no. 31 (July 30, 1992), p. 72.

3. Secretary of Defense Donald H. Rumsfeld, news briefing, February 12, 2002.

4. The author is conscious that an exploration such as this is fraught with peril; it risks entering disputed territory and raising questions to which there exist conflicting answers. Convinced that the questions are important even if the answers may prove mistaken or incomplete, the author submits what follows with hesitation, hoping that it might provoke a conversation that would offer opportunity for correction where necessary.

5. For a recent assessment see for example Nicholas Ray, *Alvar Aalto* (New Haven: Yale University Press, 2005), pp. 175-76.

6. Porphyrios, *Classical Architecture*, p. 37. If it is true that many hard-line classicists are obsessed with modernism, as the mouse is obsessed with the cat (or, perhaps, vice versa), *post*modernism is clearly not yet a popular term on either side of the debate.

7. *Ibid.*, p. 82. "In the 19th century, history became synonymous with the antiquarian revival of the past; one picked at the carcass of history and used it in whatever fashion one wanted" (quoted in Jeff Stein, "A Traditional Revolution: Demetri Porphyrios Talks with Jeff Stein, AIA," *Architecture Boston* 7, no. 5 [September/October 2004], p. 48).

8. Porphyrios, *Classical Architecture*, p. 93.

9. George Kubler, *The Shape of Time: Remarks on the History of Things* (New Haven: Yale University Press, 1962), pp. 12-13.

10. Daniel Brook, "Old School: Princeton Visiting Professor Peter Eisenman Throws Down the Gauntlet over a Gothic-Style Dorm," *Metropolis* 22, no. 10 (June 2003), pp. 52 and 76.

11. In a 1904 article on the architecture of Cope and Stewardson, Cram referred to Blair Hall (1896) and Stafford Little Hall (1902) as "poetic, collegiate, racial and logical" (Ralph Adams Cram, "The Work of Messrs. Cope & Stewardson," *Architectural Record* 16, no. 5 [November 1904], p. 423)—paraphrased by W. Barksdale Maynard, ("Something Old, Something New," *Princeton Alumni Weekly*, February 13, 2008) as "the perfect expression of the Anglo-Saxon heritage." Reading the full article might suggest a more nuanced interpretation than this quotation alone would imply; Cram's position should be compared to other contemporary attempts to identify architectural character; and it might be noted that reference to race and to place is also present in the early narratives of modernism. Elsewhere in the same article, in language similar to that of Kubler, Cram distinguishes between architects and "copyists" (p. 417); he refers to Princeton's gymnasium (no longer extant), also by Cope & Stewardson, as "an attempt to clothe a modern proposition in 'Monk Latin'" (p. 418); in comparison, he writes of "the turbulent affectations of Harvard, a 'rogues gallery' of discredited architectural superstitions; of Yale, where new

wine is put into old bottles and old wine into new bottles and the uncongenial receptacles jostle cheek by jowl," and of "the subtle obsession of the ivied Old World" (p. 411).

12. For an account that ties Cram's Princeton architecture to the collegiate architecture of Yale and back to the secular Gothic architecture of Bristol and of Oxbridge, see Gavin Stamp, "Dreaming Towers," *Apollo* 170, no. 570 (November 2009), pp. 62-63.

13. Porphyrios, *Classical Architecture*, p. 93. One of the characteristics of Porphyrios' writing, and perhaps of his generation more broadly, is a Heideggerian penchant for justifying his theory with linguistic and etymological parallels, sometimes to the point of suggesting that proof of an etymological relationship between two concepts implies a fundamental connection that it would be perverse to ignore.

14. Porphyrios, correspondence with author, April 19, 2010.

15. Adam's house in Paradise, as Karsten Harries has noted, was non-existent (*The Ethical Function of Architecture* [Cambridge, MA: MIT Press, 1997], p. 137); architecture appears only in Genesis 4 as a response to the Fall, to the homelessness of humanity.

16. For a thought-provoking discussion of that despair as an alternative to apathy, see Robert Jan van Pelt, "Apocalyptic Abjection," in Carroll William Westfall and Robert Jan van Pelt, *Architectural Principles in the Age of Historicism* (New Haven, CT: Yale University Press, 1991), 317-81, and especially the closing paragraphs, subtitled "In Conclusion," at 379-81.

17. Brook, "Old School," p. 76. Porphyrios sees institutions such as Princeton as radical in a different sense: that is, their long-term perspective permits them to challenge the impulse for short-term profit that drives Western consumerism, and therefore allows them to build in a way that questions contemporary disposable culture: "There are pockets of resistance in our culture. Cultural and collegiate institutions are pockets of resistance, not because they are revolutionaries, but because they want to have buildings that will last for a long time" (quoted in Stein, "A Traditional Revolution," p. 50).

18. Brook, "Old School," p. 76.

19. Fred Bernstein, "One Campus, Different Faces," *Princeton Alumni Weekly*, December 18, 2002.

20. Contrasted in turn, perhaps, with the history of Rem Koolhaas' native city of Rotterdam.

21. See "The Opposite of Architecture," *Diary of a Filmmaker: Observations by Thomas Ball of Telos Productions*, September 28, 2008, http://telos.tv/blog/?p=251.

22. Fred Bernstein, "One Campus." Porphyrios studied under Michael Graves, Alan Colquhoun, and Kenneth Frampton, and acknowledges the particular influence of the art historian David Coffin, the social historian Carl Schorske, and the architectural historian Anthony Vidler, who "opened up [his] mind" and introduced him both to classical architectural history and theory, and to social theory and the history of ideas (conversation with Porphyrios, June 9, 2010).

23. Mark F. Bernstein, "Demetri Porphyrios *80," *Princeton Alumni Weekly*, October 24, 2007.

24. Quoted in Colin St John Wilson, "Open and Closed," *Perspecta* 7 (1961), p. 97. This conception of a revolution that started with enthusiasm and ended in dictatorship would surely have struck a chord with Porphyrios. Even if he himself was "never really an activist" (conversation with Porphyrios, June 9, 2010), he was attracted to the project of sociohistorical analysis ("critical history") that was popular within the intellectual avant-garde culture of the mid-1970s, and he is remembered as having co-founded a reading group while at Princeton which approached the subject from the perspective of his compatriot Nicos Poulantzas, a leading Structural Marxist of the 1970s alongside Louis Althusser. The tendencies of a socialist critique might be naturally sympathetic towards an architecture of ready legibility, contrasted with modernism's enduring opacity; and indeed, such undertones are present in Porphyrios' book on Aalto. That said, any speculation as to early Marxist leanings must contend with the fact that between 1979 and 1982 Porphyrios would rely heavily on commissions from Greek shipping owners in London.

25. St John Wilson, "Open and Closed," p. 97.

26. Anthony Vidler, Porphyrios' Ph.D. advisor, remembers that "we were all looking for ways to reconstrue the *horror vacui* of vulgarized modernism" (conversation with Vidler, December 10, 2009).

27. Charles Jencks, *The Language of Post-Modern Architecture* (New York: Rizzoli, 1977), p. 9.

28. Demetrius Porphyrios, "The 'End' of Styles," *Oppositions* 8 (Spring 1977), p. 119. By 1991 he could state without qualification that "the modernist city has tragically failed" (*Classical Architecture*, p. 81).

29. "When I was a student at Princeton, . . . I had a neo-Corbusian education, led by Michael Graves and Peter Eisenman in their so-called 'white' period. And I was perplexed" (quoted in Stein, "A Traditional Revolution," p. 51).

30. Porphyrios notes that he had a great respect for Graves, although their positions were increasingly at odds. "We used to have arguments; . . . we were always at loggerheads" (conversation with Porphyrios, June 9, 2010).

31. Conversations with Léon Krier, October 9, 2009, and with Porphyrios, June 9, 2010.

32. Fred Bernstein, "One Campus."

33. Stein, "A Traditional Revolution," p. 51. Porphyrios remembers that Kahn, in a lecture, made reference to Aalto's work at Otaniemi—but it was not expected to be used as precedent (conversation with Porphyrios, June 9, 2010).

34. Aalto died on May 11, 1976, leaving Porphyrios with the reputation of having been "Aalto's last employee." Porphyrios recalls that the office was at the time working on the project for Santa Maria Assunta, Riola; although Aalto himself was not always present, Porphyrios was given full access to his drawings, not yet archived (conversation with Porphyrios, June 9, 2010).

35. Conversation with George Knight, September 29, 2009.

36. Stein, "A Traditional Revolution," p. 51.

37. Conversation with Krier, October 9, 2009.

38. Porphyrios, *Sources of Modern Eclecticism: Studies on Alvar Aalto* (London: Academy Editions, 1982), p. vii.

39. The island of Lefkas, where Porphyrios had summered in previous years (correspondence with author, April 19, 2010).

40. Demetrius Thomas Georgia Porphyrios, "Traditional Earthquake-Resistant Construction on a Greek Island," *Journal of the Society of Architectural Historians* 30, no. 1 (March 1971), pp. 31-39. The article is mentioned in John Fitchen, Building *Construction Before Mechanization* (Cambridge, MA: MIT Press, 1986), p. 261. A number of Porphyrios' earlier publications, such as his contribution to *Oppositions* 8 (1977), appear under the name "Demetrius."

41. Bernard Rudofsky, *Architecture Without Architects: A Short Introduction to Non-Pedigreed Architecture* (New York: Doubleday, 1964). Rudofsky, who had himself studied the vernacular architecture of the Greek islands as a young man, opened the way to its reapplication to contemporary practice in stating that "no architecture, it seems to me, is outdated that works for man rather than against him" (*The Prodigious Builders* [New York: Harcourt Brace Jovanovich, 1977], p. 5). This is surely the traditionalist's most basic response to those who would accuse him of obsolescence.

42. Porphyrios, "Traditional Earthquake-Resistant Construction," p. 31.

43. Porphyrios, *Classical Architecture*, p. 73. Conversely, Porphyrios contends that architecture must exceed the requirements of engineering; otherwise it remains "a symbolically mute gesture" (*ibid*, p. 23).

44. Porphyrios, "From Techne to Tectonics," in Andrew Ballantyne, ed., *What is Architecture?* (London: Routledge, 2002), p. 134.

45. *Ibid.*, p. 37.

46. Quoted in Ed Dorrell, "Hooked on Classics," *The Architects' Journal*, June 10, 2004.

47. Demetri Porphyrios, "House at Virginia Water," *Architectural Design* 49, no. 12 (1979), p. 339. One might note also that this project did not represent the last time that Porphyrios would refer to Aalto: to jump forward for a moment, one could single out his research centre library in Oxford (1999-2001), which, according to the firm's website, "pays homage to the Viipuri library of Aalto"—and, perhaps, to the asymmetrical, detached side-portico of Sigurd Lewerentz's Resurrection Chapel in Stockholm.

48. There is good precedent for this typology—such as a 1938 project at Windsor (near Virginia Water) for King George VI, by Raymond Erith, who after the war would remain a lonely classicist in a very non-classical England [FIGURE 21]. Erith took a different position on the value of working drawings: "As the job was for the King, I took a lot of trouble with the working drawings so they are really rather a show set" (quoted in Lucy Archer, *Raymond Erith Architect* [Burford, Oxfordshire: Cygnet Press, 1985], p. 118). One is reminded also of Karl Friedrich Schinkel's 1830 Tea Pavilion in the garden of the Charlottenhof, Potsdam-Sanssouci.

49. See, for example, Nicholas Penny's assessment in his review of *Demetri Porphyrios: Selected Buildings and Writings, in AA Files*, no. 26 (Autumn 1993), p.105. "Compared with Krier, Porphyrios is a sober architect, but he too has a tiresome pedagogic streak and some of his garden buildings, for instance, seem designed as an illustration to a lecture on the historical origins or the practical and symbolic fundamentals of architecture." Penny proceeds to suggest of Porphyrios that "there is no hint of whimsy in any of his work;" this much at least might seem more difficult to deny.

50. Stein, "A Traditional Revolution," p. 48. Porphyrios has noted that "there are three didactic pavilions from that period: the Highgate Tea Pavilion of 1981, the Propylon in Surrey of 1985, and the Battery Park City Pavilion of 1989" (Porphyrios, correspondence with author, April 19, 2010).

51. See Kubler, *The Shape of Time*, p. 13.

52. Porphyrios compares the discipline of classical architecture to the game of chess (he might equally have chosen any sport), pointing to the freedom of expression that is made possible by playing within rules. He describes a "profound affinity between play and order"—"as is the case with all artistic fictions, tectonic fiction creates its own supreme order where the least deviation 'spoils the game'" (*Classical Architecture*, p. 38). Here his language echoes quite closely that of Huizinga: "Here we come across another, very positive feature of play: it creates order, is order. Into an imperfect world and into the confusion of life it brings a temporary, a limited perfection. Play demands order absolute and supreme. The least deviation from it 'spoils the game,' robs it of its character and makes it worthless. The profound affinity between play and order is perhaps the reason why play . . . seems to lie to such a large extent in the field of aesthetics" (Johan Huizinga, *Homo Ludens: A Study of the Play-Element in Culture* [New York: Roy, 1950], p. 10).

53. Porphyrios, *Classical Architecture*, p. 25ff.

54. *Ibid.*, p. 94. The chapters of Porphyrios' *Classical Architecture* were initially delivered as lectures in 1987 and 1989 at the University of Virginia and at Yale University; versions of these lectures were given to students in note form.

55. *Ibid.*, p. 98.

56. Notice also the reading list that is included at the back of the volume to provide unfamiliar students with an explicit philosophical and theoretical context, ranging from Plato and Aristotle through Hegel and Quatremère de Quincy (*On Imitation*) to Tessenow.

57. Note that this argument is not dissimilar to the argument, as adopted by Krier, that architecture should be subjected to the test of Kant's Categorical Imperative: that we should act only according to that maxim that we can will as a universal law.

58. The author is grateful to Peter Eisenman (discussion, December 3, 2009) for suggesting an assessment of Porphyrios' work in these terms. On the face of it, Porphyrios privileges the Roman over the Germanic spirit; but as A. J. Herbertson observes, the two are never disconnected: "The spirit of a place changes with the spirit of the time. . . . The historian has to reckon with both" ("Regional Environment, Heredity and Consciousness," *Geographic Teacher*, vol. 8 [1915-16], p. 153).

59. Conversation with Léon Krier, October 9, 2009.

60. Mies van der Rohe discussing the Seagram Building, quoted in Peter Carter, "Mies van der Rohe: An Appreciation on the Occasion, this Month, of his 75th Birthday," *Architectural Design* 31 (March 1961), p. 100.

61. In an article for *Country Life's* 1992 equestrian issue, Giles Worsley noted the deliberate reference to Scotney Castle in Kent, "the epitome of the English Picturesque tradition" (Giles Worsley, "Homes Fit for Houyhnhnms," *Country Life* 186 no. 42 [October 15, 1992], p. 54).

62. St John Wilson, "Open and Closed," p. 99.

63. Porphyrios notes that over the course of his career he has done little in the way of fully elaborated classical work: "I have always been very shy in using the orders" (conversation with Porphyrios, June 9, 2010). He attributes this shyness to an appreciation for Greek antiquity's reservation of full classical articulation for the most august of building programmes only: he himself has "never had to do a temple."

64. See, for example, Nicholas Ray's censure of the Krier-Porphyrios position in Ray, *Alvar Aalto*, p. 192. Krier's polemic is tied to Aldo Rossi's *Architecture and the City*, published in Italian in 1966 but not translated into English until 1982.

65. Porphyrios has described this as "a fast-track structure and a slow-track envelope" (quoted in Richard Sammons, "Leaving the Dark Ages," *Traditional Building* 21, no. 1 [February 2008], p. 24).

66. St John Wilson, "Open and Closed," p. 99.

67. Fred Bernstein, "Building Whitman College," *Princeton Alumni Weekly*, December 18, 2002.

68. Conversation with Porphyrios, June 9, 2010.

69. For a reminder of the importance of hybrid systems within the broader history of architectural innovation, see the assessment of Porphyrios' work in Philip Arcidi, "Learning by the Rules," *Progressive Architecture* 74, no.12 (December 1993), pp. 42-49. Porphyrios acknowledges the contribution of his engineers, Arup, to his twenty-year research into the possibilities of such hybrid structures.

70. Léon Krier, "*Architectura Patriae*; or The Destruction of Germany's Architectural Heritage," *Architectural Design* 54, no. 7/8 (1984), pp. 101-102.

71. Porphyrios, Driehaus Prize acceptance speech, quoted in James P. Cramer and Jennifer Evans Yankopolus, eds., *Almanac of Architecture and Design*, 6th ed. (Atlanta, GA: Greenway, 2005), pp. 14-16.

72. "I cannot build because I am an architect." Léon Krier, *Drawings 1967-1980* (Brussels: Archives d'Architecture Moderne, 1980), p. 82.

The Allied Arts

Grand Central Academy of Art

The Grand Central Academy of Art (GCA) at the ICAA offers classical training to serious students. Taught by professional, exhibiting artists, the GCA offers a positive environment for classical instruction in drawing, painting, and sculpture. The GCA is home to the following programs: The Water Street Atelier, a program in classical painting; The Sculpture Atelier, a program in classical sculpture; The Hudson River Fellowship, a summer landscape painting school in the Catskill Mountains; and the GCA's Drawing and Classical Figure Sculpture Competitions.

The goal of the Academy is to train a generation of highly skilled, aesthetically sensitive artists in the humanist tradition. The program is built on the skills and ideas that have come from classical Greece and Rome, the Italian Renaissance, and the Beaux-Arts tradition of the nineteenth century.

Further, the mission of the Grand Central Academy is to offer a public place for the revival of the classical art tradition, to foster and support a community of artists in pursuit of aesthetic refinement and a high level of skill and beauty. The Grand Central Academy of Art is an integral part of the ICAA whose mission is the advancement of classical art and architecture in America.

Cast Drawing
Beginning Core Program students spend their first year in the Cast Hall learning to draw from the casts. Drawing from the antique cast, a classically rendered stationary object—using a limited palette under controlled light—teaches students to address the fundamental questions of composition, gesture, light direction, and value construction. Cast drawing encourages a slow, calm, thoughtful approach to gaining a

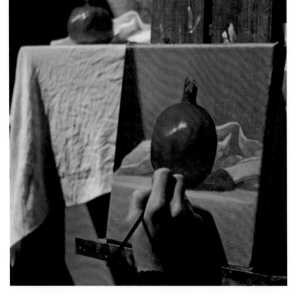

deep three-dimensional understanding of the cast. Students are trained to think sculpturally, to make more accurate decisions, and to create drawings that are true to life.

Students are required to draw each feature cast (ear, eye, nose, and mouth) and at least one head and figure. Each student works at his or her own pace, generally to the end of the first year to complete excellent examples of each.

Figure Drawing
Towards the end of the first year, students begin to draw the figure from life. Applying lessons learned by drawing the casts, they work on a series of linear figure drawings. The focus here is on accurate shapes, proportion, and dynamic gesture, without any finish or modeling. They move on to a series of drawings that show finished lines and clear resolution of detail. With their instructor's approval, students progress to drawing fully finished, modeled figures in month-long poses.

Drawing the figure through a series of long poses, students learn to manage relationships creating an analogous balance that describes the three-dimensional experience on the flat page.

Figure 1 (above): Student Carla Crawford in the Still Life Oil Painting Class, 2010.

Figure 2 (opposite): "Diadoumenos" by Katie Whipple, 2010, Graphite on Paper, 12 x 13 in.

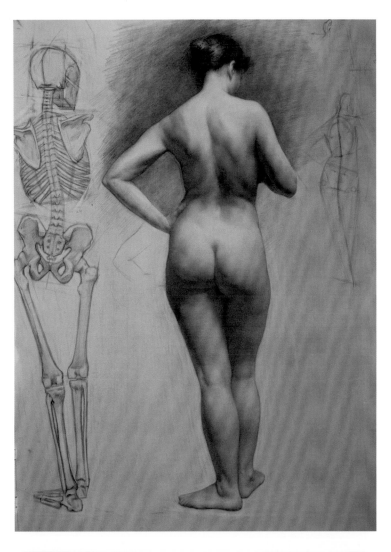

Painting

As students gain fluency with the pencil, they may proceed to utilize these principles in paint. First, students work in grisaille (monochromatic painting in shades of gray), painting from the casts, copying master paintings, and then figures and portraits from life. Students showing facility in grisaille will progress to the use of a color palette. Students must produce at least six finished, excellent month-long-pose figure paintings in color to show mastery.

Sculpture

A traditional emphasis on clarity of form, simplicity of action, balance, and harmony are woven through the sculpture program. Meticulous copying of antique sculptures, rigorous study of anatomical figure structure (including a year-long study of écorché), and extensive modeling from life are emphasized.

Painting students are required to study sculpture alongside dedicated sculpture students. Likewise, sculpture students study cast and figure drawing and painting alongside painting students. Although all students are required to model casts, half-life-size figures, portraits, and an écorché, sculpture students go on to model a life-size torso and figure.

Ecorché is an advanced anatomical study of the human body as a whole. Students begin with an armature and sculpt the skeleton one bone at a time. Then the muscles are added layer upon layer as the human form is built up from the inside out. Study of the origin, insertion, and action of the muscles helps students develop an understanding of the body's overlapping forms and the portrayal of motion. Toward the end of the process, a live model is used to further the conception of the model's anatomy as a single system.

Figure 3 (opposite top left): "Female Nude Study" by Colleen Barry, 2009, Graphite on Paper, 18 x 24 in.

Figure 4 (opposite right): "Discobolus," First Place, Morris and Alma Schapiro Prize by David Troncoso, 2010, Graphite on Paper, 18 x 24 in.

Figure 5 (opposite bottom left): Student Colleen Barry and model John Forkner in the Long Pose Oil Painting Class, 2010.

Figure 6 (right): "Jessica" by Angela Cunningham, 2010, Oil on Linen, 18 x 24 in.

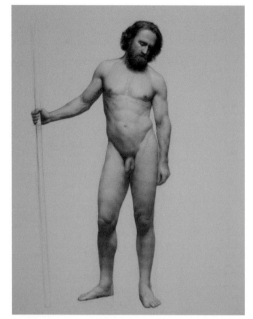

THE HUDSON RIVER FELLOWSHIP

The Hudson River Fellowship is intended to build a new movement of American art, modeling itself after the artistic, social, and spiritual values of the Hudson River School painters. It brings together the reawakening enthusiasm for the old American painters, the vigorous but unfocused scene of contemporary landscape painting, and the urgent need for a renewed reverence of the land. By bringing back the skills and spirit of the pre-impressionist landscape painters, the program gives direction to a new generation of painters. As the students learn to carefully study and reflect on the trees and clouds, blades of grass and cliffs, their paintings become beautiful. Ideally, these artists and their representations of nature will help to lead the culture back to a stronger connection to the landscape. The fellowship seeks to make a contribution both to the art world and the conservation movement.

The Hudson River Fellowship is offered by the Institute of Classical Architecture & Art in partnership with the Catskill Mountain Foundation's Sugar Maples Center for Creative Arts and is made possible by a leadership grant from the Morris and Alma Schapiro Fund.

Figure 7 (top left): "Tramskoy" by Colleen Barry, 2010, Oil on Linen, 20 x 27 in.

Figure 8 (top middle): "Male Figure," Third Place, GCA First Annual Drawing Competition by Carla Crawford, 2010, Graphite on Paper, 18 x 24 in.

Figure 9 (top right): "Jimmy," Honorable Mention, GCA Third Annual Figure Sculpture Competition by Angela Cunningham, 2010, Water Clay, 33 in.

Figure 10 (above): Students Connie Netherton and Neal Esplin in the Still Life Oil Painting Class, 2010.

Figure 11 (opposite): "Laocoön" by Colleen Barry, 2010, Oil on Linen, 18 x 24 in.

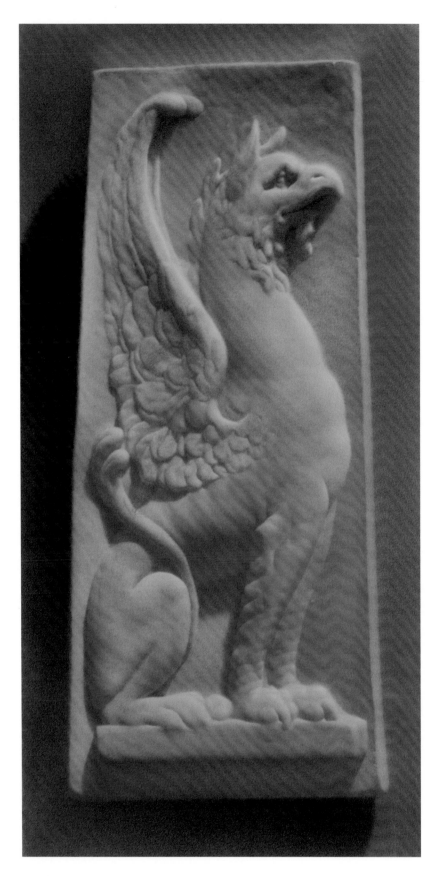

First Annual Drawing Competition at the GCA

The First Annual Drawing Competition gathered together the greatest draftsmen to work on a single figure drawing over the course of five days. Drawings were done from one model and one pose.

Drawing skills are the bedrock of good painting, and the foundation on which form and color can most truthfully be expressed. It is incumbent on the artist to routinely sharpen and develop these skills from life. The intent of this competition is to bring greater prestige and honor to those artists who have devoted time and energy to honing these abilities. It is a pure test of drawing skills.

The draftsman who executes the most beautiful drawing is awarded the Grand Prize accompanied by the title, Apelles. The second place prize includes the title, Protogenes. The winning draftsmen will hold these titles until the next annual competition. Cash prizes accompany the awards.

Participants are selected on the basis of a portfolio submission consisting of five images, including at least three figure drawings. All artists, from students to professionals, young and old, are encouraged to apply. There is no entrance fee, and no fee to compete.

2010 Winners of the Annual GCA Drawing Competition
Grand Prize, Apelles: Darren Kingsley
Second Prize, Protogenes: Will St. John

Figure 12 (left): "Griffin" by Devin Cecil-Wishing, 2009, Graphite on Paper, 13 x 7 in.

Figure 13 (opposite): "Dying Man" by Will St. John, 2010, Water Clay, 36 in.

The Story of Apelles and Protogenes (as retold by Guillaume Apollinaire)

Apelles and Protogenes were renowned painters of Ancient Greece during the time of Alexander the Great. They were rivals but also advocates of each other's work. Stories tell of their precise daily practice of outlining, and the laboriously fine finish they brought to their work, whether drawings or paintings. Their rivalry tested who could draw the finest, steadiest line and this has famously been recorded in an anecdote in Pliny's *Natural History*.

Apelles travelled to Protogenes' home in Rhodes to make the acquaintance of the painter about whom he had heard so much.

Arriving at Protogenes' studio, he encountered an old woman who told him that Protogenes was out and asked for his name so she could report who had enquired after him.

Observing in the studio a panel Protogenes had prepared for a painting, Apelles walked over to the easel, and taking up a brush told the servant to tell Protogenes that "this came from me," and drew in color an extremely fine line across the panel.

When Protogenes returned, and the old woman explained what had taken place, he examined the line and pronounced that only Apelles could have done so perfect a work; Protogenes then dipped a brush into another color and drew a still finer line above the first one, and asked his servant to show this to the visitor should he return.

When Apelles returned, and was shown Protogenes' response, ashamed that he might be bettered, he drew in a third color an even finer line between the first two, leaving no room for another display of craftsmanship. On seeing this, Protogenes admitted defeat, and went out to seek Apelles and meet him face-to-face.

Miscellanea

Reflections on Practice

By Scott Merrill

Those of us who practice traditional or classical architecture do so for a lot of very different reasons—for its expressiveness, for its capacity for development and refinement, for its promise to mitigate the harshness of life, for its affinity with our natures, and for its transcendence. I appreciate all these qualities very much. But the way I want to talk about it here is the way in which classical and traditional architecture—in my view—is most often found wanting, and that is in its faithfulness to modern life.

When I was an insufferable graduate student in the early- to mid-eighties, my classmates would sniff with unmistakable graduate student disapproval at anyone who stooped to work for developers. Maybe it was for this reason that I remember so clearly that both Arquitectonica and Duany Plater-Zyberk & Company (DPZ), each in their own way, had the courage to work in the belly of the beast. Andrés Duany, in a typically provocative aphorism, said that developers were the Medicis of the twentieth century. Of course, this was an affront to our delicate student sensibilities, which is no doubt what he intended. Arquitectonica's work seemed more glamorous at the time than DPZ's and so it was a better hook for students. My über-cool studio teacher loved Miami Vice and there was the Arquitectonica-designed Atlantis on Brickell Avenue in the fly-over opening sequence [FIGURE 1].

Everyone knew that yellow hole in the building, the aerial atrium with the palm tree, the pool and the red spiral stair like a water slide against the blue sky, just the way everyone from up north wanted to imagine Miami. This iconic image allowed us to forget that it was a very small, but intelligently concentrated part of a large gridded façade that was otherwise all South Florida brute commerce. I understand better now that the design of the Atlantis presented a different standard. In graduate school we talked ceaselessly about enlightened clients, by which we meant clients who would see how brilliant we were. But in a singularly unsentimental state built by speculators, the Atlantis is a good reminder of an architect's limited impact on large, indifferent forces, and an example of how architects might still leverage whatever small influence they do have just by being reasonably worldly.

The Atlantis possesses admirable self awareness, if I can say that of a building, and a very sly and subtle verisimilitude.

I mention the Atlantis because Florida is receptive, to a degree, of carefully calibrated flights of fancy but, believe me, it is completely disabused of untoward innocence. We are all given at times to a "disastrously glamorous imagination,"[2] but there is not enough glamorous material or enough "enlightened" clients willing to make a statement in Palm Beach or South Beach. Flannery O'Connor said of writing that it "is about everything human and we are made out of dust, and if you scorn getting yourself dusty, then you shouldn't try to write fiction. It's not a grand enough job for you."[3] We will have to make the rest of Florida from some pretty unpromising material and we will get dusty in the process. Windsor, I am aware, must seem a strange place to try to make this point, but so is Brickell Avenue.[4]

I

Whether we describe it in these terms or not, we have reservations about certain buildings because they lack "verisimilitude," which very roughly means something that is convincing to us to the degree that it conforms to our knowledge and our experience. There's actually a second definition that might apply better to the reality of Windsor—something that accords sufficiently with our knowledge and experience that we are willing to suspend our disbelief about certain other unreal aspects.

Verisimilitude in either sense requires a basic consonance with the modern world. Most people have an intuitive sense of verisimilitude. If buildings possess it, verisimilitude lends them a sort of natural authority. Without it, buildings can invite dismissal or even scorn.

Verisimilitude, or the lack of it, can be thought of at the trivial level of a detail—a long brick lintel, for example, held up only by a hidden steel angle. It can be thought of in terms of how money is spent, like a building with a complex and expensive shell forced to use impoverished materials, or a building that is all beautiful stairs and lobby and mean, ugly back offices; or a needle skyscraper that is all core; or a building whose massing requires fifty exit stairs. It may be a building with a very inefficient envelope, or the opposite, a super wide office park building where the work spaces near the core are in perpetual twilight so the developer can save more money.

Verisimilitude, or its absence, can be thought of at the level of construction integrity, like a building with an aesthetic of excessively exposed surfaces that we know will dissolve in the rain and the steam of the sub-tropics. It can come from the blindness of good intentions, like a LEED-certified building with all R-4 glass walls; or a design that demands very tight construction tolerances in a labor market where everyone is undertrained and underpaid, and where masonry, as an example, is laid like rubble. These all strike us viscerally as being wide of the mark, and as having a slightly unbecoming lack of worldliness.

A lack of verisimilitude can derive from unrealistic ideas about how change occurs, or from overestimating the possible extent of our knowledge or capabilities. It may derive from insufficient regard for the physical world, or from an unrealistic appraisal of human nature. It may come from abstractions belied by experience and observation. It may follow from an overreliance on purely deductive reasoning. It may come from completely separating an effect from its cost.

It may come from the vanity that places us, as architects, at the center of ideas, or from the fear of missing the train leaving the platform. It may come from framing everything in terms of either optimism or pessimism. It may come from a pretense to the exactitude and authority of scientific method. It often involves an implied promise that can't possibly be kept. It almost always comes from thinking that architecture can be imposed on life, rather than the other way around. Not only does all this diminish the standing of a building, but in the long run it has a corrosive effect on the trust between people who design buildings and those who commission them and use them.

Flat out dishonesty on these matters is rare. I assume that most people seek verisimilitude in their work, but because we have such wildly varying ideas of what the world is like and how it works, it's not surprising that we can't agree on what modern architecture should look like. This renders the idea very difficult to discuss. Whenever someone says that classical architecture is not "of its time," they are essentially saying that it lacks authority or standing in our world because it lacks verisimilitude. When Léon Krier warns, on the other hand, that Disney proffers two twin types of fantasies—Main Street and Tomorrowland—he is saying that if you are enthralled by a golden age of the future, it is as unworldly as if you have an undue fealty to a golden age in our past.

For me, classical or traditional architecture is seriously compromised if it is not fundamentally faithful to the modern world.

II
So what is this modern world like? To what, exactly, do we pledge our faithfulness? F. Scott Fitzgerald said that "the test of a first rate intelligence is the ability to hold two opposed ideas in the mind at the same time, and still retain the ability to function."[4]

In 2006, well before any whiff of an economic collapse, I remember reading the following passages—on the very same page—from *New York Times* editorials by Thomas Friedman and Paul Krugman regarding the prospects posed by globalization.[5] Friedman concludes a typically

breathless piece: "If more countries can get just three basic things right—enough telecom and bandwidth so their people can get connected: steadily improving education and decent corruption-free economic governance; and the rule of law—and we can find more sources of clean energy, there is every reason for optimism that we could see even faster global growth in this century, with many more people lifted out of poverty."

In the adjacent column—and this was not a coordinated juxtaposition of opposing sensibilities; its resonance came from its randomness—Krugman, a dour man who should only be read on a sunny day, wrote this of globalization: "…we became a nation in which people make a living by selling one another houses, and they pay for the houses with money borrowed from China. Now that game seems to be coming to an end. We're going to have to find other ways to make a living—in particular, we're going to have to start selling goods and services —not just I.O.U.s to the rest of the world, and/or replace imports with domestic production."

Of course, this kind of disagreement occurs all the time and in all fields. I remember a story about Ted Turner at a Silicon Valley conference at which the CEOs were enthusing about the prospect of all the children of the world owning computers, and Turner, who is known for his impatience and doesn't suffer fools, remarked upon the fact that a third of the world was without electricity. And of course where Donald Rumsfeld famously saw shock and awe, Carl von Clausewitz just as famously saw fog and friction. So we learn to live with our experts disagreeing in dismaying ways.

I practice architecture in Florida and I am with Clausewitz. But my experience makes me incline more toward Paul Krugman's grumpy insistence on fundamentals than toward Friedman's sunny credulity. Building in Florida is a spectacularly flawed process. It remains crude and construction is still remarkably vulnerable to deterioration.

Wood rots, re-bar scales, and concrete spalls. Rough trades have limited tolerances. Labor is often low paid, untrained, and illegal. Materials move, glass squanders energy. Cantilevers sag, beams deflect, lawyers sue.

Floridians are vain and a little unrealistic about their place in the greater scheme of things. Typically during hurricane season, when the barometer drops and New Providence is washed over by storm surge, those of us living on the low, shifting sandbars off the coast of Florida, pack up our families and we try to flee our homes on choked, dead flat inland highways. In the millions, we form a retreating convoy of urban assault vehicles—Suburbans, Expeditions and Hummers, of course, but more improbably, Yukons, Tundras, Denalis, Sierras, Armadas, Armanis, Infinities, Infidelities, and Intifadas. When we flee we won't even acknowledge that we flee. We affect what Saul Bellow described as "the imaginary grandeur of insects."[6]

Floridians have the oldest European settlement in the country but their state was the last to be connected to the rest of the country by railroad, some decades after the golden spike was driven at Promontory Summit in Utah. We elect mosquito commissioners but despite an industry and a bureaucracy dedicated to their eradication, there are half a million mosquitoes for every person. We clear the oak hammocks to make golf courses, but snakes and alligators are poised on the edges of the greens, ready to reassert themselves when the golfers stop hacking and the chemicals stop flowing.

With great effort, over a long period of time, and to disastrous effect, we have drained the vast interior of the state, destroying the Everglades in the process. And now at great expense and with federal money that itself threatens to dry up, we are endeavoring to flood the interior of Florida again. From Windsor's beach you can see NASA's shuttle launches rise, arc and lean into the upper atmosphere, but you can also see washed up on shore the crudely lashed together rafts of Haitian refugees seeking a better life at great personal risk. You can also still see salvagers just off shore bringing up silver from wrecks of ships sunk in the hurricane of 1715 as they were taking New World treasure back to Spain.

Florida has the largest Congress for the New Urbanism chapter in the country for the same reason that diseased bodies have high white blood cell counts. Our children all have Toshiba notepads in school, but many of them wheeze audibly from the air conditioning in musty classrooms. The principal technical initiatives on our Fort Pierce federal courthouse are resistance to mold and to bomb blasts. We have cleared the natural habitat of the eastern diamondback

rattlesnake for the depressing torpor of moldering sub-tropical suburbs. Water, the universal solvent, starts to dissolve buildings from the day we take occupancy.

My office worked on an urban design project in Port St. Joe, Florida, near Apalachicola. In 1838 St. Joe was the largest city in Florida and the site for the territorial convention that anticipated Florida statehood. But five years later in 1843, it was completely wiped from the face of the earth, a victim of yellow fever, a hurricane, and a fire. Our client there, who owns land in sum that is equal to the state of Delaware, moved a federal highway to build the commercial core of the project, but the project was laid low by the bursting of the most recent land bubble, and the site now sits in eerie, isolated quiet, waiting for the tar balls to come ashore. Incidentally, the French briefly had the first crude settlement at this location, named Crevecoeur, or Broken Heart.

Most everything I describe here is a rebuke to our sense of modern life, but from all these antediluvian considerations Florida architects must make modern buildings and places.

III

In trying to think about what modern architecture might look like I find examples from writing to be helpful. My old boss, Pat Pinnell, an architect and an English major, said that "form is form," and sometimes I think you have to look in places where you don't have a horse in the race.

James Wood, a literary critic, wrote a review for *The New Republic* in which he described the "hysterical realism" in a certain type of modern novel.[7] He wrote: "The big contemporary novel is a perpetual motion machine that appears to have been embarrassed into velocity. It seems to want to abolish stillness, as if ashamed of silence…Stories and sub-stories sprout on every page, as these novels continually flourish their glamorous congestion. Inseparable from this culture of permanent storytelling is the pursuit of vitality at all costs. Indeed, vitality is storytelling as far as these books are concerned."

"The conventions of realism are not being abolished, but on the contrary exhausted, overworked…One is reminded of Kierkegaard's remark that travel is the way to avoid despair…Their mode of narration seems to be almost incompatible with tragedy or anguish." "Again and again," Wood continues, "books like these are praised for being brilliant cabinets of wonders. Such diversity! So many stories! So many weird and funky characters! Bright lights are taken as evidence of habitation…It does not lack for powers of invention. The problem is there is too much of it."

Wood has, elsewhere, characterized big postmodern novels as "curiously arrested books that know a thousand different things—the recipe for the best Indonesian fish curry! The sonics of the trombone! The drug market in Detroit! The history of strip cartoons! But [the novels] do not know a single human being."[8]

Leon Wieseltier was Wood's editor at *The New Republic*, a magazine founded during the Progressive Era by Herbert Croly. I was interested in an unlikely comparison he once made between two very different writing styles—the voluble loquaciousness of the characters of the television screenwriter Andrew Sorkin (*West Wing*, etc.), and the halting, inarticulate prose of the characters of *The Sopranos*, the series about venal New Jersey gangsters.

Wieseltier writes:

> In Sorkin's shiny nonsense, people speak in repartee, and always find the words they need, and nothing insignificant or tedious is ever uttered. They talk as nattily as they look. Even their afflictions are oddly high-spirited, as coolness conquers all. There is not an unmordant or unmoralized second in anyone's day. Sorkin's phony people go from portentousness to hipness and back. They are figments of a disastrously glamorous imagination, the polished puppets of a shallow man's profundity. In The Sopranos by contrast, there is no eloquence, even when there is beauty. Silences abound. These people speak the way people actually speak; they lie, and lie again; they hide; they repair gladly to banalities and to borrowed words; they struggle for adequacy in communication; they say nothing at all. Their verbal resources are cruelly lacking for their spiritual needs. They cannot say what they mean. Their obscenities are their tribute to the power of their feelings: the diction of their desperation. When they reach for sophistication they mangle it. Their metaphors are awkward and homely…Yet all this inarticulateness is peculiarly lyrical, and deeply moving. It is also a relief from the talkativeness that passes for thought in fancier places. Words should be fought for.[9]

I hope this is not too great a transition. Abraham Lincoln, notably, was not the first to speak at Gettysburg. He was not even the featured speaker. Edward Everett, a friend of Daniel Webster's, was the featured orator at Gettysburg, preceding Lincoln, who was scheduled only to make a few "remarks." Everett spoke volubly, rapturously for two hours. But, after Lincoln spoke for three minutes, a total of 272 words, Everett's high church style was obsolete, replaced forever by the vernacular cadences of Lincoln's pared rhetoric.

When Walker Percy was given the National Book Award he was asked why the South had produced so many fine writers. He said, somewhat enigmatically, that it was because the South had lost the war. Flannery O'Connor expanded on this. "It is because we have had our fall," she said. "Because we are born with an inburnt sense of human limitations, and with a sense of mystery that we would not have had in our first state of innocence."[10]

In Florida, I observe conditions that improve steadily, if erratically, and not without considerable and sustained effort. But I am almost always impressed as much by the limits of knowledge as by the extent of it. My feeling is that our capacity for greatness—as writers, or politicians, or doctors, or soldiers, or scientists, or architects, will more likely come from knowing just those limitations that also frustrate and

humiliate us so much; that it will come from battles that we have lost, and from battles we have won, like Lincoln, at too high a cost.

Modern building is like anti-poetry or anti-theory, which I suppose is why I so appreciate Wieseltier's description of *The Sopranos*. Buildings are built, or fail to be built because of ambition, intrigue, duplicity, lack of faith, lack of sufficient ambition, vanity, fear, generosity, sniping, perseverance, patience, laziness, luck, talent, timing, stubbornness, largeness of heart, fatigue. Everything human.

For me to speak of great leaps forward, or of transformations, or change agents, of risk taking, of frictionless global markets, of invisible hands, of the ends of history, of paradigm shifts, would render me like a circus barker calling the suckers into the tent; or like one of those guys who used to spin plates on the end of sticks. The glamorous view of the world teeters constantly like those plates, and it requires constant spin. It takes a furious and unflagging effort to force an abstract idea on a world that stubbornly refuses to conform to it. It requires a credulity that I personally can't muster every day.

IV

From 1988 until 1990 my wife and I lived in Seaside, a project designed almost 30 years ago now by Elizabeth Plater-Zyberk and Andrés Duany in the Panhandle of Florida [FIGURE 2]. We arrived about seven years after Robert Davis started building beach bungalows on Tupelo Street, and four years after *Architectural Record* published the sort of Victorian cottages on Rosewalk by Orr and Taylor. These two initiatives—Robert Davis' rude bungalows and the pastel cottages of Rosewalk—established, probably unwittingly, competing visions for Seaside's architecture.

In his 1852 pattern book, *The Architecture of Country Houses*, Andrew Jackson Downing wrote that "men of imagination" will seek "houses with high roofs, steep gables, unsymmetrical and capricious forms… any and every feature that indicates originality, boldness, energy, and variety of character."[11] Downing seemed prescient in anticipating the Gilded Age and our fascination with the cartoon vanity and swagger of the self-described iconoclast. By 1988 when my wife and I arrived, Seaside was, for the New South iconoclasts, everything that Downing had imagined and foreseen for their Victorian forebears.

In contrast, I had been an architectural field historian in Vermont, a state that has not developed architecturally on the whole since Downing wrote his pattern book. A Vermont town was typically comprised of the same three or four house types and so I had come to appreciate a taciturn urbanism, repetitive and laconic, and architecture that had an admirably low cost of entry.

What Downing argued for was much more flashy and expensive, but Downing was psychologically astute and Seaside homeowners were well off. Downing's ideas tickle the vanity of the owner and the architect at once, and for the most part he carried the day in Seaside. In terms I have already tried to establish, the difference between Davis' first bungalows and the fancy houses that came to dominate Seaside was the

Figure 2 (opposite): Chapel, Seaside, FL, 2001, by Merrill, Pastor & Colgan Architects. Photograph by UGArdner.

difference between more and less glamorous worldviews, and between the more or less voluble vocabularies that give them expression.

Windsor was conceived by DPZ in 1989 in charettes in Vero Beach and Toronto. I was invited to the charettes by Lizz and Andrés, and ultimately invited by the Westons to come to Vero Beach to help implement the plan. Windsor, for me, has been an ongoing effort to step out of Downing's long shadow. Careers and even some lives seem to oscillate in a pattern of over-correction, and though it is unfair to both, I can't help but think of Windsor as a sort of inversion of Seaside, a counterweight to some of its tendencies.

I will suggest a purely personal and probably painfully earnest list of epigrammatic principles on which I think Windsor's architectural guidelines were based. Designing buildings from architectural guidelines is like freeze-drying food and then adding water back. It's a tricky business prone to failure or abuses at two points—the reduction of building antecedents to words, and the reconstitution of buildings from words.

What these principles all have in common, I hope, is that they start with an attempt to understand life and then proceed to architecture. People who try to start with architecture and impose it on life tend to have tin ears and heavy boots. Corbu once visited a housing project of his that had been severely altered by residents in a way that must have disappointed him badly, but he responded only that "life always wins." This is the most graceful sentiment I have ever heard attributed to an architect. We will fail to bend the world to our will.

In no particular order then, here are some principles on which I think Windsor's guidelines were written:

1. Balance the private pleasures of freedom with a modicum of public restraint. Freedom is subtle and not always what you think it is. In his writings about manners, James Fenimore Cooper suggested that the real choice one typically faces in life is not between freedom and restraint, but between self-restraint and imposed restraint. He allied himself with manners, which he thought of as self-restraint, the more dignified of the two options. It is interesting to me that Cooper anticipates somehow the trivial tyrannies to which we constantly submit—homeowner associations, Architectural Review Boards, and co-op boards. The real argument for self-restraint, of course, is freedom from busybodies.

2. Solve recurring problems with models rather than singular problems with masterpieces. Andrés Duany said "we decided for the Model T rather than the Bugatti. The Bugatti is in the Museum of Modern Art but the model T changed the world." On another occasion, I think he said that there is Thomist beauty and there is Fordist beauty. There is an informal utilitarian calculus going on here about the most effective models for change. The Bugatti model says the masterpiece transforms our lives at a stroke. The Ford model assumes that change is slow and incremental, a tough, unglamorous slog, and best aimed at recurring problems. When Pat Pinnell says that progress in classical architecture is measured by the perfection of the type, this is what he means. Windsor's great contribution in this regard is the introduction, refinement, and mainstreaming of the courtyard house in a real estate market that had marginalized it altogether.

3. Provide meaningful variety, where it is affordable, based on the vagaries of the site and the program. When variety is not affordable or justifiable, ennoble repetition. Resist gratuitous variety based on the grotesquely personal. It is so very hard to be inventive without being exaggeratedly so.

4. A corollary to point 3: Hype is corrosive. To avoid two inverted forms of hype, do not use classical or traditional forms to lend gravity to the merely callow, and do not use extreme formal invention to disguise the unremarkable or the pedestrian. The unremarkable can be attractive but it can't be remarkable. Adapt, refine, develop, and innovate when you are dealing with uniquely modern problems, but do not try to disguise the degree to which we deal with the same intractable problems as our forebears.

5. Balance the archetypal in the plan, with the specifically regional in the detailing. Develop a regional language based on climate, materials, and the tolerances and skills of each trade. Resist the hegemony of all international styles including those that descend from Mies and Palladio.

6. Look for new languages in the detritus and cast-offs of our back yards. Stanford White was said to have discovered the forms of the shingle style in the rude ancillary roofs behind the colonial houses of New England. One of the projects I most enjoyed doing at Windsor was a small structure based on the beautiful and simple statics of the grapefruit sorters of the fruit packing houses of Indian River County. A hundred such traditions, if studied, could help reinvigorate traditional forms by increasing the DNA pool from which it drew.

7. As a corollary to looking in your back yard, look for pertinent models throughout the world. Long before Jared Diamond claimed in *Guns, Germs, and Steel* that ideas and inventions migrated readily along lines of latitude, and long before Thomas Friedman declared the world to be flat, Lizz Plater-Zyberk and Andrés Duany presciently proclaimed the Mediterranean and the Caribbean to be two shores of the same sea.

We need to develop new languages and get new life out of old ones that have been prematurely cast aside. Languages are big games, our innocent pleasures, and imagination is central to what makes us human. The promises of new languages will have to be judged by how much they can be developed and refined, and by how expressive they can be. Some languages are too personal for others to advance, others are too minimal, and still others will reward our efforts almost endlessly.

Le Corbusier, late in his career, was said to have been unsatisfied with his houses of the twenties, so we are fortunate that Richard Meier loved them so much. The language proved to have an almost unimaginable capacity to develop further. How many other languages are needlessly cast off long before they are fully developed or refined? In Florida alone I think of Marion Manley's work at the University of Miami, Paul Rudolph's small hovering houses in Sarasota, and Henry John Klutho's attempt to introduce the Prairie style to Jacksonville, where it would have made great sense. Some of us can range broadly with language; most of us, like Meier, will have to go deeper, and refine like classicists.

8. Be concrete. Architects reflexively curtsey to abstraction but we must not miss the pleasures of the concrete. Our heads are attached to our bodies and hearts. At Windsor we sought visible evidence of the weight of the roof coming to the ground, of the uplift of strong winds, and of the brutality of the sun. It was especially fun to think, for example, of a column type, a classical order in tension that could express the fact that columns in Florida had to hold roofs down as well as up. Classical architecture is so incredibly expressive and adaptive in this way.

9. Reserve monumentality for public buildings, which are often much smaller than houses or commercial buildings. Some of Seaside's houses reflect an untoward and overweening ambition. Windsor is full of world-beaters who live in taciturn houses. I think we all liked the idea of a place where there appeared to be less going on than there actually was, which is the opposite of what you come to expect.

10. Search for origins, for the archaic, for Paestum as well as the Parthenon. When Inigo Jones designed St. Paul's Covent Garden for a London developer in 1631 he reputedly said that he would design "the handsomest barn in England [FIGURE 3]."[12] If Jones was making a virtue of necessary economy, he was also placing his Protestant church in opposition to the high church tradition of the Counter Reformation.

Whether true or apocryphal, the idea that Inigo Jones could think of an early Protestant church as a beautiful barn is still an incredibly expressive form of protest against periodic excess. In Windsor there has been a similar wariness of the high tradition, and incidentally a predisposition toward barns as a useful expression of that wariness. See Cooper Robertson's beach club if you can, or Jorge Hernandez's tennis pavilion. Or see the boat hull of Léon Krier's Town Hall.

Some projects are just plain dowdy by nature. Windsor is consciously lacking in glamour, which is a different matter altogether. Andrés once described it as high cost, low luxury. It is suspected of loquaciousness, and glibness and shiny nonsense. It is wary of high church styles; it is wary of most all high traditions, including those that derive from Palladio. It expresses poetry and prose in appropriate measure, but it is weighted toward the prosaic because that is what swamps our boat most of the time. As Mario Cuomo once said, "we campaign in poetry but we govern in prose."

V

Windsor won't be judged here. It will be judged beyond its gates, and if it fails to plant seeds in much less fortunate and less beautiful places, we can safely judge it a noble failure. In considering Windsor's inception, think of its experimental nature, its determined practicality, the subtle generosity of the master plan, its delight in invention and refinement, its suspicion of grand gestures. I hope its influence will be felt in some unlikely places, that its influence will take forms unsuspected and facilitated by people you wouldn't guess capable of great things. I hope that it will help foment a rebellion against excess. Study Windsor, but lead your target, and as always, look ahead. ◄

Figure 3 (above): St Paul's, Covent Garden, London, UK, by Inigo Jones, 1633-38. Photograph by bthomson.

NOTES

1. The following is based on a talk given in the Town Hall at Windsor, Florida, to the local chapter of the ICAA.
2. On the source of the quote, Leon Wieseltier, see the discussion below.
3. Flannery O'Connor, "The Nature and Aim of Fiction" in *Mystery and Manners: Occasional Prose.* Selected and edited by Sally and Robert Fitzgerald. (New York: Farrar, Straus and Giroux, 1969), p. 68.
4. F. Scott Fitzgerald, *The Crack-Up,* ed. E. Wilson, (New York: New Directions, 1945), p. 69.
5. *The New York Times,* May 19, 2006.
6. Saul Bellow, *Mr. Sammler's Planet* (New York: Viking Press, 1970), p. 232.
7. A review of Zadie Smith's *White Teeth*: James Wood, "Human, All Too Inhuman," *The New Republic,* July 24, 2000.
8. In a review of Jonathan Franzen's *The Corrections*: James Woods, "Abhorring a Vacuum," *The New Republic,* October 15, 2001.
9. Leon Wieseltier, "Addio," *The New Republic,* June 18, 2007.
10. Quoted by Paul Elie, "Pilgrims," *Boston College Magazine,* Spring 2004.
11. Andrew Jackson Downing, *The Architecture of Country Houses* (New York: D. Appleton & Company, 1852), p. 263.
12. According to an anecdote told to Horace Walpole by the Speaker of the House of Commons, Arthur Onslow (1691–1768), Horace Walpole, *Anecdotes of Painting in England,* second edition, (Strawberry-Hill: Thomas Kirgate, 1765) vol. II, p. 175 n. The anecdote is not given in the first edition of 1762.

Architectural Drawing in the Digital Age

By Jacob Brillhart

New drafting software, such as CAD and Revit, has changed the age-old practice of hand drawing. Though invaluable tools, they are unintentionally compromising the education and creative development of the young architect. As hand drawing is eliminated in favor of CAD both in the office and in the classroom, the full extent of collateral damage has yet to be appreciated. It is, unarguably, an exciting time for architects who have at their fingertips the powerful tool of the computer. Yet, relative to the hundreds of years in which architects have traditionally practiced architecture, the technology is still very new and unvetted. Recently my personal observation of creative output in the academic setting has revealed that the computer's shortcuts unintentionally create a digital vacuum in terms of scale, diminish our understanding of designs, and weaken our editing processes.

When drawing by hand, one designs, thinks, plots, and prints simultaneously in a single process. Computer drafting is instead a two-step process: The designer captures ideas via the computer, inputting these thoughts through a series of logical commands. Still ephemeral, the work is not a drawing yet, but rather intangible, changeable, and temporary. It is only during the second step, the plotting or printing of the file—the creative filtering process—that the image takes on life, delivered from the virtual to the actual.

Although the computer functions are rapidly executed, they are nonetheless fractured and disjointed from the printing process—very different from the right brain's holistic process of creation and production in hand drawing. This time lapse between the perception or idea and the printing reduces the sense of personal ownership of the image. The ownership of the hand drawing, however, is always evident through its "real time" creation, and is not diluted by the limited vocabulary of the printer or the computer.

The phrase "I didn't know how to draw what I really wanted to do on the computer" or "when I went to print this is what happened, I am not sure why" are frequently heard from students today. Excuses such as these are commonly accepted because most people, students and teachers alike, have little understanding of the technology they are using. The norm is to blame the plotter or the computer for poor drawings, which raises the question: Who is in charge?

The blind dependence on CAD and other software tools increases after architecture school as young designers continue to design things they do not understand. Working under severe time constraints, they make maximum use of the copy and paste commands, pulling details, elevations, and wall sections from past projects and reassembling them. The drawing can be altered and then reproduced by the new author without tracing over every line. Seemingly a swift and efficient technique, it effectively undermines the apprenticeship aspect of the architect's education. When one draws,

Figure 1 (above): Detail of sculpture in Piazza Navona, Rome.

Figure 2 (opposite): Study of the Teatro Farnese, Parma.

All illustrations are by the author.

Figure 3 (left): Studies of S. Maria in Trastevere, the Tempietto at S. Pietro in Montorio, and the cortile of S. Maria della Pace, Rome.

Figure 4 (above): Horologion of Andronikos (Tower of the Winds), Athens.

Figure 5 (opposite): Ospedale degli Innocenti, Florence.

Figure 6 (following page): Vatican Palace, Rome.

one understands and remembers; when one uses the right click command, one does neither. This scenario not only inhibits the intellectual development of young designers, but also leads to a complacent architecture that is void of invention. The path of least resistance is followed, leaving the computer in charge by choosing from a menu of defaults.

Software technologies, when used to supplement or expedite processes of design, are invaluable. The computer unquestionably belongs in schools and architectural offices. However, the fundamentals of architectural design are still rooted in hand drawing. If ownership of the design shifts to the software and plotter, and the architect's grasp of scale diminishes, buildings will inevitably suffer. To balance the benefits of technology with the human component of creative design, we must consider how we process and perceive information using our right and left brains.

In my opinion, we need to encourage more use of the right brain and not continually default to the left brain activity of data entry. One of the simplest and most effective ways to engage the right brain is to encourage the use of a sketchbook as an incubator of ideas and intellectual activity. This is why, six years ago, in a feverish need to escape the confines of my computer at Columbia University, I set out on a series of European road trips to rediscover the forgotten practice of sketching in situ.

Schinkel, "Gothic Hall" or War Memorial 1816
good example of Neo Classical Architecture.
UNTER DEN LINDEN →

11·6·06

30 PACES

The great architects of the past drew by hand on site to understand directly and deeply scale, light, shadow, and form in the full, physical three dimensions of the real world. This is in marked contrast to the flat, virtual two dimensions of the computer monitor—where there is no sun, no shadow, no gravity, no weight, no material, no scale, and zero physical and cultural context. The drawings and small paintings reproduced here—selected from over 700 hundred travel sketches I have made on site in Europe, America, and Asia—are intended to sustain the physicality of history. They attempt to resuscitate the forgotten tools of the imagination and the resilient influence of drawing on design. ❧

Figure 7 (previous page): Neue Wache, Berlin.

Figure 8 (above): Museo della Civiltà Romana, E.U.R., Rome.

Figure 9 (opposite): Villa d'Este, Tivoli.

Villa d'Este, w/ Frank, Fett & Graves. 10·21·86

Administration,
Members, and Sponsors

PROFESSIONAL MEMBERS

LATROBE SOCIETY
Professional
Dell Mitchell Architects, Inc.
E. R. Butler & Co.
Electronics Design Group, Inc.
Elegant Additions, Inc.
Hailey Development Group, LLC
Reilly Windows & Doors
SBD Kitchens, LLC
Tischler und Sohn

BENEFACTOR CIRCLE
Professional
Andrew V. Giambertone & Assoc.
Architects, PC
CoorItalia
Crown Point Cabinetry
Curtis & Windham Architects, Inc.
Geoffrey DeSousa Interior Design
Historical Concepts

PATRON
Professional
Allan Greenberg, Architects
Alvin Holm, AIA Architects
Atelier AM
Balmer Architectural Mouldings
Chadsworth 1-800-COLUMNS
Charlotte Moss
Drake Construction
Duany Plater-Zyberk & Company, LLC
Eric J. Smith Architect, PC
Eric Stengel Architecture
Exclusive Cultural Travel Programs
Ferguson & Shamamian Architects, LLP
Foster Reeve & Associates, Inc.
G. P. Schafer Architect, PLLC
Giannetti Architecture & Interiors, Inc.
Haddonstone
Hamady Architects
Harrison Design Associates - Atlanta Office
Heather Hilliard Design
Hottenroth & Joseph Architects
Hyde Park Mouldings
Ike Kligerman Barkley Architects
Insidesign, Inc.
James Doyle Design Associates, LLC
Jimenez Custom Painting, Inc
John B. Murray Architect, LLC
Jorge G. Loyzaga Arquitecto
Leeds Custom Design
Les Métalliers Champenois (USA)
Marisa Marcantonio
Mayfair Construction Group, LLC
Merritt Woodwork
Michael G. Imber Architects
Katherine Pasternack

Peter Pennoyer Architects
Project Solutions, LLC
R. D. Rice Construction, Inc.
Robert A. M. Stern Architects, LLP
Schotten Fenster
Seaside Community Development Corp.
Sebastian Construction Group
Serendipity
SilverLining Interiors, Inc.
Stern Projects
The Marker Group
Tim Barber, Ltd. - Architecture & Design
TJS Partners, Inc.
Tradewood Industries, LTD
Tucker & Marks
Vella Interiors
Vintage Millworks, Inc.
Waterworks
Woolems, Inc.
Zeluck Inc./Fenestra America
Zepsa Industries
ZFA Structural Engineers

DONOR
Professional
Apex Wood Floors
Appleton & Associates, Inc.
Architectural Millwork Installation
Architectural Nexus, Inc.
BAMO, Inc.
Barbara Scavullo Design
Bernsohn & Fetner LLC
Biglin Architectural Group
Black Mountain Construction / Development
Caccoma Interiors
Carlisle Wide Plank Floors
Charles Warren, Architect
CJNA Architects
Clark Construction Corp.
Creative Millwork LLC
Decorative Carpets
Decorators Supply Corp.
Distinctive Remodeling Solutions
Florian Papp, Inc
Fuller Construction Services
Fondation de Coubertin
Halper Owens Architects, LLC
Heartwood Fine Windows and Doors
Judith F. Hernstadt
Hilton-VanderHorn Architects
Historical Arts & Casting, Inc.
Interior Management, Inc.
Kais Custom Builders, LLC

Ken Tate Architect, PA
Klise Manufacturing
Laczko Studio, Inc.
Lawrence H. Randolph, Architect
Leonard Porter Studio, LLC
Leonard Woods, Architect
Lichten Craig Architects, LLP
Lifescape Associates, Inc.
Lisa Singleton
Mark P. Finlay Architects, AIA
MATT Construction
McCoy Construction
Newington-Cropsey Cultural Studies Center
Page Duke Landscape Architects
Parc Monceau Antiques
Patricia McCarthy Smith Interior Design
Paul Stuart Rankin, Inc.
Peter Cosola, Inc.
Planning Partners Limited
Portola Paints & Glazes
Restore Media, LLC
Richard Manion Architecture, Inc.
Rockwood Door & Millwork
Eleanor Schapa
Scofield Historic Lighting
Scott Group Custom Carpets
Shears & Window
Snyder Diamond
St. Charles of New York
The Green-Wood Cemetery
Thomas M. Kirchhoff Architect, AIA, PA
Thurston / Boyd Interior Design
Todd Alexander Romano, LLC
Vintage Lumber & Interiors
Warren Sheets Design, Inc.
White River Hardwoods
William Hefner Architecture, Inc.
Woodstone Architectural Windows & Doors

SUSTAINER
Professional
Acanthus Press, LLC
AJ.T Architect, PC
Alexandros C. Samaras & Associates, SA
Alisberg Parker Architects
Alison Crowell Interior Design
Amalfi Stone & Masonry
Amanda Webster Design, Inc.
Andre Tchelistcheff, Architect
Andrew Nuzzi Architects, LLC
Andrew Skurman Architects
Archer & Buchanan Architecture, Ltd.
Arnn Gordon Greineder Architecture
Artistic Painter of Decorative Plaster Mouldings
Athalie Derse, Inc.
Austin Patterson Disston Architects, LLC
Baltazar Construction, Inc.
BAR Architects
Barbara Tattersfield Designs, Inc.
Benchmark Design International, Inc. Architects & Planners
Berndsen Company, Inc.
Bertolini Architectural Works
BKSK Architects, LLP
Brekhus Tile & Stone, Inc.
Brian Dittmar Design, Inc.
BSF Properties, Inc.
Budd Woodwork Inc.
Burdge & Associates Architects, Inc.
Bush Interiors, Inc.
Calhoun Design and Metalworks, Inc.
Camille Charles Interior Design
Cannon Design
Carbine & Associates, LLC
Carpenter & MacNeille, Architects & Builders, Inc.
Catlin Interiors, Inc
Chalet
Charles Luck Stone
Charter Homes and Neighborhoods
Chestnut Specialists, Inc.
Chris Barrett Design
Chris Carson, Architect
Chris McNeely House Designs, Inc.
Christian Rogers Architect
Christine G. H. Franck, Inc.
Christine Haught, Ltd. Interior Design
Chryssanthou, Inc.
Cindy Grant Architecture, Inc. AIA
Classic Tile & Mosaic, Inc.
Classical Decorative Arts
Clawson Architects, LLC
Columbian Model & Exhibit Works, Ltd.
Contreras Residential Design
Cooper, Robertson & Partners

Cornerstone Architectural Precast
Couture Design Associates, Inc.
Cronk Duch Architecture
H. Beck Crothers
Cullman & Kravis, Inc.
Cumberland Architectural Millwork, Inc.
D. C. Williamson General Contracting, Inc
Daniel Du Bay Interior Design, Inc.
David D. Harlan Architects, LLC
David H. Ellison, Architect
David Jones Architects
David Scott Parker Architects, LLC
Debra Antolino Interiors, Inc.
DecoCraft USA
Dennis Brady, Architect
Derrick Architecture
Di Biase Filkoff Architects
Dianne Warner, Fine Artist
Dibello Architects, PLLC
Domani Architecture + Planning, Inc.
Don B. McDonald Architect, AIA, Ltd.
Donald Whittaker - The Design Guy
Douglas Durkin Design, Inc.
Drake Design Associates
DSC - Design Solutions Company, Inc.
DSI Entertainment Systems
Duncan McRoberts Associates
E. F. San Juan, Inc.
E. Frank Smith Residential Design, Inc.
Eberlein Design Consultants, Ltd.
Elleco Construction
Engineered Environments
Ervin, Lovett, & Miller, Inc.
Escobedo Construction, Ltd.
EverGreene Architectural Arts, Inc.
F. H. Perry Builder, Inc.
Finton Construction
Florez Lopez Architects
Flower Construction
Folger & Burt Architectural Hardware
Ford Drywall & Stucco, Inc.
Franck & Lohsen Architects, Inc.
G. Morris Steinbraker & Son, Inc.
Galice, Inc.
Genesis Architectural Design
Genesis Elevator Company
Geoffrey Mouen Architect, LLC
George Penniman Architects, LLC
Georgina Rice & Co., Inc.
Gewalt-Hamilton Associates, Inc
Gold Coast Metal Works, Inc.
Golenberg & Company Construction
Goodchild's, Inc.
Goodwin Classic Homes
Graphic Builders, Inc.
Gregory Lombardi Design, Inc.
Gretalogie

Griffiths Constructions, Inc.
Group 3 Architecture-Interiors-Planning
GSBS Architects
Hadley's Custom Millwork
Hartman-Cox Architects
Hawtof Associates
Hayslip Design Associates, Inc.
HBRA Architects, Inc.
Helga Horner, Inc.
Herrmann Masonry
Historic Doors, LLC
Horizon Builders, Inc.
Horizon General Contractors, Inc.
Horizon Houseworks
Hubert Whitlock Builders, Inc.
Hull Historical, Inc.
Italy Adagio
Jack deLashmet & Associates
Jack Herr Design Associates
Jackson & Ryan Architects
Jacquelynne P. Lanham Designs, Inc.
James Bleecker Photography
James Leslie Design Associates Corp.
James Marzo Design, Inc.
Jan Gleysteen Architects, Inc.
Jaycox Reinel Architects
Jeff Allen Landscape Architecture
John Canning Studios
John Milner Architects, Inc.
Jonathan Browning Studios, Inc.
Jonathan Lee Architects
Joseph A. Buchek, AIA
Joseph Minton, Inc.
Juarez & Juarez Residential Design LLC
KAA Design Group, Inc.
Kaese & Lynch Architecture
Kaiser Trabue Landscape Architecture
Kaplan Gehring McCarroll Architectural
    Lighting
Kass & Associates
Kate Johns, AIA
Keesee and Associates, Inc.
Knight Architecture, LLC
Lambert Garden Design
Lane - McCook & Associates, Inc.
Lantern Masters
Lawrance Architectural Presentations
Lenkin Design, Inc.
Leonard Metal Art Works, Inc.
Leverone Design
Logoluso Design Studio
Loop Worx
Lucia Benton Interiors, Inc.
Ludowici Roof Tile

Lundy Flitter Beldecos & Berger, PC
Lyn Muse Interiors, Inc.
Malatesta & Co., Inc.
Marmi Natural Stone
Mary Follin Design
Materials Marketing
McCrery Architects, LLC
McKinnon and Harris, Inc.
McRoskey Mattress Company
Medusa Stone Studio
Meier / Ferrer
Merrill, Pastor and Colgan Architects
Merrimack Design Associates
MH Akers Custom Homes
Michael Goldman Architect, PC
Michael Rouchell, Architect
Michael Whaley Interiors, Inc.
Milam & Co Painting
Millworks, Etc.
Minor L. Bishop, Architect
Mitchell Studio, LLC
Moberg Fireplaces, Inc.
Molly Isaksen Interiors, Inc.
Mona Hajj Interiors
Montag Windows & Doors
Morales Design Studio, Inc.
Mosaic Architects
Mykonos Corp.
Nancy Boszhardt, Inc.
Nanz Company - Los Angeles Showroom
Nanz Company - New York Showroom
John R. Neal
Neal Johnson, LTD
Nelson Daniels
Neumann Lewis Buchanan Architects
New World Millworks, Inc.
Nicholas Custom Homes, Inc.
Noble Interiors, Inc.
North Shore Architectural Stone
Oak Grove Restoration Company
Oatman Architects, Inc.
Oehme, Van Sweden & Associates
Offenhauser Associates, Inc.
Ore Designs
Orentreich Family Foundation
Orleans Realty, LLC
P. E. Guerin, Inc.
Paskevich & Associates Architects
Patricia Benner Landscape Design, Inc.
Pauline Kurtides, AIA
Penelope Rozis Interior Design
Peninsula Custom Homes
Period Architecture, Ltd.
Perry Guillot, Inc.
Peter Block & Associates Architects, Inc.
Peter Zimmerman Architects, Inc.
Platner & Associates Interior Design

Polhemus Savery DaSilva Architects
    Builders
Portera Antique Spanish Doors
Portuondo Perotti Architects, Inc.
Pursley Architecture, Inc.
Pyramid Builders
Quintessence
R. G. Architects
R. S. Granoff Architect, PC
R. Scott Javore & Associates Ltd.
R. L. Connelly and Co., Inc.
Ralph L. Duesing, Architect
Randall Architects, Inc.
Raymond Goins
Real Illusions, Inc.
Rebecca Bradley Interior Design
Remains Lighting - LA Showroom
Remains Lighting - NY Showroom
Renaissance Molding & Design
Rent Charleston.Com
Revival Construction, Inc.
Richard Ferson Barrett, Architect
Richard Holz, Inc.
Richard Skinner & Associates, PL
Robert Bump Construction
Robert C. Magrish, Architect
Robert E. Woodworth Jr., Architect
Robert Frear Architects, Inc.
Robert S. Bennett Architect
Robert Wadginski, Architect
Robinson Iron Corporation
Ronald Bricke & Associates, Inc.
Ronald Frink Architects
Rose Tarlow Melrose House
Rugo / Raff Architects
Russell Taylor Architects
Ryall Porter Architects
Samuel Furr, Architect
Sanchez & Maddux
Sater Group, Inc.
Sawyer/Berson
Schenck & Company
Schooley Caldwell Associates
Sheldon Richard Kostelecky, Architect
Silvio Luca Architect
SLC Interiors
Sloan Architects, PC
Smiros & Smiros Architects
Smith Ekblad & Associates
Spitzmiller & Norris, Inc.
Sroka Design, Inc.
Stancil Studios
Staprans Design

Steichen Interior Design
Stewart Design UK, Ltd.
Strocker Hoesterey Montenegro
  Architects
Stonemark Construction
  Management
Summerour & Associates
  Architects, Inc.
Susan Masterman Architects, Inc.
Suzanne B. Allen Design, LLC
Suzanne Furst Interiors
Suzanne Lovell, Inc.
Suzman & Cole Design Associates
  Landscape Architecture
Sylvester Construction Services, Inc.
Synergy Builders, Inc.
Tanglewood Conservatories
Taylor Development
The Bonfoey Gallery
The Galileo Group
The Grand Prospect Hall
The I. Grace Company
The Lotus Collection
The Rosen Group
  Architecture - Design
The Taylor & Taylor Partnership
Thomas Callaway Associates, Inc.
Thomas Gordon Smith Architects
Thomas Jayne Studio
Thomas P. Matthews,
  Architect, LLC
Thomas Riley Artisans' Guild
Timothy Bryant Architect, PLLC
Town & Country Conservatories
Tracie Butler Interior Design
Tradewood Windows
  and Doors, Inc.
Traditional Architecture, Inc.
Traditional Cut Stone, Ltd.
Trapolin - Peer Architects
Trellis Interiors
Turncraft Architectural
Tyler Tinsworth, Ltd.
Vander Zee Group, LLC
VanWert Technology Design
Village Homes
Vincent Jacquard Design
Volz & Associates, Inc.
Von Morris Corporation
Waterworks - Dallas
Weil Friedman Architects

Westye Group Southeast
White Construction Company
Wiemann Metalcraft
William D. Litchfield Residential
  Design, Inc
William H. Childs, Jr. &
  Associates
William R. Eubanks Interior
  Design, Inc.
Wilson Kelsey Design, Inc.
Winchester Construction
Windham Builders
Wright Brothers Builders, Inc.
Zivkovic Connolly Architects, PC
Zoho Stone, LLC.

INDIVIDUAL
Professional
Laura Abramson
Timothy Adams
Ian Agrell
Anne Marie Alexander
Rene Alonso
Frederick L. Ames
Brad Anderson
Christine Anderson
Marvin Anderson
Richard Anderson
John G. Arnold
Lorna Auerbach
William T. Baker
Nan Baldwin Procknow
Robert F. Ballard
Trinidad Baquero
Janice Barker
Anthony Barnes
William D. Barnes
Charlie Barnett
Barry Johnson Design
Glennis Beacham
Bob Becker
Deborah Belcher
Charles Belson
Judy R. Bentley
Joseph Bergin
Jill Biskin
Frederick L. Bissinger
David J. Black
Nora M. Black
James Blakeley
Kent Bloomer
Sam Blount
Glen B. Boggs
Adam Bonosky
Margaret C. Bosbyshell
James Boyd
John Bracey
Martin Brandwein
William Briggs
Jean-Luc Briguet
Ernesto Buch
David Buchta
Thomas Anthony Buckley
Michael Burch
Charles Burleigh
Ken Burney
Daniel Busbin
Greg Busch
Gerald Buxbaum
Fredrik Bystedt
Dale Cadrecha
Brian P. Calandro
Joanne Campbell

Frank J. Capone
Matthew L. Carlton
Thomas Carr
Darcy Anne Carroll
James F. Carter
Michael Carter
Braulio Casas
Castro Design Studio, LLC
Catalano Architects
Barbara Chambers
Tommy Chambers
Susan Christman
Ray W. Clarke
Carl Close
John H. Cluver
Mark Cole
Samantha Cole
Cate Comerford
Franklin B. Conaway
Roger M. Cooner
James Cooper
David Cornelius
Chad M. Cox
Warren J. Cox
Tim Cronin
Gerry Crouch
Linda D'Orazio MacArthur
Kathryne Dahlman
Elizabeth Dain
John Dale
Jennifer Dallas
Thomas David
Maria de la Guardia
Anne Decker
Vanessa Decker
Charles DeLisle
Spencer Denison
Charles Denning
Laura DePree
Curt DiCamillo
Elizabeth Dinkel
Gregory Dixon
Stan Dixon
Larry Donnell-Kilmer
Lindy Donnelly
John F. Dorr
Judy Drake
Lise Dube-Scherr
Liam Duffy
Teri Duffy
Bryan Dumas
Susan Durrett
Danielle Eber
Janet Edwards
Chris Eller

Annette English
Coburn D. Everdell
David A. Ewald
Ruth Falkenberg
Ralph W. Fallon
Marlene Farrell
John Feldman
Ellen Finch
Ned Forrest
Gerald Forsburg
Leta Foster
Thomas E. Fox
Rosemary Battles Foy
Carolyn L. Franklin
Darren Franks
Violanda Franzese
Edward Fraughton
Angela Free
Carrie Fundingsland
Oliver M. Furth
Jake G. Gaffigan
Danielle Galland
Kathleen M. Galvin
Kaja Gam
Gary William Justiss, Architect
Anne Gauthier
Frank W. Genello
William Gerstner
Frank Giacchetto
Donald Giambastiani
Thomas W. Gibb
Grant Gibson
Lisa Gielincki
Donald Glockner
Charles Paul Goebel
Guillermo Gomez
Wayne L. Good
Steven Goodwin
Dan K. Gordon
Keith Granet
Christopher Gray
William Green
Maxine Greenspan
Matthew Grode
Terry S. Gross
Donald J. Grubb
Max M. Guenther
Mario Guertin
Ron Haase
Maureen Hackett
Shannon Hall
Kristen J. Haller
Wayne D. Hand
Eliza Hart
Laura Hattrup
Brandt Hay
Constance Haydock

Mary M. Heafey
James Hellyer
Charles Henkels
Allison Hennessy
Stephen Hentschel
Richard Hershner
William Heyer
Patrick Hickox
Colleen Higgins
Jeffrey Hitchcock
Steve Hogden
Kelly Hohla
Chery S. Horacek
Jean Horn
Bradford R. Houston
Curt Howser
Mark A. Hutker
Antonia Hutt
Barbara Israel
Ann James
Roger Janssen
James M. Jech
Jeff Jenkins
Meg Joannides
John E. Johnson
M. D. Johnson
Rhett Judice
Claudia Juestel
Daniel Kahan
Robert Kaler
Kristine P. Kamenstein
Mark Kaminis
Rachel Karr
Louis Kaufman
Trevor Keetley
Robin Kencel
Philip S. Kennedy-Grant
David Kensington
Douglas A. Kertesz
Glenn KnicKrehm
John F. Koncar
Regina Konet
Brent A. Kovalchik
James Kunz
Judy Kushner
Monique Lafia
Lucien Lagrange
Salem R. LaHood
Sandra Lamer-Seres
C. D. Lane
Bree LaNoue
John LaPolla
Jean Larette
Joel Laseter
Anthony Latino

Kathryn Le
Katie Leede
Kathleen O. Leeger
James Leslie
Isaac Lewin
Frank Lewis
Salvatore A. Liberti
Allison Lindeman
Anne Linville
Carolyn Llorens
Edward Lobrano
Gregory Lombardi
Thomas E. Low
Joseph Lucier
Hugh Luck
Molly Luetkemeyer
James Lumsden
Robert C. Lyles
Madison Spencer Architects
Aliza Majid
Rosario S. Mannino
B. T. Kinsey Marable
John P. Margolis
Jennifer Markanich
Robert Martignoni
David Martin
André Martinez
John M. Massengale
William M. Massie
Arnaud Massonnat
Michael Matrka
W. Travis Mattingly
David M. McAlpin
Steven L. McClain
Peter McCourt
Kirsten McCoy
Charles F. McLarty
David B. Meleca
John Melhorn
Michael Merrill
Gary Mertz
Michael Mesko
John Meyer
Alec Michaelides
Eric Milby
Travis Mileti
Jeffrey L. Miller
Kimberly Mockert
Eliza Montgomery
Murphy Moon
Nicholas Moons
Peter D. Moor
Martha Moos
Ricardo Morales
Maria Morga
Shelley Morris
Susan C. Morse

Aidan Mortimer
David Mourning
Jackie Naylor
Alfred Nazari
Bradley S. Neal
Adrienne Neff
Noelle Newell
Paul Niski
David M. Novak
Maria Nutt
Dan O' Brien
Sean O'Connor
Brendan T. O'Neill
Joseph Odoerfer
William D. B. Olafsen
Ruthann Olsson
Rita Orland
Dan Ouellette
Yong S. Pak
Arturo Palombo
Manuel Palos
Daniel Parish
Ernest C. Parker
Janice Parker
Neill E. Parker
Daniel Parolek
Jan M. Peck
John Peixinho
Linda Pellegrini
Frank K. Pennino
Theresa Pergal
Kirk E. Peterson
Van Pond
Frank Ponterio
Wendy Posard
Donald W. Powers
Joseph Pozzuoli
Daniel Prior
Anthony M. Pucillo
Michael Purser
Tony Quinn
Willem Racke
James Radin
Thomas L. Randleman
Hugh J. Randolph
Randy Ratcliff
David W. Rau
John Reagan
A. M. Redd
Nicholas S. Reed
Dave Reichert
Richard Swann Architect
William D. Rieley
Mitchell E. Right

Dan Ritosa
Melinda Ritz
Ladd B. Roberts
Nina Roefaro
Christopher Rose
Dara Rosenfeld
Paul R. Rousselle
Aaron Ruby
Lynne Rutter
Thomas Ryan
Alireza Sagharchi
Daphna Salimpour
David D. Samuelson
Daphne Scarbrough
Gladys Schanstra
Helen S. Schatiloff
James Schettino
Michael Semenza
Steven W. Semes
Brad Shapiro
David Shaw
Timothy Sheehan
Barbara Shelton
Marla Sher
Charles Shipp
Stephen Shriver
Robert Shure
L. M. Silkworth
Robert Sinclair (CO)
Robert Sinclair (CA)
Samuel Sinnott
Howe K. Sipes
Catherine Sloan
Jeffrey Small
Cole Smith
Philip K. Smith
Susan S. Smith
Jeremy Sommer
Belinda Sosa
Maureen Sowell
Cheryl Ann Spigno
John B. Springer
Ian Stallings
J. O. Stamps
Leland Stone
Nina Strachimirova
Debbie C. Stuart
Robert Sussenbach
Stephen Sutro
Andrea P. Swan
Hal Swanson
Lori Swanson
J. Huddleston Tackett
Cheryl Tague
Charlotte Temple
Clark Templeton
Eduardo Tenenbaum

Dan Thompson
Lisa M. Thompson
John B. Tittmann
Robert Tobiason
Richard J. Torres
Michele Trout
William B. Tucker
Virginia W. Kelsey, AIA
Arthur Vitoch
M. L. Waller
James P. Walsh
Marigil M. Walsh
Doug Walter
Peter Walter
Brad Walters
Stephen Wang
Issac Wantland
Mary E. Watkins
Kirk Watson
Peter Watson
Stanley Watts
Amy Weaver
James Scott Weaver
Mark Weaver
Beth Webb
David Webster
John H. Wells
Bob White
David White
Matthew White
Charlie H. Whitney
Dan Wigodsky
Kendall Wilkinson
Kevin Wolfe
Robie Wood
Delta Wright
Lowell Wynn
Karen S. Yannett
Joshua Youngner
Randall Zaic
Juan Zorrilla
Dayle Zukor

GENERAL MEMBERS

LATROBE SOCIETY
Maja K. Armstrong
George J. Gillespie

BENEFACTOR CIRCLE
Louise Beit
Suzanne Rheinstein
Mary Ann Tucker

PATRON
Martha O. Alexander
Mary M. Ballard
Paul Beirne
Charles P. Bolton
Gary L. Brewer
Deborah Brightman Farone
Kevin P. Broderick
Adele Chatfield-Taylor
David Dowler
Emily T. Frick
Alicia Hammarskjold
Anne K. Mann
Lisa Mosbacher Mears
James R. Utaski

DONOR
Betsy Allen
Constance G. Baron
Patsy A. Bell
Catherine Cahill
Frances & John Cameron
Michael Carew
Sandraline Cederwall
John S. Clark
Edward A. Cross
Elana Donovan
David Emery
Patricia Fast
Todd Furgason
Dick Goodsell
Christabel Gough
Edmund Hollander
Mike McClain
James T. Mitchell
Paula Naraf
Gregory L. Palmer
Octavia Randolph
Stephen Salny
Jan Showers
Peter J. Talty
Richard Trimble
Phyllis Washington
Gail Whelan

SUSTAINER
Emerson Adams
Donald Albrecht
Eleanor Alger
Shelley G. Belling
Thomas E. Bishop
Morrison Brown
Robin Browne
Chris Carson
Scott R. Dakin
Eric I. Daum
Angelo Davila
Hornor Davis
Ron de Salvo
Timothy Deal
Seth Faler
Cherie Flores
Christopher Forbes
Mary Campbell Gallagher
Mark J. Gasper
David H. Gleason
James C. Goodfellow
Peter Louis Guidetti
Stephen Harby
Thomas S. Hayes
Kirk Henckels
Sarah & Ozey Horton
William B. Irvine
Michael Jefcoat
Margaret Jensen
David Karabell
Joseph Keithley
Richard Kossmann
Catesby Leigh
Alan P. Levenstein
David Lewandowski
Calder Loth
Sandra Mabritto
Helen Marx
Victoria McCluggage
Mark W. McClure
Lucy McGrath
Chas A. Miller
Richard D. Miller
Jon Morrison
Joseph Murin
David Orentreich
Suzanne Rahll
Lawrence H. Randolph
Alan J. Rogers
Shulim Rubin
Stanley D. Scott
Salli Snyder
L. Caesar Stair
David E. Stutzman
Jack Taylor
David M. Wood
Fred S. Zrinscak

CONTRIBUTOR
Malouf Abraham
Mark Addison
Michael Allen
Lawrence Angval
Michel Arni
Brent Baldwin
Steve Bass
Marguerite Bierman
Russell Bloodworth
Louis H. Blumengarten
Michael Bolasna
William Bruning
David Brussat
John Burgee
Christian B. Calleri
Helen A. Cook
Andrew Cullinan
Leslie B. Davidson
Rysia de Ravel d'Esclapon
Antoinette Denisof
Alden Lowell Doud
Diane Dunne
Carter Ellison
Paul W. Engel
Carolyn Foti
Stephen Fox
Malin Giddings
Lynn Gilbert
Joan G. Grier
Mac Griswold
G. William Haas
Janice L. Hammond
Tom Hanahan
Philippe Hans
Jane Havemeyer
W. A. Heath
Peter Hodson
Richard Holt
Mark Howard
Mark Jackson
Roger P. Jackson
Barry Jenkins
Richard John
Joseph F. Johnston
Raymond Kaskey
Thomas W. Kendrick
Bruce G. King
Fred Kramer
Scott R. Layne
Benjamin Lenhardt
Silvina Leone
Ernest Lipscomb
Michael Lykoudis
Christopher Macklin
William Malmstedt

Isabelle Manuel
Tripp March
Arturo Marti
Denis McNamara
Albert G. Martin
Clinton Miller
Orloff Miller
Elizabeth Moore
Grace Mynatt
Sean O'Kane
H. Craft O'Neal
Suzanne M. Oberlin
Lee Pritchard
Jonathan D. Rabinowitz
Johnathan Redditt
Robert W. Rich
Donald H. Roberts
Allyson Evans Roebuck
Samantha Salden
Kibby Schaefer
Jack Schreiber
Ann G. Seidler
Alfred R. Shands
Harold R. Simmons
John Sinopoli
Kim Smith
Michael Smith
Stephen R. Sonnenberg
Michael J. Spalding
Joseph Peter Spang
Daniel Stan
Eric P. Svahn
Maria Elena Torano
Paul D. Trautman
Paul R. Tritch
Nancy R. Turner
Andrew von Maur
William B. Warren
Michael Watkins
Katharine Webster
Seth J. Weine
Lucy Weller
Carroll William Westfall
Roby Whitlock
Thomas Wigley
Isidora P. Wilke
Nalla Wollen
John K. Wynpardn
Richard Zini

DUAL
Nancy Allerston
Jennifer Amundson
Norman D. Askins
Steven Ballenger
Edward S. Barnard
Sharon B. Barnard
Clara Bartlett
William H. Bates
Karen H. Bechtel
Myron Beldock
William Bell
Raffi R. Berberian
William Biondolino
Burke Blackman
Elizabeth Bramwell
Sandra Breakstone
Alex Brodsky
Pamela Bryan
Richard T. Button
Torrey S. Carleton
John P. Casarino
Alice Caskey
Thomas A. Cassilly
Paul Chapman
George Clemens
Steven R. Cohen
Aaron Cook
Richard D'Attile
Nat Day
Claudio De Lourenco
Nicolas de Meyer
Hendrikus A. de Waart
Stewart Desmond
Alan Doft
Michael Doniger
Richard P. Donohoe
Kathleen Duane
Robert G. Dyck
Laura I. Egelhoff
James N. Evans
David Flaharty
Laura W. Fleder
Jason Flemming
Donald T. Fox
Barbara Freeman
Patrick Gaughan
M. Barry Goldman
Kay Golitz
Maxine Graham
Nancy Greenberg
Richard Greene
John A. Gunn
Nancy Gunther
Gary Guthrie
James Haas
Helen Haje

Charles Haworth
Franklin Headley
Douglas Heckrotte
James Hunnewell
Diane O. Jacoby
John M. Jascob
Henry Pinckney Johnson
Sharon Jones
Majda Kallab
Dorothy Kamenshine
Chris Kascsak
Lawrence Kasdan
Rose Kenny
Ron Kerridge
Marieanne Khoury-Vogt
Isabel Kilroe
Linda Kirchner
Bradford Kolb
Barbara Kraebel
Richard Landry
Rick Larson
George Lewis
Bob London
Margot London
Catherine Lynn
Hannah Marks
Shelley Marks
John D. Mashek
Heath Massey
James R. McKeown
Antony M. Merck
Newton Merrill
Brenda H. Mickel
Briana Miller
Michelle Moody
Steve Moreland
Robert Mueller
J. Mark Nelson
James S. O'Barr
H. Drexel Patterson
Edward Pollak
Annabelle F. Prager
John W. Rae
Viggo B. Rambusch
Stephen Renton
Rosalie W. Reynolds
Colleen M. Rogers
Molly Schaefer
Beverly M. Schnur
George Secor
Bailey Sharp
Teresa Power Silverman
Priscilla Smith May
Martin Avery Snyder
Michael Sovern

Sara Ann Spooner
Sally Swing
James W. Sykes
Raun Thorp
Jeffrey Tilman
P. C. Townsend
Peter B. Trippi
Matthew Turner
Wesley R. Vawter
Sophie Vittoz
Scott Watson
Robert L. Woodbury
John Woodward
Michael J. Young
Victoria Yust

INDIVIDUAL

Annatina Aaronson
Debra Abdalian-Thompson
Dawn Abrecht
Lee Abuabara
Ted Adams
Jacob Albert
Margaret M. Alessi
Beverly Allen
Suzanna Allen
Rita Amendola
Chris Andersen
Edward D. Andrews
Mason Andrews
Marie-Rose Andriadi
Martha Angus
Jane Antonacci
Joshua Arcurio
Alissa Ardito
Charlotte P. Armstrong
Paul Armstrong
Walter S. Arnold
Anu Arora
Kevin Asbacher
Ann Ascher
Frederick W. Atherton
Judith Auchincloss
Katherine Austin
Terry Bailey
Sheryl Ball
William W. Ball
Thomas M. Ballentine
Leonora M. Ballinger
Betsy Barbanell
Frank Barham
Robert M. Baron
Russell Bartels
Ann Barton
Sara E. Beam
Maria Becerra
David A. Beckwith

Gerard J. Beekman
Don Behrstock
Jack Belcher
Paul Belotti
Merrill Benfield
Ronald Bentley
Ivan Bereznicki
Meredith Bergmann
John L. Beringer
Ian Berke
Inez Bershad
Daniel Betsill
John Bews
Elaine Biser
Philip Blocklyn
Richard Blumenberg
Carlos Bonilla
Dori Bonn
Valerie J. Boom
Erik Bootsma
Ellen Borker
Richard Bouchard
Doug Bowman
Linda Boyce
Holland Brady
Diane Brandt
Gail L. Breece
Jack Breithaupt
Charles Brindley
Pascal Brocard
Stephen Brodheim
Nathaniel Brooks
Harry P. Broom
Barbara Brown
Lisa Brown
Vance Browning
Liza Bryan
William D. Buckingham
Barbara B. Buff
Thomas Burton
Jonathan P. Butler
Ralph Cadenhead
Helene Cagan
James A. Campbell
William Cannady
Caroline Capell
Christopher M. Carrigan
Rocco Ceo
Thomas Cerruti
Margaret K. Chalk
Karla Champion
Carl Chapman
Winston B. Chappell
Eri Chaya

Pinares Childers
Lucylee Chiles
Ji Yeon Choe
Aaron Chupp
Blanche Cirker
James M. Clark
Melanie Coddington
Etienne Coffinier
Lori Cohen
Mary H. Cole
Todd Cole
Susan Collins
Scott Collison
Barbara Colvin-Hoopes
Faye Cone
Daniel W. Cook
John Cotugno
Hunter Crabtree
Rex Crook
Gabriella Cross
Richard Crum
Kevin G. Crump
Art Curtis
Ramsey Dabby
Paul Dalmazio
David Dalton
John Danzer
Nicholas Daveline
John E. Day
Helen E. Dayton
George De La Nuez
Daniel P. DeGreve
Ana Maria Delgado
Joseph Dennan
Christopher Deorsay
Mary DePasquale
Christopher Derrington
David Desmond
Peter F. Dessauer
Gina DeWitt
Benjamin Dhong
Nancy DiFrancesco
Elizabeth Dillon
Mason H. Disosway
Kim Doggett
Robert F. Domergue
Paige Doumani
Stuart A. Drake
Robert W. Drucker
Susan Ducey
Frances Duffly

Rebecca Dungan
Molly M. Dunlap
Saranne Durkacs
Timothy Eaton-Koch
Don Edson
Ruth Edwards
Sari Ehrenreich
Anne Ellington
Elizabeth Elsey
Janette Emery
Stephanie Enright
Laura Errico
Kay Evans
Julie R. Exley
Laura Falb
Diane E. Farrar
D. J. Farris
Marsha Faulkner
Laura M. Fay
Pledger Fedora
William P. Feldkamp
Laurie G. Fellows
Curtis Fentress
Val Fiscalini
Jennifer Flanagan
Neil Flax
Sheryl Fleischer
Peter D. Fleming
Ronald L. Fleming
Ruth Frangopoulos
Tobias Freccia
Charles J. Frederick
Eric Furan
M. Jane Gaillard
Jim Galloway
Brooke Gardner
James Garrison
Susan Gee-Wilson
Kathy Geissler Best
Heidi K. Gerpheide
Marlene Gidaro
Richard Giesbret
Raymond Givargis
Jessica Goodyear
Justin Gordon
Kristine Gould
Suzanne Graham
John L. Gray
Bryan Green
Gail Green
Nancy Green
Eric Greenberg
William Greene
Connie Greenspan
Shane Griffin
Jeff Groff
Michael Grosswendt

Catherine Gulevich
Jan Gunn
Susan Hager
Erik Haig
Edward Hall
Burks Hamner
Robert G. Hancock
Edwin Hardy
Kevin L. Harris
Mary Hays
Adriana V. Hayward
Suzanne Heer
Huyler C. Held
Julie Helfrich
Nathan Hendricks
Deborah Hershowitz
Ron Heston
Glenn D. Hettinger
Cara Highfield
Casey Hill
Damian Hils
Tim Hine
Joseph Holbrook
Tom Holifield
H. R. Holmes
E. R. Hooks
Thayer Hopkins
Carter Hord
Nancy Hornstein
Chris Hotze
Carolyn Howard
James Howard
Neil Hoyt
Joan Hughes
James Hunter
Marianne Hunter
Sari Imber
Laura Isabelle
Siegfried Ising
Alfred Izzo
Richard H. Jenrette
Marion Johnson
George R. Johnston
Andrew B. Jones
Brianna Jones
Marianne Jones
Timothy Joslin
Hetty Joyce
Diana Justice
Eve M. Kahn
Susan Kahn
Edward J. Kammerer
Gersil N. Kay
Jerry Kearns
David Keiter
Mark Kelleher
Arthur Keller

David Kelly
Sheila Kelly
Margaret Kendrick
Philip Kessler
Margaret D. Ketcham
Kourtney Keys
Jacquelann Killian
David Kim
Michelle Kinasiewicz
Theodora Kinder
Lauren S. King
Gregory R. Kingsley
Shannon Kirby
Catherine L. Kirchhoff
Grant Kirkpatrick
Dawn Kirkwood
William Kirwan
Stephen Klimczuk
Raymond Knowles
Gregory P. Koester
Trian Koutoufaris
Joseph Kowalski
Brian Kramer
Richard L. Kramer
Sara Kramer
Laura Krey
Cameron Kruger
Eric Kuchar
Lisa Kurzner
Brian N. LaBau
Jonathan LaCrosse
Rocky LaFleur
Christopher Lagos
Janice Langrall
Chris LaNoue
Robert R. Larsen
Dana Laudani
Ian Lauer
Andrew Laux
Anne C. Lawrence
W. J. LeBlanc
Michael Lee
Jennifer Levin
Sally Levine
Linda Lottie
Erin Liedle
Barry Light
Timothy L. Lindsay
Kent Lineberger
Charles Lockwood
David Long
Mariann Lotenero
David Lowden
David Garrard Lowe
John B. Lunday

Elaine Luxemburger
Melissa Mabe-Sabanosh
Joe Mabry
Donald MacDonald
Carl Magill
Mariah Magill
Elizabeth Maier
Christine Mainwaring-Samwell
Gina Maisano
Robert Maisano
Suzan Makaus
John D. Malick
Eric Mandil
Laurence E. Mansfield III
David B. Marable
Thomas F. Marble
Ernie Marjoram
Robert C. Marks
James C. Marlas
Brenda Martin
John Martin
Van Jones Martin
Marilyn R. Masaryk
Eleanor Mascioli
Susan Mason
Richard Massa
Doris L. Master
Patricia J. Matson
Zach J. May
John Mayfield
Diane Maze
Virginia S. McAlester
Mary R. McCarthy
Benita McConnell
Thomas A. McCrary
Mark R. McCrerey
Meriwether McGettigan
Mary McGrath
Stephen McLaughlin
Daniel McMillan
Brian McNally
George McNeely
Christie McRae
Susan C. Meals
H. Park Melahn
Marcelo C. Mendez
Ruth A. Mepham
Jean Mercier
Margo W. Merck
Amy Merello
Manuel Mergal
Emily Merrill
John Mesick
Juszi Meskan
Pauline Metcalf
Robert Meyers
Christina Michael

John F. Millar
Jonathan Miller
Pat Miller
Ariadne Milligan
Debra Mills
Justin F. Minieri
Eric Mitchell
Kenneth M. Moffett
Wendy Moonan
Daphne More
Mar Morosse
Elise Morrissey
David Morton
Eric Moser
Andy Moszynski
Stephen Mouzon
Ralph Muldrow
Sarah Muller-Chernoff
Beverly Mullins
James Mundy
Andrea Murphrey
Jessica Murphrey-Olson
Mark A. Murphy
George Murray
Meg Murray
Christine Myres
Vickie Nash
Merise Nelson
Tom Nelson
Mark W. Nester
Deborah Nevins
Chester Nielsen
Doris Nieves
Sudie Nostrand
Jennie Nunn
Mark Odell
Kevin K. Ohlinger
Crystal Olin
William L. Oliver
Kristin D. Olson
Patricia Ostrander
Wendy Owen
Rose Pappas
Peter Paravalos
David Park
Susan Parker
Bret Parsons
Edward J. Pass
Lenore Passavanti
Patricia Paterna
Richard Paulson

Katherine Pearson
Betty Perlish
Finley H. Perry
Carolyn Peterson
Hugh D. Petter
Noble Gregory Pettit
M. D. Petty
Laura K. Pfaff
H. L. Pharr
Louis Pietrocola
Thomas Pike
Brian Pinkett
Patrick Pinnell
Ross Piper
Daniel Pisaniello
Christopher M. Pizzi
Stephen Poe
Carol Poet
Patricia Poundstone
Catherine Powell
Jane Cheever Powell
Robert Pulliam
Donna Punj
Maria Quiros
George A. Radwan
Natasha Rahban
Jan S. Ramirez
Mark Ramsey
Andrea Raynal
Riley Reagan
Ben Reeves
Devin Reid
Heather Reid
Diana Reising
Gregory M. Richard
William K. Richardson
Robert C. Ripley
Michael L. Ritchie
Tommie Robertson
Helen Rockwell
Eleanor Rodgers
Frank Rogers
Kathleen Rogers
Sheila Rogers
Thomas Romich
Marion Rose
Jane E. Rosen
D. Crosby Ross
Frank A. Ross
Patricia Allen Ross
Barbara Rossi
David Rowland
Donald H. Ruggles
Pamela L. Rumble
Robert C. Russek

Lynn Russell
Matt Russell
William Rutledge
William Sacrey
Marguerite Saith
Nikos Salingaros
Richard Salomon
Siamak Samii
Anne Samuel
Alina Sanchez de Myklebust
Frank Sardone
Gilbert P. Schafer, Jr.
Barbara K. Schaffel
Dick Schnar
Jim Schram
Jennifer K. Schreiber
Victoria Schreiber
Janet Schwartz
Joel A. Schwartz
Kent Scott
Theresa Seabaugh
Thomas B. Segars
Tor Seidler
June Shapiro
Steve Shard
Leslie Sharp
Louise Shaw
Mary Shepard
Lisa Shire
Jeffrey Shopoff
Lawrence Sicular
Nathan R. Silverstein
Roger Simmermon
Leo Simone
Daniel Sinclair
Diane Sipos
Margaret Skinner
Dale Wayne Slusser
Scott Smissen
Alex Smith
Dean Smith
Susanne Smith
Sandra Sobel
Elizabeth L. Sobota
Jeffrey P. Soons
Randy J. Soprano
Jack Soultanian
Helen Spalding
Steven Spandle
Brian Speas
Joann S. Speas

Clayton E. Spence
Barrie C. Spies
D. Scott Springer
Carl Stearns
Carl Steele
Thomas Stegeman
Catherine B. Stein
Emily Stenger-Schwartz
Alan H. Stenzler
Martha Roby Stephens
R. Craig Stevens
Edward Stick
Jennifer Stinson
David W. Stirling
Kristin Stone
R. Adam Storch
Robin Storie
Holly Street
Arlene Sullivan
Gerald Sullivan
Leonard Sussman
Matt Swaim
Stephanie Swann
Anita Sweeney
Caroline Taggart
Joelle Tambuatco
John Tankard
Mia Taradash
Jay Tartell
Michelle P. Tate
Henrika D. Taylor
Mark Taylor
Karen Taylor-Hajek
Stephanie Tegnazian
E. Clothier Tepper
Melissa Terefenko
Charlotte Terrell
Barbara Teuscher
Michele Thackrah
A. J. Thomas
William G. Tinsley
Gary Tisdale-Woods
Margaret A. Tockarshewsky
Ruth Tooker
Betty R. Torrell
William Tregoning
Marina Trejo
Douglas Trimmel
John S. Troy
Stephen Trudic
Helen S. Tucker
Andrew Tullis
Christine Ussler
Gregory Van Boven
Clayton Vance

Michael Vecchione
Raymond Vinciguerra
Shepard E. Vineburg
Peter Vitale
Sandra Vitzthum
Benjamin L. Walbert
Susan B. Wallace
Sandra Warshawsky
Suzy Wasserman
Joan Watkins
Sam Watters
Joe Wayner
Lamar T. Webb
Robert Weinstein
Kathryn Welch Howe
Margot Wellington
Luanne Wells
Frank Wen
Paul Whalen
Timothy Whealon
Elizabeth J. Wheeler
Bruce W. Whipple
Brooks S. White
B. F. Williams
Jann Williams
Jerry Williams
Stephanie Williams
Scott Wilson
Christine Wolfe Nichols
Rebecca Woodson
John M. Woolsey
Cynthia Wright
Douglas C. Wright
Gregory L. Wyatt
Cornelia Wyma
Howard Yaruss
Geoff Yovanovic
Nancy Zito
Bob Zoni
Rosemary Zraly

STUDENTS

Sylvester Bartos
Reid Burgess
Emily Cafarelli
Anthony Catania
Elizabeth Deans
Taksit Dhanagom
Rosalie Dixler
Justin Dothard
Juwon Eom
Whitley Esteban
Kathryn Garrison
Michael Gibbs
Philip Gill
Pamela L. Goodrich-Yohe
David Hathcock
Sanna Heald
Kathleen Hotze
Craig Kelly
Paul Knight
Kaitlyn Luzader
Andrew Lyman
Jennifer Macdonald
Peter Miller
Megaran Morris
Connie Netherton
Lyubov Nicholls
Luke Paskevich
David Payne
Kimberly Pittman
Robin Prater
Susie Ranney
Paul A. Ranogajec
John Reyna
Philip Rhea
Andrea Rivera
Talia Rubin
Brian M. Scandariato
Nicholas Schroeder
Joshua Shearin
Emily Smith
Robert Smith
Huaxia Song
Elizabeth Stageman
Ailene Steinberg
Keith Stevens
Elise Stirzel
Nathanial Walker
Claire Watson
Paige Wineinger
Qing Xue
Silvio Youla

Current membership roster as of
September 1, 2011

SPONSORS

The publication of *The Classicist No. 9* has been made possible thanks to the generous contributions of the following.

University of Notre Dame School of Architecture

———

Jamb
Peter Pennoyer Architects

———

ABC Stone
Austin Patterson Disston Architects, LLC
Balmer Architectural Mouldings
Chadsworth Incorporated
Clark Construction Corp.
Curtis & Windham Architects, LLC
Dyad Communications, Inc.
E. R. Butler & Co.
Eric J. Smith Architect, PC
Fairfax & Sammons Architects PC
Ferguson & Shamamian Architects, LLP
Fondation de Coubertin
G. P. Schafer Architect, PLLC
Gold Coast Metal Works, Inc.
Haddonstone
Harrison Design Associates
Ike Kligerman Barkley Architects
James Doyle Design Associates, LLC
John B. Murray Architect, LLC
Juárez & Juárez Residential Design LLC
Ken Tate Architect, P.A.
Leonard Porter Studio, LLC
Les Metailliers Champenois (USA)
Mark P. Finlay Architects, AIA
McKinnon and Harris, Inc.
National Monuments Foundation
Northern Roof Tiles
Oliver Cope, Architect
Peter Pennoyer Architects
Peter Zimmerman Architects, Inc.
Precision Stone
R. D. Rice Construction
Reilly Windows & Doors
Robert A. M. Stern Architects, LLP
SBD Kitchens, LLC
Timothy Bryan Architect, PLLC
Town & Country Conservatories
Vela Interiors
Waterworks
Zepsa Industries

Brockschmidt & Coleman, LLC
Flower Construcction
Hyde Park Mouldings
Michael G. Imber Architects
Historic Doors, LLC
White River Hardwoods

———

Griffiths Constructions, Inc.
Traditional Cut Stone

———

Antonia Hutt & Associates, Inc.
McCrery Architects, LLC

———

© Jeff McNamara

AUSTIN PATTERSON DISSTON

ARCHITECTS

Connecticut
Southport (203) 255-4031
New Milford (860) 210-7852

New York
Quogue (631) 653-1481
apdarchitects.com

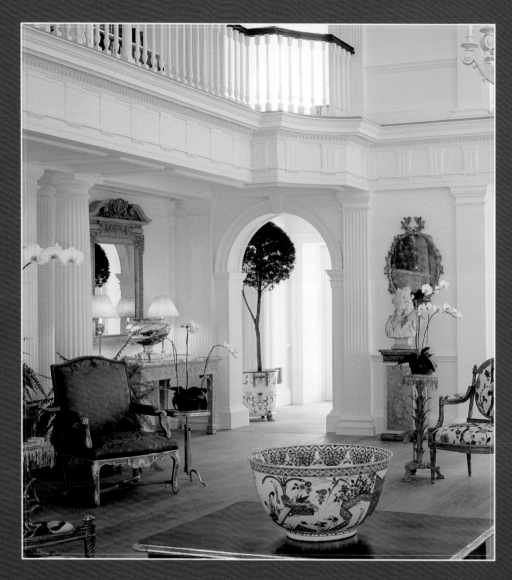

Balmer Architectural Mouldings Inc.

271 Yorkland Blvd. Toronto, ON, M2J 1S5 Canada
Tel: 416 491 6425 Fax: 416 491 7023
www.balmer.com

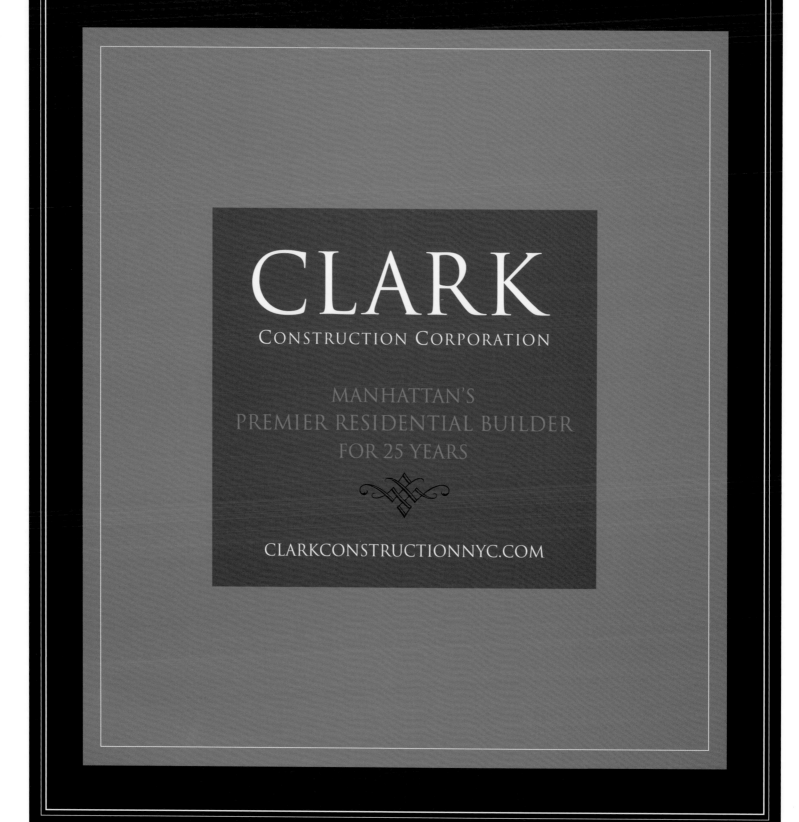

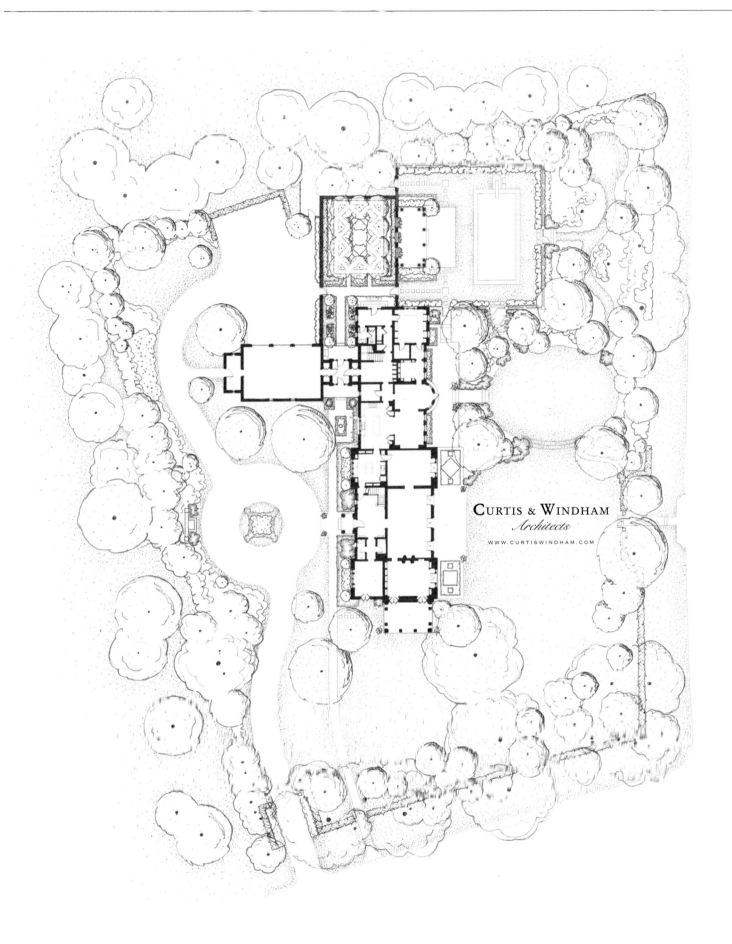

CURTIS & WINDHAM
Architects

WWW.CURTISWINDHAM.COM

DYAD COMMUNICATIONS *design office*

IDENTITY, PRINT AND WEB / *dyadcom.com* / 215-636-0505

B̈

E.R. BUTLER & CO.

MANUFACTURERS

WWW.ERBUTLER.COM

CATALOGUES AVAILABLE TO THE TRADE · SHOWROOMS BY APPOINTMENT ONLY

FINE ARCHITECTURAL, BUILDERS' AND CABINETMAKERS' HARDWARE

FAIRFAX & SAMMONS
ARCHITECTURE

PHOTOGRAPHY BY DURSTON SAYLOR

NEW YORK ~ PALM BEACH ~ CHARLESTON

WWW.FAIRFAXANDSAMMONS.COM

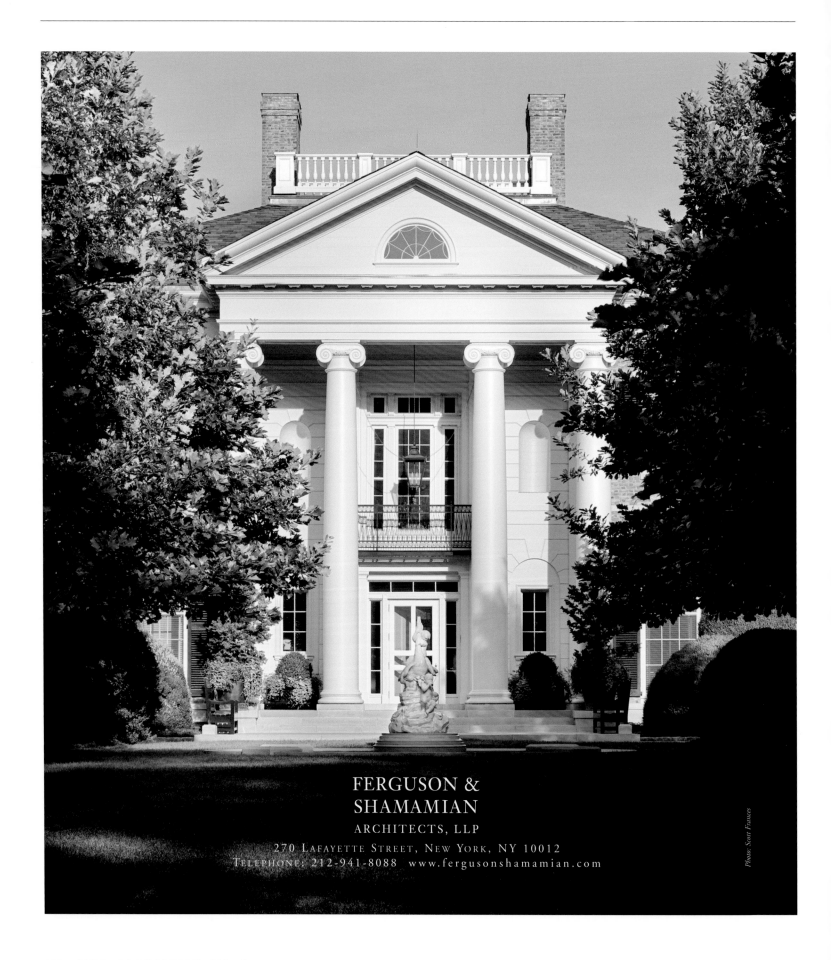

FERGUSON & SHAMAMIAN

ARCHITECTS, LLP

270 LAFAYETTE STREET, NEW YORK, NY 10012
TELEPHONE: 212-941-8088 www.fergusonshamamian.com

Photo: Scott Frances

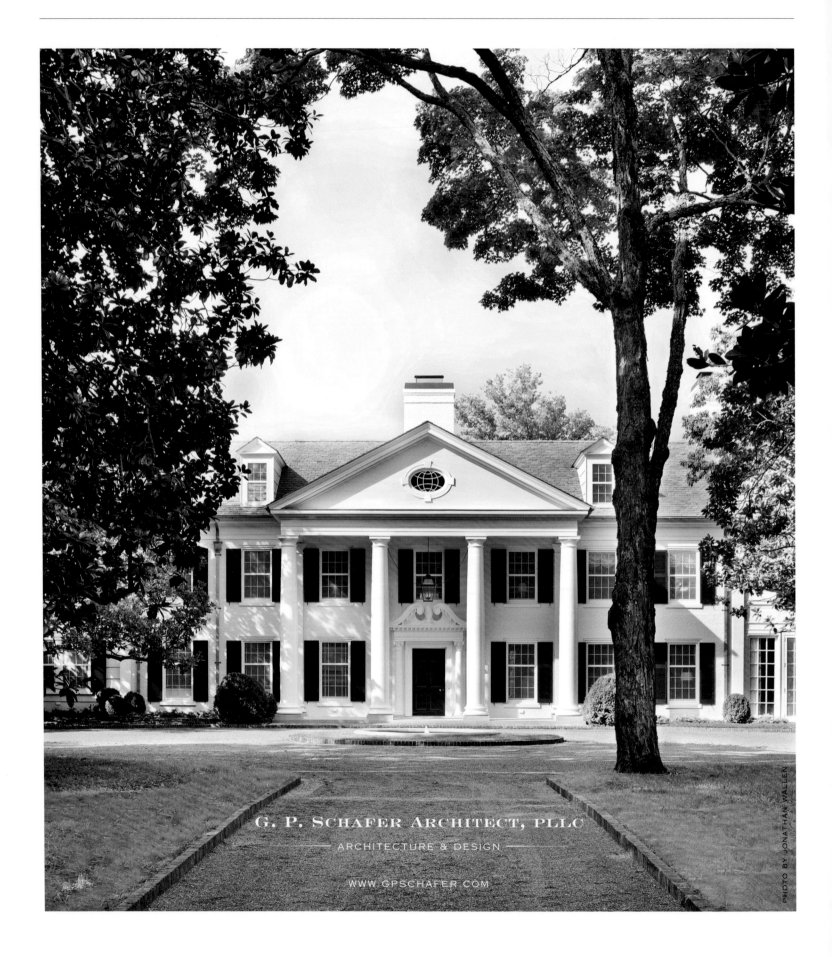

G. P. Schafer Architect, PLLC

—— ARCHITECTURE & DESIGN ——

WWW.GPSCHAFER.COM

PHOTO BY JONATHAN WALLEN

Gold Coast Metal Works, Inc.
Fine Architectural Ironwork, New York Olomouc

Gold Coast Metal Works, Inc.
118 Bay Avenue, Huntington Bay, NY 11743
Phone: 631-424-0909, Fax. 001 131 1967
e-mail: info@gcmw.com
www.gcmw.com

HARRISON DESIGN ASSOCIATES
ARCHITECTURE & DESIGN

www.harrisondesignassociates.com
866.688.3988

Atlanta   Beverly Hills Santa Barbara St. Simons

IKE KLIGERMAN BARKLEY ARCHITECTS P.C.

330 WEST FORTY-SECOND STREET • NEW YORK NY 10036 • 212 268 0128
645 HARRISON STREET, SUITE 101 • SAN FRANCISCO CA 94107 • 415 371 1850
WWW.IKBA.COM

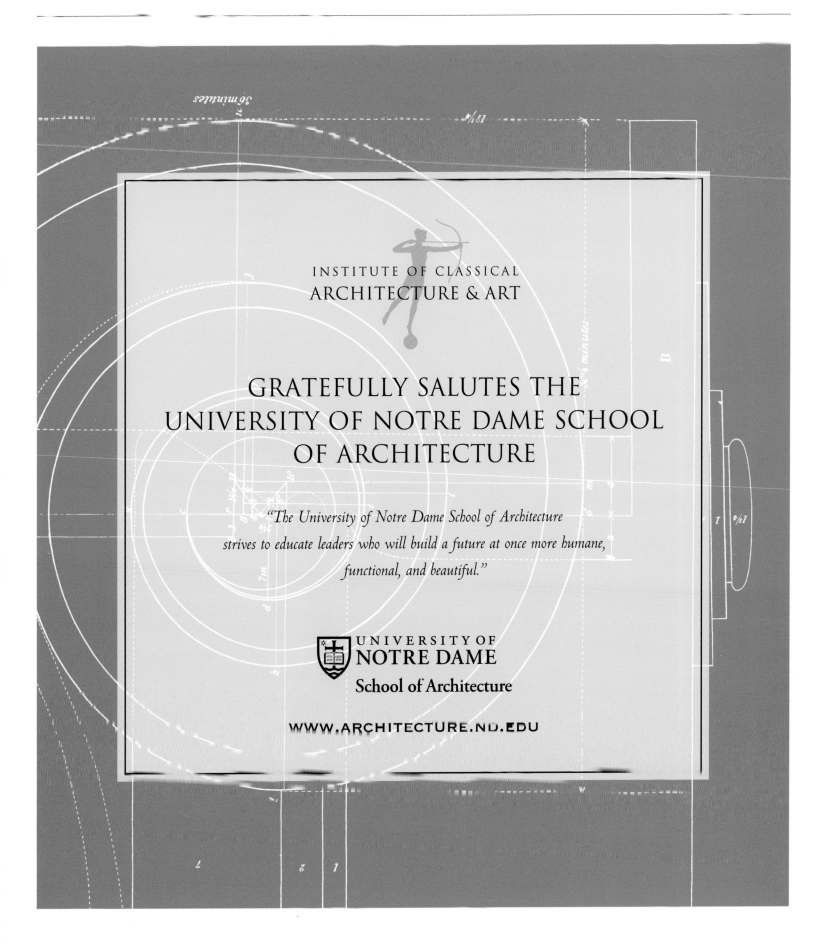

INSTITUTE OF CLASSICAL
ARCHITECTURE & ART

GRATEFULLY SALUTES THE
UNIVERSITY OF NOTRE DAME SCHOOL
OF ARCHITECTURE

*"The University of Notre Dame School of Architecture
strives to educate leaders who will build a future at once more humane,
functional, and beautiful."*

UNIVERSITY OF
NOTRE DAME
School of Architecture

WWW.ARCHITECTURE.ND.EDU

Jamb.

107A Pimlico Road, London SW1W 8PH, UK
T +44 (0) 20 7730 2122 www.jamb.co.uk

Traditionally hand-crafted lighting

Jamb.

107A Pimlico Road, London SW1W 8PH, UK
T +44 (0) 20 7730 2122 www.jamb.co.uk

Traditionally hand-crafted stone and marble
mantles, grates and accessories

Doyle Herman Design Associates
LANDSCAPE DESIGN

125 GREENWICH AVENUE | GREENWICH CT 06830 | PHONE 203 869 2900 | DHDA.COM

JOHN B. MURRAY ARCHITECT, LLC

48 West 37th Street, 10th Floor, New York, New York

212•242•8600

JBMARCHITECT.COM

Ken Tate Architect

433 N. Columbia Street, Suite 2 Covington, LA 70433   985. 845. 8181   *kentatearchitect.com*

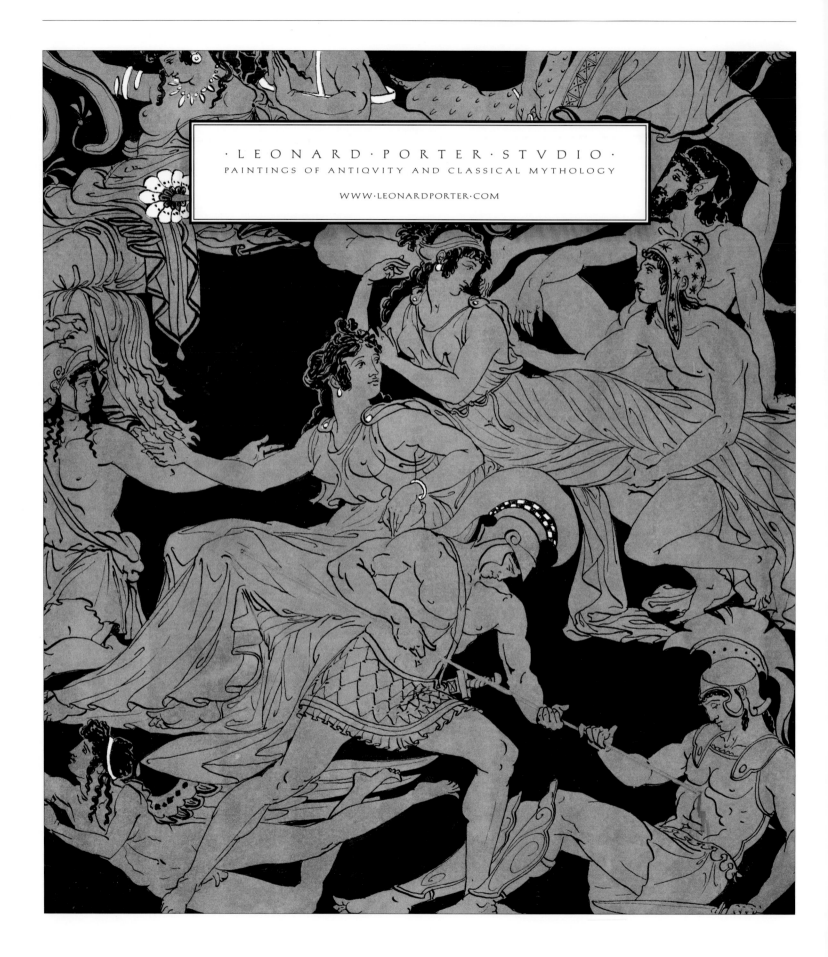

·LEONARD·PORTER·STVDIO·
PAINTINGS OF ANTIQVITY AND CLASSICAL MYTHOLOGY

WWW·LEONARDPORTER·COM

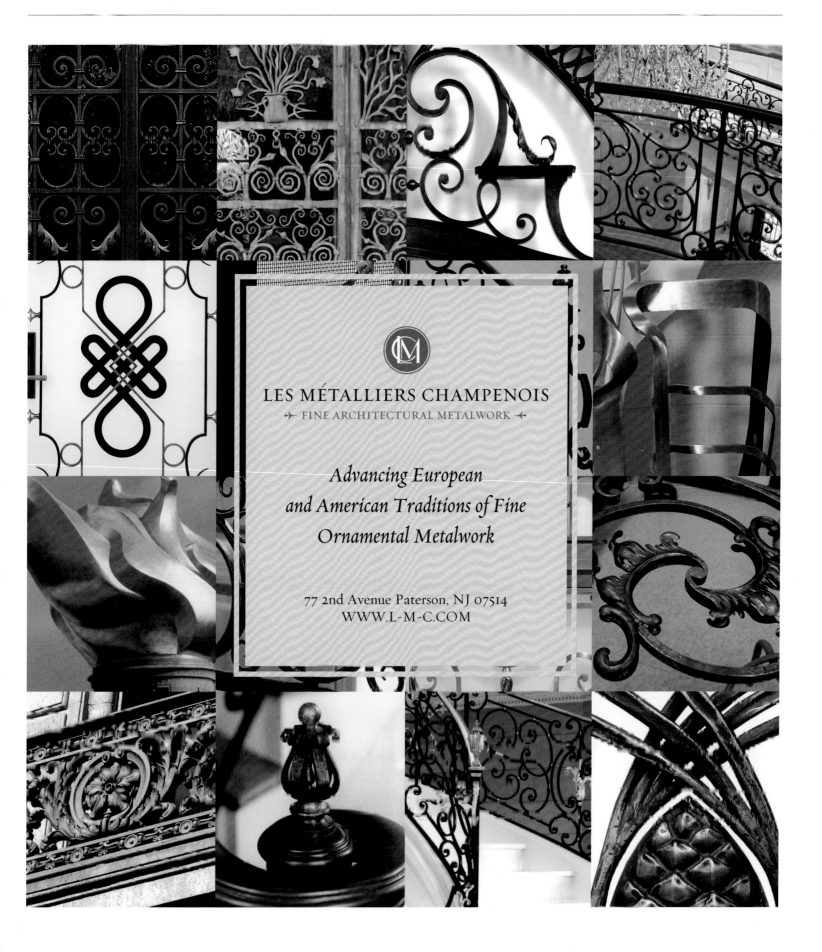

LES MÉTALLIERS CHAMPENOIS

↠ FINE ARCHITECTURAL METALWORK ↞

Advancing European
and American Traditions of Fine
Ornamental Metalwork

77 2nd Avenue Paterson, NJ 07514
WWW.L-M-C.COM

MARK P. FINLAY ARCHITECTS, AIA

ARCHITECTURE   •   INTERIOR ARCHITECTURE   •   MASTER PLANNING

96 OLD POST ROAD, SUITE 200
SOUTHPORT, CT 06890
(203) 254-2388

60 EAST 66TH STREET, SUITE 4B
NEW YORK, NY 10065
(212) 933-4834

WWW.MARKFINLAY.COM

SUBLIMIS · VIRTUS · SEMPITERNA

211 E. 59TH STREET · NEW YORK, NEW YORK 10022 · TO THE TRADE
212.371.8260 · www.mckinnonharris.com

OLIVER COPE · ARCHITECT

151 WEST TWENTY-SIXTH STREET, NEW YORK, NEW YORK 10001

www.olivercope.com   *(212) 727-1225*

PETER PENNOYER ARCHITECTS

PPAPC.COM

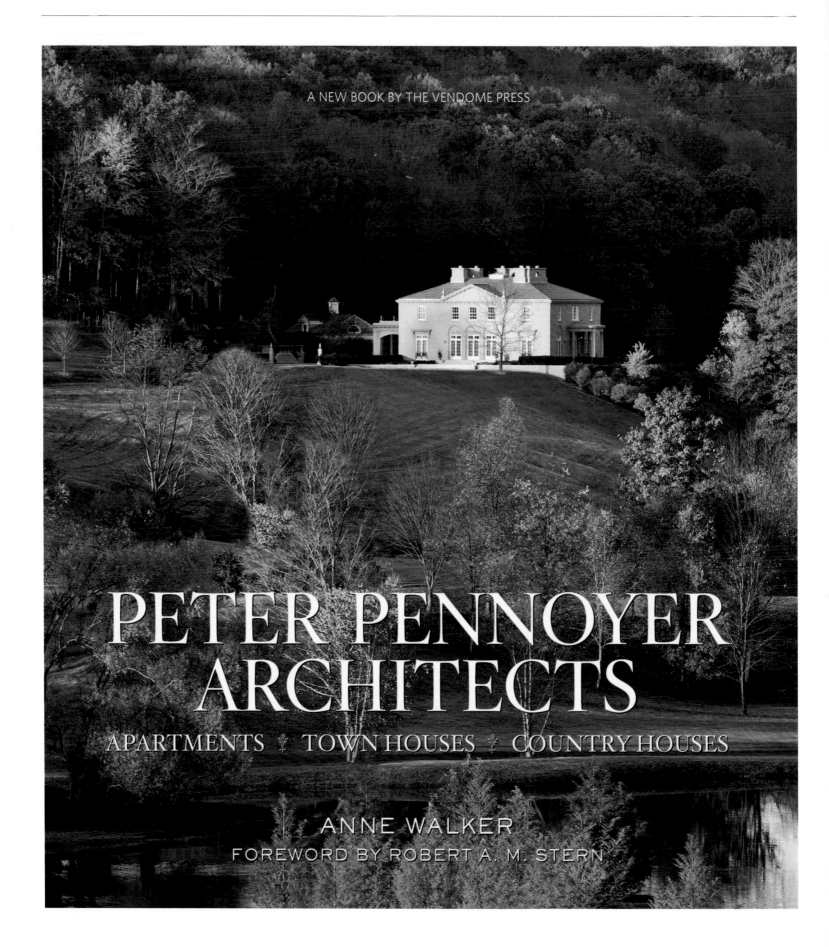

A NEW BOOK BY THE VENDOME PRESS

PETER PENNOYER ARCHITECTS

APARTMENTS ❧ TOWN HOUSES ❧ COUNTRY HOUSES

ANNE WALKER

FOREWORD BY ROBERT A. M. STERN

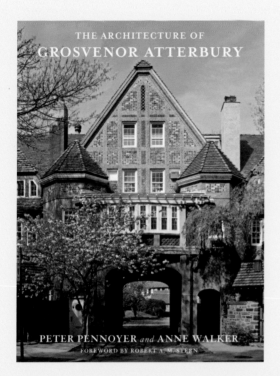

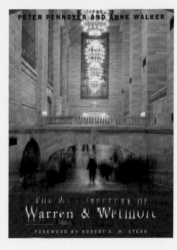

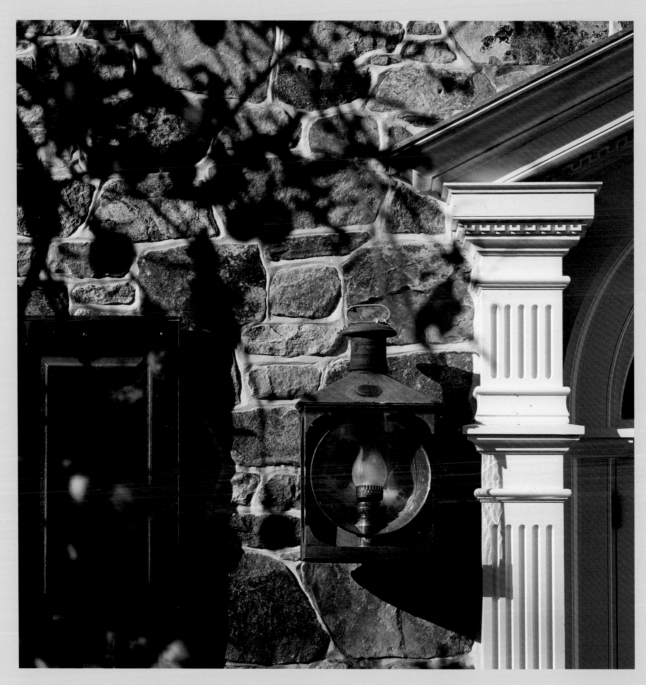

PRECISION STONE, INC.
CUSTOM STONE INSTALLATION

95 HOPPER STREET, WESTBURY, NY 11590 516.997.6190 INFO@PRECISIONSTONE.NET

RD RICE

BUILDING HOMES OF DISTINCTION

INNOVATIVE APPROACH
FLAWLESS EXECUTION
IMPECCABLE CRAFTSMANSHIP
UNPARALLELED SERVICE

CONTACT STACEY BLUME
SBLUME@RDRICE.COM
212 268-1414 | RDRICE.COM
NEW YORK CITY

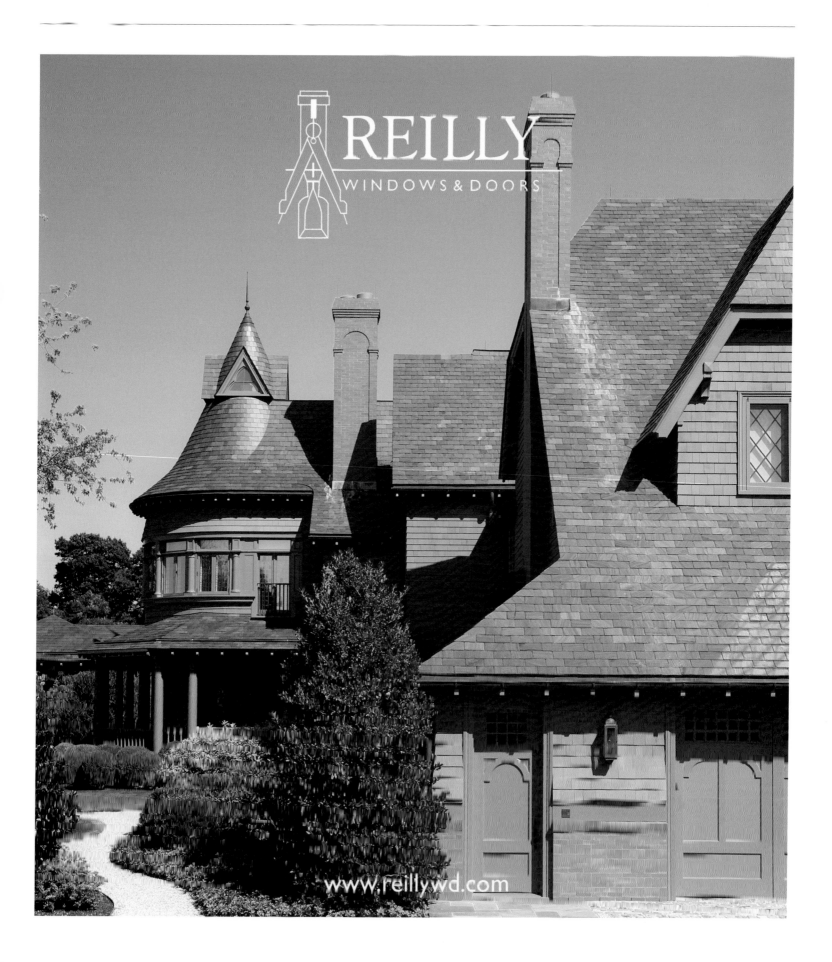

REILLY
WINDOWS & DOORS

www.reillywd.com

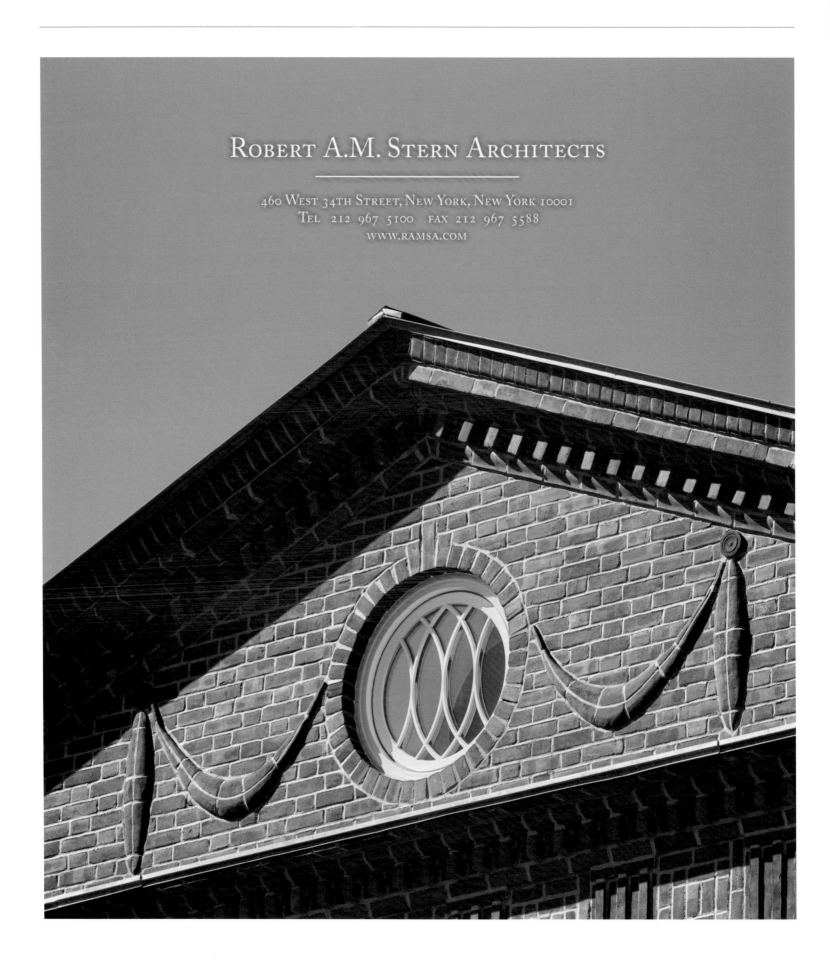

ROBERT A.M. STERN ARCHITECTS
—————————
460 WEST 34TH STREET, NEW YORK, NEW YORK 10001
TEL 212 967 5100 FAX 212 967 5588
WWW.RAMSA.COM

Timothy Bryant Architect

66 West Broadway · New York, New York 10007 · timothybryant.com

VELLA INTERIORS
BUILDERS OF EXQUISITE RESIDENCES

New York City ~ Long Island's Gold Coast ~ Shelter Island
718-729-0026 ~ VellaInteriors.com

INTRODUCING

HENRY FITTINGS
& GROVE BRICKWORKS

DESIGN AUTHENTICITY, QUALITY, AND CRAFTSMANSHIP

HENRY LOW PROFILE ONE HOLE DECK MOUNTED LAVATORY FAUCET
WITH GROVE BRICKWORK IN MIDNIGHT BLUE GLOSS

WATERWORKS

WWW.WATERWORKS.COM | 1 800 899 6757

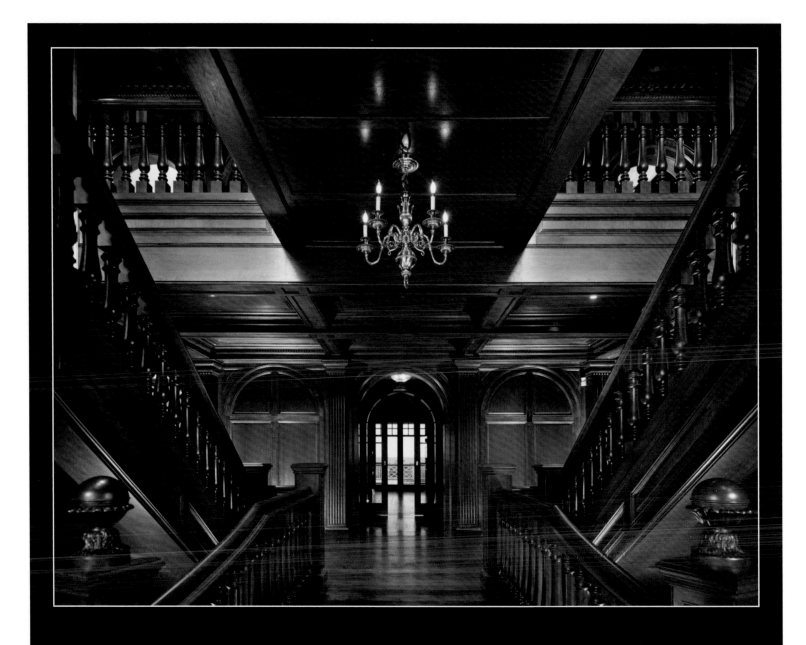

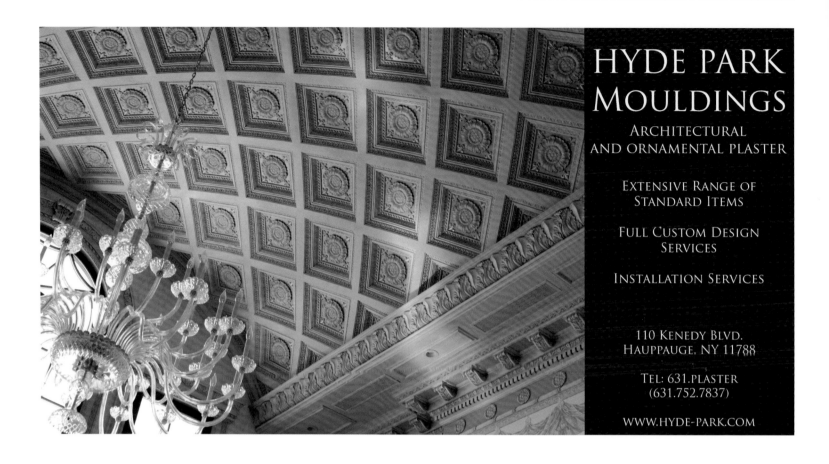

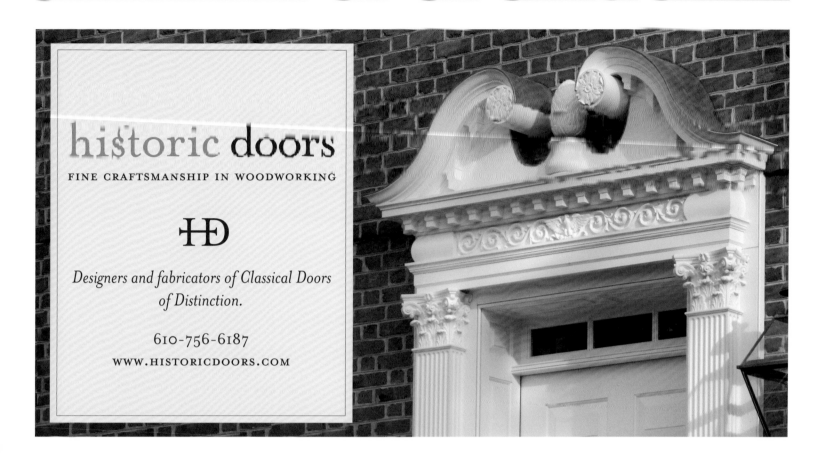
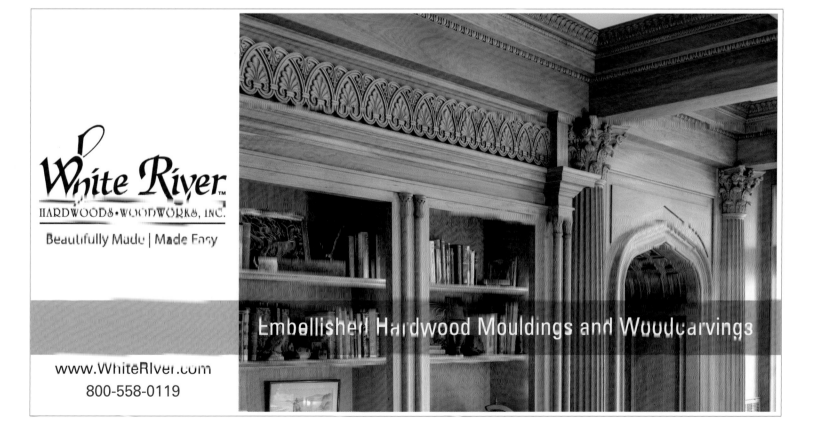

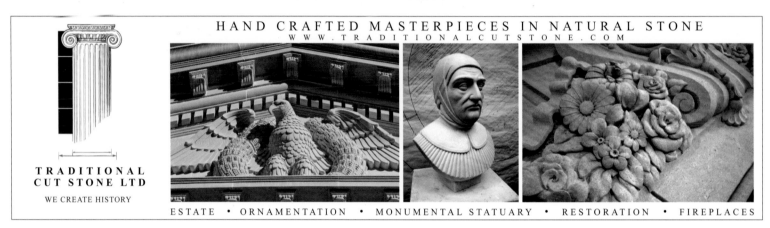

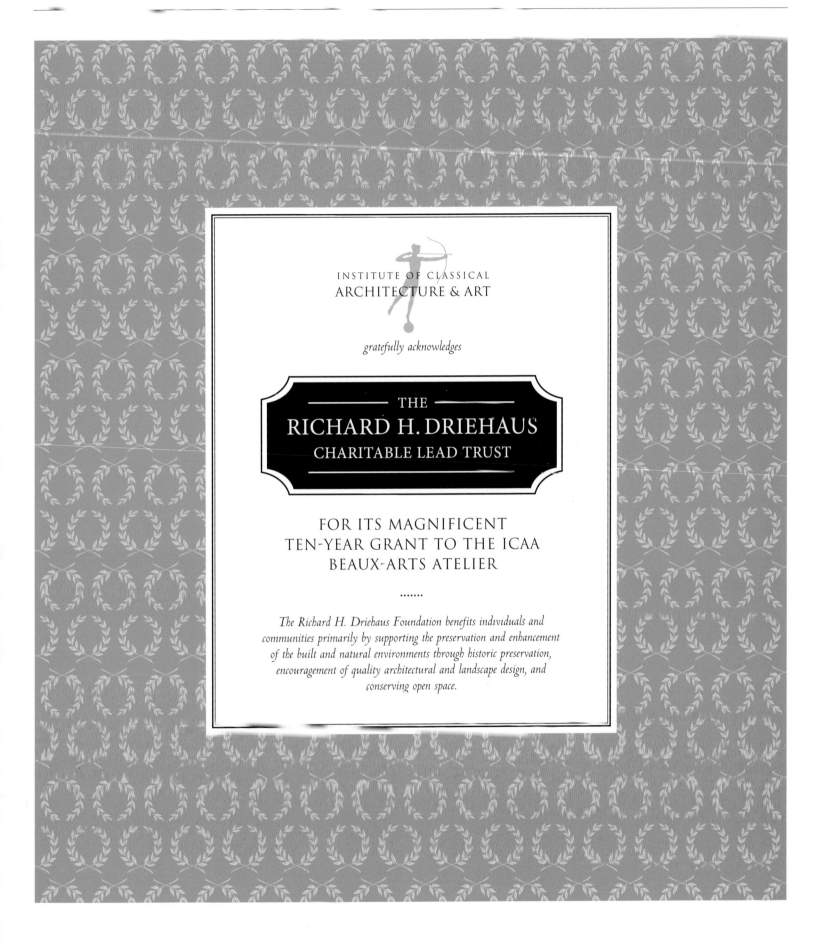

INSTITUTE OF CLASSICAL
ARCHITECTURE & ART

gratefully acknowledges

THE
RICHARD H. DRIEHAUS
CHARITABLE LEAD TRUST

FOR ITS MAGNIFICENT
TEN-YEAR GRANT TO THE ICAA
BEAUX-ARTS ATELIER

········

The Richard H. Driehaus Foundation benefits individuals and
communities primarily by supporting the preservation and enhancement
of the built and natural environments through historic preservation,
encouragement of quality architectural and landscape design, and
conserving open space.

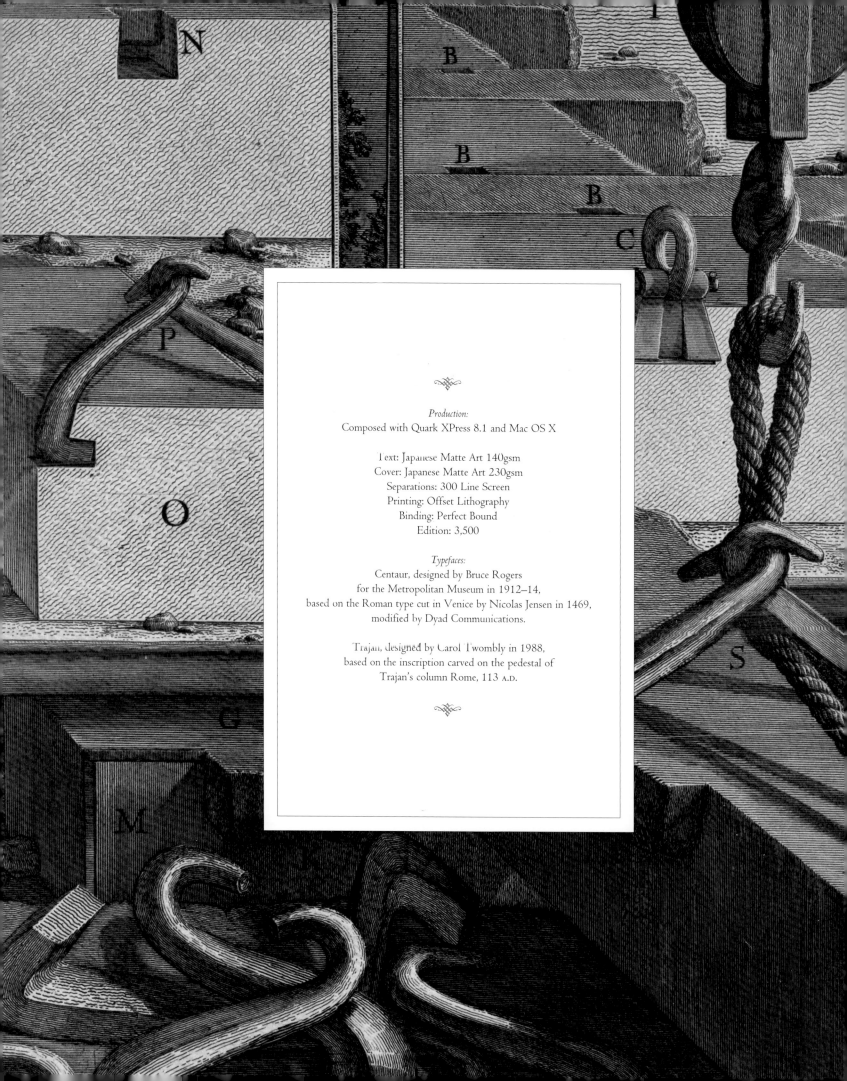

Production:
Composed with Quark XPress 8.1 and Mac OS X

Text: Japanese Matte Art 140gsm
Cover: Japanese Matte Art 230gsm
Separations: 300 Line Screen
Printing: Offset Lithography
Binding: Perfect Bound
Edition: 3,500

Typefaces:
Centaur, designed by Bruce Rogers
for the Metropolitan Museum in 1912–14,
based on the Roman type cut in Venice by Nicolas Jensen in 1469,
modified by Dyad Communications.

Trajan, designed by Carol Twombly in 1988,
based on the inscription carved on the pedestal of
Trajan's column Rome, 113 A.D.